Property of R.J.



# Rearwin

## A Story of Men, Planes, and Aircraft Manufacturing During the Great Depression

# Rearwin

*A Story of Men, Planes, and Aircraft Manufacturing During the Great Depression*

*by*

*Bill Wright*

Printed in the United States of America on acid-free paper.

The publication of this book has been arranged through the joint cooperation of Kenneth R. Rearwin, La Jolla, California, and the Airpower Museum, Inc., Blakesburg, Iowa.

Photos courtesy of the Rearwin Family unless otherwise noted.

ISBN 0-89745-207-0 pbk
ISBN 0-89745-208-9 hdbk

Edited by Lisa Jankoski
Layout by Lori L. Daniel

*For*
*Laura,*
*"J. J."*
*and*
*Bridgette*

*It is such a secret place, the land of tears.*
— Antoine de Saint-Exupéry

# Contents

## Part Three — Finesse and Finality



## Part Four — Appendices

# Acknowledgments

*RAE REARWIN, the central figure of this book, did not design, build, and sell aircraft by himself; likewise, this book is not the product of one person. It is the collective effort of many who generously contributed their time, energy, and resources. I am grateful and indebted to them all, but especially to Ken Rearwin, the driving force behind this project; his brother, Royce; Robert L. "Bob" Taylor, of the Airpower Museum, Inc.; and Robert W. Rummel, Chief Engineer of the Rearwin Aircraft and Engines, Inc., for some five years. Without their input, records, recollections, photographs, and dedication, this project would still be only an idea.*

*Just as they helped design and build aircraft more than 50 years ago, many former Rearwin employees also participated in this endeavor. They include, in no particular order, Viola Becker Bourland, John E. "Jack" LeClaire, Robert C. Faris, George Stark, Eugene Salvay, George Hyde, Keith Dentle, Tony Slobodnick, John F. Roche, Charles W. Nixon, John J. "Jack" Clark, William Henry Weeks, Jack Bucher, Joel A. Firman, and James Combs. The families of many of those who have "gone West," including William E. "Bill" Miller, Troy Keys, Lester Naylor, Marvin Forman, Fred Landgraf, Tom McCullough, and Alfred Haase, also contributed important background information and rare photographs.*

Others with no connection to the Rearwin aircraft firms or family also graciously responded to pleas for help. They include Margie Reed, Salina Historical Society, Salina, Kansas; Judy Lilly, Campbell Room of Research, Salina Public Library, Salina, Kansas; Dan Hagedorn, Archives Division, National Air and Space Museum, Washington, D.C.; Nancy Thaler, Manuscripts Librarian, Pikes Peak Library District, Colorado Springs, Colorado; John Nichols, Archivist, Wyandotte County Museum, Bonner Springs, Kansas; Mary Douglas, Curator of Collections, Smoky Hill Museum, Salina, Kansas; Mary Ann Townsend, Kansas Aviation Museum, Wichita, Kansas; Gerald Knox Bishop, Curator, Frontiers of Flight Museum, Love Field, Dallas, Texas; Ray Wagner, San Diego Aerospace Museum, San Diego, California; Lori Calcaterra, Parks Air College, East St. Louis, Illinois; Sandra Keist, Kansas Wesleyan University, Salina, Kansas; Lester E. Hopper, Colonel, Civil Air Patrol; Gordon Fiedler, *Salina Journal*; Willis M. Allen, Jr., Allen Airways; Denise Morrison, Archivist, Kansas City Museum, Kansas City, Missouri; Paul H. Poberezny; Neil LaFrance; Rob Bach; Marion McClure; Jill Mosley Sandow; Roger Freeman; Betty Fineman; Alan Buchner; and the family of the late Oscar Cooke.

Needless to say, I am also indebted to my wife Bridgette, who gently prodded me; to Jodi Dubots, who patiently typed a number of drafts; to mentor Don Downie, for friendship; and to a mother who received fewer telephone calls than usual from an errant son.

Bill Wright
September 1996

# Preface

*A CHRONICLE of human activity is by definition the story of men — the early years that forged them, their strengths and foibles, their quests for opportunity, and the will with which they faced the obstacles in their way. The chronicle of Raymond ("Rae") Andrew Rearwin, the founder of the various firms and aircraft bearing his name, is one typical of the brave businessmen who devoted their energies to, and risked their resources in, aviation enterprise from the historic stock market crash of 1929 through the start of World War II.*

*Unfortunately, the recording of such fleeting events is imprecise, virtually always tainted by subjectivity and error. Records can be located and dates verified, films and recordings viewed and heard, writings researched and studied, and witnesses and participants alike examined and cross-examined. As yet, however, there is no way to harvest the human thought process, to validate all that has been set down before, or to ensure that memories have not been eroded or corrupted. Even the chronicler must interpret, assess, and choose. As Rae Rearwin might have said, and without apology, all one can do is his best.*

*Part One*

# The First Half Century

Rae Andrew Rearwin (1878-1969).

## Chapter 1

# Let's Build an Airplane!

*THERE WAS never a better time to design and build a new flying machine than the spring of 1928 — or so it must have seemed to those who did.*

*The Air Commerce Act of 1926, through the licensing of pilots and mechanics and the airworthiness certification of aircraft, had ushered in an era of respectability, responsibility, and growing public confidence in aviation. The new Aeronautics Branch of the Department of Commerce, headed by William P. McCracken, was backlogged with thousands of license applications from prospective pilots, mechanics, and manufacturers — almost 10,000 by mid-1928.*

*McCracken proclaimed it was "the duty of every municipality to own an airport . . . ," while notables such as one-eyed pilot Wiley Post and humorist Will Rogers cajoled the citizens of every city, town, and hamlet they visited, including Salina, Kansas, to build one lest they be left behind in the "Age of Aviation."[1] Many did, sometimes on land only recently purchased by city fathers for resale.*

*The fragile and underpowered planes — the Jennys, DH-4s, and Standards — as well as the once-plentiful OX5, Hisso, and Liberty engines were wearing thin and fading from the skies. At the same time, the U.S. Post Office, which had awarded airmail contracts since 1925, was granting even more routes to contractors who demanded faster and more reliable aircraft that could carry even larger payloads.*

Salina's first airport was located east of town and opened in 1929. The site was purchased shortly after the American Legion sponsored the Salina appearance of Wiley Post and humorist Will Rogers in 1928.
Kansas Room, Salina Public Library

No lesser a figure than Henry Ford himself had entered aviation by rescuing designer/builder Bill Stout's floundering Trimotor aircraft project in 1924, establishing freight service between Detroit and Chicago in 1926, and bidding on airmail routes. Everyone knew what Ford had accomplished in the automobile industry. Will Rogers had said, "Ford wouldn't leave the ground and take to the air unless things looked pretty good to him from up there."

But aviation's undisputed catalyst was Charles Lindbergh's trans-Atlantic flight to Paris in May 1927, followed by his six-month, 48-state tour in the *Spirit of St. Louis* sponsored by the Guggenheim Foundation.[2] It heightened enthusiasm in aviation to a new and sustained pitch that still interests students of hero idolatry.

In Wichita, Kansas, the self-proclaimed "Air Capital of the World," Swallow, Travel Air, Cessna, and Stearman aircraft were soon back-ordered. Pilots across the country played cards and pitched pennies waiting to take delivery of new planes. Aircraft securities tripled and quadrupled, and new firms sprouted up almost overnight, from New England to California.

Men called "barnstormers" dashed across the skies in propellered chariots, alighted briefly, and offered a heavenly view of the "south forty" for two dollars cash. Something called the "aerial circus" also came to town, or to the next one over, where brave men — or lunatics — defied the very deaths they had escaped in the skies over Europe just a few years earlier. Young angels climbed from wing to wing and plane to plane and sometimes "fell," miraculously saved by a billowing canopy called a parachute.

The front pages of the nation's newspapers were filled with headlines of endurance and long-distance flights, races, tours, records, and other daring exploits. Hollywood brought aerial thrills to local theaters even before sound,[3] and passengers trickled to the fledgling airlines in increasing numbers.

Any businessman with foresight, it seemed, wanted in on the aviation explosion ignited by Lindbergh's flight. Bill Skelly, the president of Skelly Oil, bought Mid-Continent Aircraft of Tulsa, Oklahoma, and changed the name to Spartan Aircraft Company, while A. A. Durant, the founder of General Motors, bought 48 percent of the Kansas City-based American Eagle Aircraft company headed by Ed Porterfield.[4] E. E. Nordquist, the owner of the Butler Metal Building Company, also joined the Blackhawk airplane project with cash. Others followed.

Coincidentally, it was also a time for Rae Andrew Rearwin, age 50, a successful lumberyard dealer, property owner, and investor from Salina, Kansas, to cast about for a fresh source of income — "diversification" it would be called today. Collecting rents, cashing dividend checks, and processing orders for lumber, coal, and fuel oil were respectable endeavors, but they hardly offered the challenge a man of Rearwin's considerable energy needed to keep occupied.

Many men at the half-century mark with about a half-million dollars in assets would have been content to coast, but not Rearwin. A man worked until he was 65 or so, and then took stock of his situation. That was just the way things were in 1928, but for Rearwin, age 65 was still a fortune or two away.

A few years earlier Rearwin had enjoyed stopping the flow of red ink from an ailing Salina flour mill controlled by his in-laws. It had sparked a curious satisfaction. Bushels of wheat were transformed into railroad cars of flour. Production, he discovered,

This publicity photo, apparently taken before Lindbergh's flight in May 1927, hyped the fuel and oil sponsors. Lindbergh is third from right.
American Aviation Historical Society, Santa Ana, CA

Later, on February 23, 1929, Charles A. "Slim" Lindbergh and early Kansas barnstormer Tex LaGrone appeared at Fairfax Airport, Kansas City, Kansas. Kansas City Museum, Kansas City, MO

was creation, and somehow was more gratifying than retailing.

So it was that Rearwin decided to build and sell aircraft. It was a fateful decision made by many others. There were only 30 manufacturers building government-certified aircraft when Lindbergh flew the Atlantic in 1927; two years later there were 132. None, of course, envisioned the Great Depression, and by 1934, only 48 were left.

What set Rearwin apart from many of his contemporaries was that he had no time to ruminate over the sudden misfortune that beset them all. He was too busy attacking the calamity at the throat. He may have fared better financially had he followed those who withdrew, or were forced out of aircraft manufacturing for the duration. Retreat, however, was unthinkable. He would not submit to so-called "hard times" or "bad luck." He was too determined — "bull-headed" actually. But he was also a survivor: of the Kansas frontier that had claimed two brothers; of a plot to bankrupt him; of the machinations of finance and financiers; of fierce competition and sabotage; of the Great Depression; and, for 91 years, 8 months, and 9 days, of life itself.

A limestone fence post “manufactured” by John Rearwin in the 1880s still stands in rural Lincoln County, Kansas.

## Chapter 2

# From the Beginning . . .

*FEW HORSE-AND-BUGGY drivers from the era of outlaw Jesse James were privileged to witness the unfolding of heavier-than-air aviation from the sand dunes of Kill Devil Hill in 1903 to the lunar Sea of Tranquility. Not only was birth required before James' death in 1882, but one's exit had to be delayed until at least July 20, 1969, when Neil Armstrong took his "giant leap for Mankind" on the moon. Fewer still had a role in that 66-year epic drama. One such player was a tall Kansan who never piloted or designed an airplane, yet built and sold more than 500 during the Great Depression.*

*Raymond Andrew Rearwin, or Rae, as he chose to spell his name, was born March 10, 1878, near Rushford, New York, a farming crossroads located about a day's buggy ride southeast of Buffalo. Rutherford B. Hayes was President of 38 states, and the first commercial automobile would not be sold for nearly two decades. Years later, Rae's elder sister would have to verify his date of birth by attesting under oath that she was present at the event.*

*Rushford was less than a half-day's ride west of Hammondsport, where aviation pioneer Glenn Hammond Curtiss was born just ten weeks after Rae. The pair would never meet. Curtiss left aviation for Florida real estate ventures before 1928 and died of a pulmonary embolism in 1930.*

The Teutonic stature and countenance Rae developed with adulthood was the result of dual Germanic ancestry. His paternal grandfather, Wilhelm Rührwein, was born in Prussia in 1812 and emigrated to Philadelphia in 1836. He settled first in Rensselaer County, New York, and then near Clarence Center in Allegany County where he joined a brother, Earle, and worked as a cooper, or barrel maker. Wilhelm's wife, Catherine (née Croll) was also born in Germany, but in 1808. She emigrated separately and married Wilhelm in 1843.

Wilhelm (d. 1890) and Catherine (d. 1891) had five children who survived mid-19th century infancy: William (1844-1926), a Civil War veteran of Company K, 26th Regiment, New York Cavalry; John, Rae's father, born in Clarence Center on February 16, 1849 (d. 1932); Sophia (1852-1938); and twin sons born in 1854, Levi (d. 1953) and Eli (year of death unknown). Except for John and Eli, all remained and died in New York State.

It was Wilhelm who anglicized the family name of Rührwein, meaning wine from Germany's Rühr Valley, to "Rearwin." Nearly a century later the change would confuse customers of his grandson's aviation business, which occasionally received mail addressed "Rearwind," "Rearwing," and "Rear Win."

Rae's mother, Elizabeth Bohnét, was born in Grambach, Württenburg, Germany, on March 27, 1845. Her father was a bridge builder employed by the government in the Alsace-Lorraine region, an occupation that indirectly led to her life in the so-called "New World." Elizabeth helped a younger brother emigrate to the United States to avoid military conscription. But upon learning of the indiscretion, the embarrassed civil servant sent his daughter packing after her pacifist brother. He had settled in Michigan and was delayed meeting Elizabeth's debarkation in New York. Fortunately, she was befriended by a group of German emigrants she met on the crossing, and went with them to Erie County, New York. It was during Elizabeth's stay there that she met John Rearwin, who, at 21, was 4 years younger.

Several months elapsed before Elizabeth arranged to join her brother in Michigan. She did not stay long. A romance with John had developed in New York, and he followed her to Michigan and proposed. They were married in Waterloo, Michigan, on May 21, 1870, and returned to Allegany County, New York, in 1872 where they farmed rented land.

Elizabeth and John had five children other than Rae. Willie, the eldest, was born in Michigan in 1871. Dora, the next, was born in Angelica, Allegany County, on August 13, 1872; and Sophia was born in Bear Creek, Allegany County, in 1874. Eli, another brother, followed two years later. Rae came along in 1878, and a younger sister, Josephine, was born July 29, 1882.

John learned of the Homestead Act passed by Congress in 1862 during the Civil War. Government land was available to any man or woman at least 21 years of age (except "Rebs," who had fought for the South) in a distant place called Kansas. All one needed to do to become an owner of 160 acres was stake a claim, build a home, and work the land for five years. John could not resist the lure. With the same trepidation his parents had experienced as they crossed the Atlantic, John and his family crossed the Mississippi.

How the young pioneers accumulated the funds to make the trip, and how they traveled to Kansas, is not known. Typically, the unpropertied saved for years and, with final contributions from family and friends, headed West with a mule team and wagon. If they could afford it, they traveled by railroad and purchased a team and wagon at the end of the line or point of settlement. Still others floated along inland rivers on paddle-wheelers, barges, and rafts.

By the time the John Rearwins arrived in the Lincoln, Kansas, area in 1880, the fertile bottomland had been gone for years. Some had been taken by settlers who "sat the land" the required time, received their patents, and then dutifully deeded their homesteads to the Eastern "benefactors" who had supported them.

The best property available was a hilly tract about three miles northeast of Lincoln Center, not far from the geographical mid-point of what would become the lower 48 states. The acreage was rocky in places, and mature trees, if any had existed, had been stripped from the land by others for timber and fuel. Nevertheless, John believed it would support his family and filed Land Patent Application 53489.

From the comfort and plenty of more than a 100 years later, it is impossible to understand how the pioneer John Rearwin family survived that first Kansas winter with only about $200 of savings. Sadly, not all of the Rearwins did. Willie was caught in a snowstorm returning from school, contracted pneumonia, and died in 1881 before his tenth birthday.

Kansas homesteaders of the 1880s struggled for basics: food, water, clothing, and shelter. John planted wheat and, later, corn for livestock feed that was sold or traded until he could afford a few cattle of his own. Elizabeth tended vegetables and a small orchard, raised chickens, and bartered surplus eggs.

Winters were spent improving the land, building and repairing structures, making and mending tools, protecting livestock, and preparing for the planting season. During the growing months, barbed-wire fencing was needed to keep the grazing livestock separated from the wheat and corn. But wooden fence posts were available only at a high price. With help from his sons, John "manufactured" posts for his own needs and earned winter dollars selling the excess. He developed a quarry on a particularly rocky section of the land and fashioned stone posts about five feet high and six to eight inches square from the horizontal limestone layers. The work was hard, but nature helped. Two parallel lines of small holes were drilled or chipped into the limestone about two inches apart for a distance of some five feet and filled with water. The stone cracked when the water froze. The result resembled a fence post, which John boasted was guaranteed "for a lifetime and beyond."

The finished stone posts were carried to the fields on wagons, spaced in holes dug 90 to 100 feet apart, and strung with a single strand of barbed wire that was supported by branches from small trees. Many such posts still dot the farmlands of rural Lincoln County. Others, now collectors' items, are used in Lincoln, Salina, and nearby communities to hold mailboxes, bird houses, and signs.

Records of the First Presbyterian Church of Lincoln show that John and Elizabeth, who was sometimes called Mary, became members on April 24, 1881, and that a three-year-old son, Raymond Andrew, was baptized the same day and became a member at age 15 on July 16, 1893. The children, as they grew, were assigned chores that became as routine

PATENT RECORD.

C. B. Hamilton & Co., Printers and Binders, Topeka.

*Homestead Certificate No.* 10026 *Application* 23489.

THE UNITED STATES OF AMERICA,

To all to Whom these Presents shall Come, Greeting:

**Whereas,** There has been deposited in the General Land Office of the United States a Certificate of the Register of the Land Office at Salina Kansas. , whereby it appears that pursuant to the Act of Congress approved 20th May, 1862, "To secure Homesteads to actual Settlers on the Public Domain," and the acts supplemental thereto, the claim of John Rearwin has been established and duly consummated in conformity to law, for the South West quarter of Section twenty eight in Township eleven South, of Range seven West of the sixth Principal Meridian in Kansas, Containing one hundred and sixty acres.

according to the Official Plat of the survey of the said Land, returned to the General Land Office by the Surveyor General.

**Now know ye,** That there is, therefore, granted by the United States unto the said John Rearwin the tract of Land above described: TO HAVE AND TO HOLD the said tract of Land, with the appurtenances thereof, unto the said John Rearwin and to his heirs and assigns, forever.

**In Testimony Whereof,** I, Benjamin Harrison , President of the United States of America, have caused these letters to be made Patent, and the seal of the General Land Office to be hereunto affixed.

(seal)

**Given** under my hand, at the City of Washington, the Twenty Eighth day of September in the year of our Lord one thousand eight hundred and Ninety One and of the independence of the United States the one hundred and Sixteenth.

BY THE PRESIDENT: Benjamin Harrison

By Ellen Macfarland Asst Secretary.

Recorded Vol 21 Page 35

~~Filed for record on the~~ ~~day of~~ ~~18~~

I. R. Conwell. Recorder of the General Land Office.

Filed this 4 day of November 189 at 9 o'clock a M. Ad interim

J M Burnt

*Register of Deeds.*

John and Elizabeth Rearwin.

as watching television would become to their counterparts in the last half of the next century. Even in the 1880s, daughters were subject to peer pressures and needed special attention. Their mother managed, without John's knowledge, to occasionally save a few cents from her egg sales for store-bought lace handkerchiefs and ribbons.

The Rearwin children attended Beaver Creek County School and, later, high school in Lincoln. To be sure, the youngsters devoted much of their time to work around the farm. However, unlike some farm-

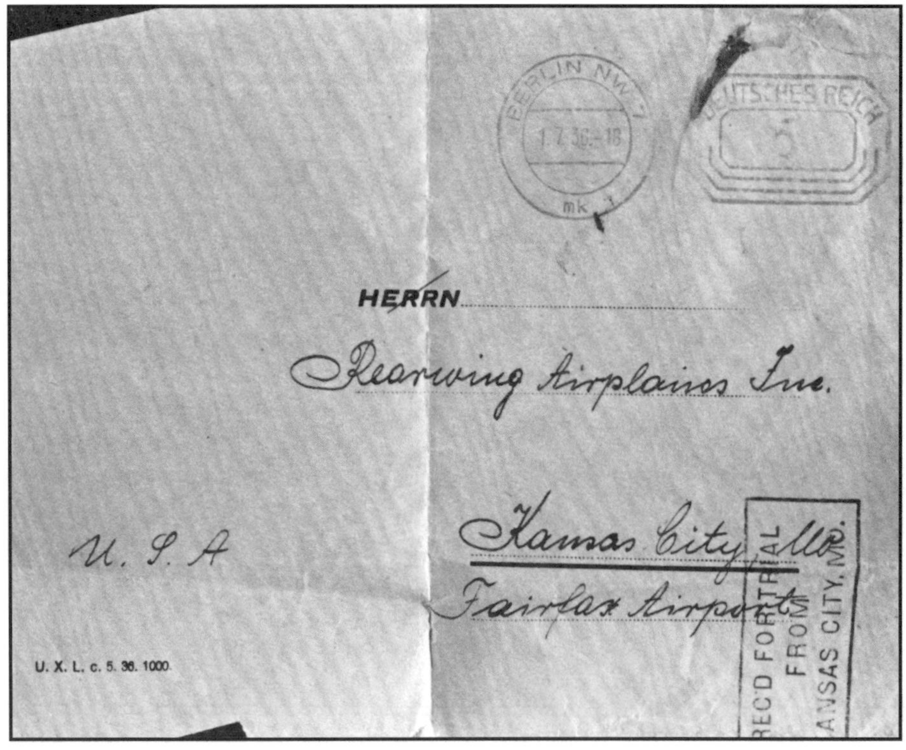

BERLIN NW 7
1.7.36.-18
mk
DEUTSCHES REICH
5
HERRN
Rearwing Airplanes Inc.
U. S. A
Kansas City Mo.
Fairfax Airport
REC'D FOR TRIAL
FROM
ANSAS CITY, MO.
U. X. L. c. 5. 36. 1000.

Above: This earliest surviving family photograph captures young Rae chauffeuring two of his sisters to church, *circa* 1895.

Left: A letter from Germany mailed in 1936 was addressed to "Rearwing Airplanes Inc."

ing parents, John and Elizabeth placed few demands on the children that would interfere with their education.

Rae was barely in high school when, as he would later tell his own sons, he vowed that farming life was not for him. It was about 1891, the same year President Benjamin Harrison had signed Homestead Certificate No. 10026 deeding John Rearwin 160 acres of Kansas land formerly owned by the United States of America. Rae was assigned to patrol the fence lines to ensure that the cattle didn't pull down the wire, as they sometimes did, and raid the crops. It was a particularly hot, dry summer day. Rae counted on older brother Eli to relieve him at an appointed time, and so he drank his water supply unsparingly. Eli, however, was several hours late, and Rae was duty-bound not to surrender the planting to the cattle. He swore to himself through parched lips that he would earn a living some other way.

As strapping youths, Eli and Rae spent much of their spare time breaking horses for local farmers at a dollar a head. It was grueling work, but the money earned was their own. In the winter of 1894, however, Eli was thrown backwards from a particularly difficult mount that landed on top of him. Both boys had been thrown many times before, but this was different. Eli went to bed and got progressively worse. A physician summoned by rail from Kansas City found no broken bones but could not diagnose the problem. Eli died three days later, on December 18th. He was just 18.

Rae, then 16, and the rest of the family were devastated by the death of a second brother and son. The brothers had been close, and the loss only reinforced Rae's resolve to escape farm life. Years later, Rae and his own eldest son, Royce, would speculate that Eli had died from a ruptured appendix — but bleeding from internal injuries was just as likely.

The future aircraft manufacturer, who excelled in math, graduated from high school in June 1895. He promptly enrolled in Kansas Christian College, then located in Lincoln,[1] and boarded with the minister of his church. Two years later he was teaching school in the Lincoln Center area to save money to finish college, his boyhood oath fulfilled.

## *Chapter 3*

# Birth of a Salesman

*RAE INTENDED TO enroll in Kansas Wesleyan College in Salina, located at the south end of Sante Fe Avenue, in the fall of 1900, earn a degree, and make teaching a career. That summer, Charles Bloss, who was married to Rae's sister Sophia, offered Rae a summer job selling new and used farm implements in Lincoln County. Rae took to selling, as they say, "like a duck takes to water." He had an innate affinity for things mechanical and kept his promises to repair the machinery he sold the next time he was by.*

*He entered Kansas Wesleyan in September, enrolled in "special courses" rather than a structured curriculum, and pledged a fraternity. Rae also taught the math class he was taking when the instructor was absent. At the same time he changed the customary spelling of his given name. A decade later he was told that he had adopted the feminine form, but he shrugged it off.*

*Rae sold farm implements again during the summer of 1901 and returned to college in the fall to finish his degree. While there he met a coed from Salina named Leila Sudendorf who, although 3 years younger, attracted his 23-year-old eyes. However, he received a letter from his brother-in-law before the term was over. The regional salesman for northern Kansas and southern Nebraska had suddenly died. The company was impressed with Rae's summer work and the job was his if he*

Lockwood Hall, Kansas Wesleyan College, Salina, Kansas. Kansas Room, Salina Public Library, Salina, KS

This portrait of Rae was taken in Omaha in 1906, while he was employed as a traveling salesman for the Beebe & Runyon Furniture Company.

Rae as a 22-year-old upperclassman at Kansas Wesleyan College, 1900-1901.

wanted it, but it could not be held open until graduation. By then, Rae realized that he had a knack for selling and that the financial rewards were greater than those of teaching. He also knew, as Bloss had counseled, that it could take three to five years to achieve a similar position and income level. The opportunity was too good to ignore.

Although Rae continued to reside in Salina, he traveled much of the time, sometimes going as far as southern Minnesota on special assignment. Within a year or two, many of the competing farm implement firms, including Rae's, joined to form the International Harvester Company. Rae was reassigned to the Columbus, Nebraska, territory but the infant company was reorganized and downsized the following year. While hundreds of salesmen across the country lost their jobs, Rae was promoted to Special Representative and was put in charge of selling used and weather-worn machinery throughout the Kansas and Nebraska regions.

The new assignment involved even more travel. The trips, primarily by rail, sometimes lasted two weeks and frequently involved three train changes in a single night. It wasn't that Rae minded the travel, the work, or the pay. Indeed, by 1905 he was averaging almost $300 a month, had an expense account, and qualified for year-end bonuses. The travel simply kept him away from Salina too much and interfered with the

Leila Sudendorf, *circa* 1905.

Above: Leila Wilhelmina Sudendorf, age 6. Smoky Hill Museum, Salina, KS

Left: Leila (front left), Henry, and Carrie Sudendorf outside the family home, 1895.

Salina pioneer Herman Henry Sudendorf.
Kansas Room, Salina Public Library, Salina, KS

Above: Leila Sudendorf, *circa* 1890.

Below: Henry Sudendorf built this home at 142 South Eighth Street in 1870 and lived in it until his death in 1913.
Kansas Room, Salina Public Library, Salina, KS

courtship of Leila Sudendorf, which he had somehow found time to initiate. Being away so often was not good for a young man planning on marrying soon. In that, Leila agreed.

It was time to look for another job that would keep Rae closer to Salina. He found it as a traveling salesman for the Beebe & Runyon Furniture Company, a large Omaha-based wholesaler. He would have the Northern Kansas Territory. That would involve substantially less travel, at most a day or two at a time. Leila would like that. And Rae would even have time to shop for an engagement ring.

Employer and employee entered into a one-page agreement dated November 25, 1905, that expired on December 31 the following year. It provided for a three percent commission "on all shipments made on orders taken, as well as on mail orders received from said territory which were influenced by the salesman." Expenses included the cost of rail transportation, hotel fare not to exceed two dollars a day incurred while in the prosecution of the company's business, and such team hire as was necessary to make points not accessible by rail. It also required orders and expense accounting to be submitted daily by mail.

Unknown to Rae, the Northern Kansas Territory was ranked 17th among Beebe's 18 sales districts. It suffered heavily from Kansas City competition. Within six months, however, sales were running neck and neck with Beebe's top district. At first, Beebe & Runyon was so surprised by the volume of orders that the firm contacted the retailers for confirmation. They were valid. By selling at that pace, Rae would earn more than $3,600 his first year.

It had not taken Rae long to discover the secret of cracking the difficult territory. The furniture, it seems, was shipped by rail. The freight charges, which were paid by the retailer, were based not on distance, but on volume. The charges for a few pieces of furniture in a freight car could be higher than those for a full car. In some cases, they approximated the cost of the furniture, a fact that did not escape Rae's notice.

Most merchants in the territory had been in the habit of ordering only a piece or two at a time or as it was sold from a catalogue. Rae, however, offered "discounts" that they found difficult to turn down. With careful planning, he was able to delay and consolidate the orders of several retailers along the same line to fill a freight car. The rates charged by the railroads for such "pool" cars were substantially less than for partial ones. How much was drop-shipped at different stops did not matter. Thus, Rae was able to significantly reduce shipping costs, and he passed the savings along to his customers. This meant more sales for both the merchant and himself. And, if one retailer in a town placed an order, it was not overly difficult to convince a rival that he also needed to place one.

Both Leila's father, Henry Sudendorf, and Herman, her paternal grandfather, were duly impressed with the shrewd young man who was courting Leila. They rightly concluded that he was not only thrifty, hard-working, and highly motivated, but also a gentleman — even if he was "off the farm." Indeed, he was rarely seen without a coat, properly starched high collar and tie, vest, and spats. Also, he did not smoke, gamble, chew, or imbibe, as far as they could discern, and a curse word from Rae had not yet reached their ears. Both approved when Rae and Leila informed them that they planned to marry. There was a bright future for young Rae Rearwin, maybe even some day in the family lumberyard business.

Like the Rearwins, the Sudendorf roots were in German soil. Herman Heinrich (H. H.), the family patriarch, had been born in Hanover on October 10, 1832, and had entered the United States at New Orleans in 1848. His family had settled in Cincinnati where he worked as a carpenter and married Wilhelmina Lizette Lange in 1852. She was born in Preusminden, Prussia, on October 20, 1826. They had eight children, but only the first and last survived to adulthood. Henry Herman Frederick, sometimes known as "H. H. F.," was born in Cincinnati on October 2, 1852. He would become Rae's father-in-law. The other survivor, Edward H., was born in Leavenworth, Kansas, on December 29, 1863, four years after the family had moved there from Seymour, Indiana.

During the Civil War, Herman and one Christopher Eberhardt, another German emigrant and a carpenter, had become close friends. In 1868, Eberhardt moved west with the Union Pacific Railroad and persuaded Herman to follow and enter the lumber business with him in Salina. Herman took the leap but cautiously left his family in Leavenworth until he was convinced that the venture would succeed. Two years later he built a new home at 142 South Eighth Street and moved his wife and sons to Salina.

In 1873, Herman and Eberhardt joined with C. R. Underwood and Eli Rittigers to purchase the Shelden

Flour Mill, which had lacked sufficient capital to finance a suitable beaver-proof dam on the Smoky Hill River. The new owners promptly built one. However, it raised the water level upstream, which interfered with the operation of the rival "Upper" or Gower Mill. Threatened with a lawsuit, the partners bought it and later consolidated both mills with one previously owned by Rittigers into the Western Star Mill, which was established as a stock company.[1]

The older of the Sudendorf sons, Henry, married Carrie Adelia Dearborn on February 11, 1879. Carrie had been born in Marlboro, New Hampshire, on June 3, 1853, the only daughter of the Reverend George Sullivan Dearborn (1823-1903) and Sarah Amelia Briggs (1825-1912). Sarah was a native of Manchester, England, and the Reverend Dearborn had been born in Compton, New Hampshire.

Henry briefly attended business college, and entered his father's lumberyard business before Herman and Eberhardt split up in 1891 after the depression of 1889. He and Carrie built a substantial home on a lot Herman gave them at 324 South Eighth Street. Their first daughter, Leila Delight, was stillborn, but their second, Leila Wilhelmina, was born into Salina society and comfort on August 30, 1881. She studied music and poetry as a young girl, and apparently enjoyed her only-child status. Unfortunately, she suffered a childhood attack of rheumatic fever, in those days an untreatable condition that frequently resulted in damage to the heart's mitric valve and a shortened life expectancy. Strenuous activity was discouraged. "Lilly," as she was called in her youth, entered Kansas Wesleyan College as a 20-year-old in 1901 and, like the tall former school teacher she met there, enrolled in "special courses," primarily piano and voice.

Between school years at Kansas Wesleyan, Leila worked in the office of the lumberyard founded by her grandfather, which was managed by her father after Herman's retirement in 1896. Henry, in a rare unfatherly gesture, persuaded her to stay on rather than return to college in 1903. After all, he had no other issue and thought that Leila should have more than a passing acquaintance with the enterprise she would someday inherit. Besides, business was not good, tuition was an unwarranted expense, and Leila's income would remain in the family.

The Sudendorf-Rearwin wedding took place on Sunday evening, December 11, 1906, at 8:30 p.m. in the parlor of the family home. The ceremony was performed by Methodist Minister Charles Coke Woods and, following a brief reception, an evening supper was served in the dining room. Rae's parents and his three married sisters, each with her husband in tow, were present. An article in the *Salina Journal* the next day reported:

Mr. and Mrs. Rae Rearwin on their wedding day, December 11, 1906.

> The young couple left at 3:45 this morning by rail for Kansas City. From there they will go to New Orleans, being absent three weeks. After returning to this city, they will make their home on South Eighth Street.

It is difficult to fathom Rae staying away from work for three weeks. At 28, he was already a borderline workaholic. However, wholesale furniture sales were sparse during the holiday season, so it was not by coincidence that Mr. and Mrs. Rae Andrew Rearwin had chosen to marry in December and would return from their honeymoon trip only after the first day of 1907.

Rae Rearwin, *circa* 1906.

## *Chapter 4*

# All in the Family

*IN DECEMBER, before his wedding, Rae had told Beebe & Runyon he would continue to work for them but that he did not want to be time-bound by a contract. His father-in-law-to-be was impressed with his drive and success. He had said so on several occasions, and it was not unrealistic to think that Rae might be offered a position in the Sudendorf lumberyard. After all, he would be family, or so he thought, and Henry was 55. Someone would have to carry on when Henry chose to retire, or died. Rae was the logical choice, and he wanted to be available if the offer came.*

*Beebe & Runyon weren't exactly sure how, but their star salesman had increased the volume of the Northern Kansas Territory from 17th place to 2nd in just a few months. Not wanting to lose him, they offered an additional two points commission if Rae would sign for another year. It didn't take the math whiz more than a second to realize that the offer translated to a 67 percent increase on the same volume of sales. He also realized that they had unwittingly dealt him a pat hand.*

*Since Beebe had offered to pay an extra two points if Rae signed a new one-year employment agreement, why shouldn't they pay the same commission if he stayed without signing? Rae played his cards and won. On a handshake he agreed to provide a month's notice of his intention to leave. Maybe, just maybe, he would also*

Henry H. F. Sudendorf, Rae's future father-in-law, *circa* 1890.

disclose "The Rearwin Sales Technique" for the Northern Kansas Territory when he left.

The Sudendorf call came within the year. The offer, however, was disappointing. Henry suggested that it was time for Rae to join the family business — but as a salaried salesman at $100 a month for the first year. It must have been difficult for Rae to mask his shock. He knew the business wasn't doing well, but the income cut he was being asked to take was substantial, if not outrageous. At the same time, however, it would be unthinkable to turn down his new father-in-law, even though he was clearly taking advantage of the family relationship. Beebe & Runyon got their one-month notice and Rae's selling secrets.

Rae was never one to fret for long. He put his displeasure with the meager salary aside and went to work in the lumber business with the same zeal he applied to any endeavor. Meanwhile, he became a Third Degree Mason of Salina Lodge No. 60, and started planning to build a home on a lot two doors north of his father-in-law, which Herman had given to his granddaughter as a wedding present. The two-story frame house would have ten rooms and would be properly set back at 310 South Eighth Street. Rae and Leila would share the cost of construction and furnishing.

Within a few months the Sudendorf lumberyard was busy enough to purchase a second team and wagon to deliver the materials its new employee was selling in the rural areas of Saline County. If Rae figured the sudden change in the firm's fortunes would be noticed and promptly rewarded, he was only half right. He waited a few months more before inviting himself into his father-in-law's office. Half-expecting Henry to fall back on his unilaterally imposed one-year salary term, Rae cited his accomplishments and suggested he deserved a raise. Rae quoted Henry's reply to his sons many years later: "Of course you do. I was just waiting to see how long it would take you to ask!" Rae's salary was doubled, but Henry's position on the issue was curious and briefly embittered Rae. He resolved never again to hesitate to ask for a raise, family or not.

Rae settled into the lumberyard business and the gentlemen's life offered to Salina businessmen in the first decade of the new century. More wagons and teams were needed at the humming Sudendorf lumberyard, and the community took notice of that young Rearwin fellow; he was a "comer," no doubt about it. Two sons appeared: Royce, named by his

Office of **H. H. SUDENDORF,**

......DEALER IN......

**Lumber, Coal, Lime, Cement, Etc.**

**Yards at** { **SALINA, McPHERSON.** **Principal Office at SALINA.**

**Salina, Kansas,**..................................................190.........

The letterhead of the Sudendorf lumberyard where Rae worked could be used for a full decade without reprinting.

Rae and Leila built this home on a 100- by 150-foot lot at 310 South Eighth Street that Leila's grandfather had given her as a wedding present. The house has since been moved.

Below: Rae frequently told his sons he spent the best ten years of his life working for his father-in-law at this Salina lumberyard.
Kansas Room, Salina Public Library, Salina, KS

mother after a cousin, in Salina, on September 18, 1910, and — as Leila's mother sighed — "another boy," Kenneth, on July 19, 1913, also in Salina. Leila had wanted to tag her second-born with "Cuthbert," but Rae prevailed and unquestionably saved the youngster from many a boyhood scrap.

Rae and his father-in-law frequently disagreed on business matters. On one occasion, a major contractor failed to pay his account within 30 days and Henry billed him an additional two percent of the balance. The contractor had been a longtime customer and was clearly good for the money. He argued with Rae over the service fee, about $60, and threatened to take his considerable business elsewhere.

Henry was still the boss, so Rae asked if he was

willing to lose one of his best customers for $60. "Well, of course not," Henry replied, thinking the query was purely hypothetical. Rae then explained the problem, and Henry did a quick reversal. "I don't care, Rae, he owes the money and should pay." Frustrated, Rae paid the $60 himself and saved an important customer for Henry, who died believing he had been right.

It did not take Rae long to learn why Henry insisted that he concentrate his selling efforts in rural Saline County. The reason involved a common practice used by lumberyards and other businesses throughout the Midwest and other regions to ensure profits. The owners of the yards orally agreed to set prices and divide the sales in a given area. Thus, competition was eliminated and the public paid whatever prices were set by the "pool" or local cartel. While the practice was clearly illegal under the Sherman Antitrust Act of 1890, old habits, especially profitable ones, are not easily set aside.

The five Salina lumberyard owners met privately for lunch once a month in the back room of a local restaurant. They disclosed their sales figures to each other, agreed on who was entitled to what sales volumes the next month, and set their bids and prices so that the lagging yards could catch up. There were frequent disputes over whether the sales figures reported were accurate, and from time to time, the conspirators would part ways for brief periods. Before long the crafty businessmen would kiss and make up. Competition not only resulted in less profits, but one had to work for them.

The Salina "pie" consisted of the city limits. Anything beyond them was fair game, which was why Rae spent 10 or 12 hours a day, 6 days a week, on the county's back roads. Even Sundays were not totally idle. It was not unusual to see the five lumberyard owners out for buggy rides reconnoitering city streets for new excavations and ensuring that one of them was accountable for the lumber by the time the framing started.

When Salina pioneer and family patriarch Herman Sudendorf died in his home of 43 years on April 3, 1913, full ownership of the Salina lumberyard, another in McPherson, several farms, and the stock controlling the Western Star Mill, then operated by Edward, passed equally to his sons. Both Henry and Edward drew comfortable salaries from the businesses they managed. While neither was active in those oper-

4896

Rae (lower left) and Leila (right) vacationing with friends before Royce was born in 1910.

ated by the other, the brothers received a fixed annual return of six percent on their ownership equities in the lumberyard and the remaining profits were divided. By 1916, Rae was receiving 25 percent of the lumberyard profits after the interest payments on ownership capital were made, and Henry and Edward divided the remaining 75 percent.

A drawing of family patriarch Herman Sudendorf appeared in the *Salina Journal* two years before his death in 1913. *Salina Journal*

Rae believed, with justification, that his efforts were responsible for the resurgence and continuing success of the lumberyard since 1907. Four additional teams and wagons had been added to handle deliveries, and interest and profit shares had been paid regularly. Although Rae ran the lumberyard and was compensated well for doing so, he had waited three years following Herman's death for an invitation to become an owner or partner — at a price, of course — but there was no such offer. Even if it would never come, Rae believed he was entitled to a larger share of the year-end profits than Edward, who had nothing to do with the success of the lumberyard or the profits it generated.

If his father-in-law was again waiting to be asked, Rae accommodated him. It was early 1916 when he approached Henry, who was then 63. Rae raised the matter as diplomatically as he could, pointing out his achievements, the fact that he was virtually managing the business, and that Edward had no impact on its success but still took home half again as much profit. At a minimum, the profits should be divided equally in thirds.

Despite the validity of Rae's arguments, Henry was unmoved. He rejected the request out of hand without even suggesting that he would consider the matter or discuss it with his brother. Henry also sought to quell the anger welling in his son-in-law with ill-chosen words: "Well, Rae, you know, Edward *is* family."

Rae would discuss the confrontation with his sons over the years, but he could not clearly recall if he had responded to his father-in-law or, if he did, what he had said — only that he left the office numb. He remembered thinking, but not necessarily saying, "Well, what am I? I've been married to your only daughter for ten years and I'm the father of your grandchildren."

## *Chapter 5*

# Family Feud

*ORDINARILY, Rae was not one to act impulsively. Even his quick decisions were seldom reached without careful thought, the balancing of pros and cons, and a back-up position. Whether he gave such consideration to resigning from the Sudendorf lumberyard is not known. Presumably, Rae had decided what he would do if his proposal was rejected. On the other hand, Rae believed that Henry's inept and impromptu rebuff had exposed his father-in-law's truest feelings. He would always be an outsider. Rae was a proud man. He had no choice but to quit. With mixed emotions of anger, trepidation, and pleasure, he did.*

*Whether Henry sought to soothe his fuming son-in-law with a belated offer, promises, or a sincere apology did not matter. The damage was done. Perhaps Henry thought Rae would come around after cooling down. Indeed, what else could he do at age 38? Rae's income, including his share of profits, was high enough that he could not match it elsewhere. Henry (albeit at Rae's prodding) had seen to that, and he now counted on it to bring Rae back. But Henry wasn't the first to misjudge his son-in-law, and this would not be the last time he did.*

*Revenge is a relentless motivator. Rae knew the Salina lumberyard business. If he could generate enough business to provide ample salaries for Henry and himself, fixed annual returns on the Sudendorf brothers' ownership equities, and addi-*

The Missouri-Pacific railroad station was one block north of the Rearwin Lumber and Coal Company.

tional profits to divide at year's end, there was no reason he could not do the same for himself. Indeed, Salina could use another lumberyard, one that R. A. Rearwin would open with about $9,000 in savings and a loan of $12,000 from the Planters State Bank.

Rae leased a vacant 125- by 250-foot livery stable on the northwest corner of Santa Fe Avenue and Elm Street from John Schippel. The site was just two blocks north of the center of town and one block south of the railroad tracks — an ideal location. It even had a small office. The R. A. Rearwin Lumber Company opened its doors in 1916, becoming the sixth lumberyard in town. Rae had no illusions that he would be welcomed by the owners of the other five, particularly his father-in-law, or that he would be invited to their monthly luncheons. It didn't matter. He wasn't fond of the "pie." He was well known and liked in the community. With hard work he would earn a fair share — maybe more — of the business, whether his competitors liked it or not. At least he planned on it.

R.A.REARWIN

LUMBER, COAL AND PETROLEUM PRODUCTS

SALINA, KANSAS

The Rearwin letterhead, 1926.

What Rae did not count on was the response of the other yards set in motion by his father-in-law. Henry would teach the ingrate a thing or two about the lumber business. Just as the five yards had agreed in the past to divide the Salina lumber business in order to avoid competition and ensure profits, they would now cut prices to the bone if necessary, and drive the upstart out of business before one could say "such tactics are illegal."

The next two years or so were a period of ironic justice for the lumber and building material customers of Salina and the surrounding area. After years of on-again, off-again price fixing, lumber prices were successively trimmed, shaved, and slashed to force Rae to close his barely opened doors. Time would prove, however, that Henry had again underestimated his son-in-law. This time he had drawn in the other lumberyard owners, although certainly without objection. They were not exactly thrilled with the idea of a sixth lumberyard in town, especially if it was owned by that "comer" who had resurrected Henry's sleepy operation a decade earlier.

Rae sized up the situation. Although he had no choice but to reduce prices and did so, he knew he could not win on their field. In the long run — and that could be very short — the other lumberyards had the resources to outlast him. What Rae needed was staying power, the ability to remain in the fray long enough to at least bring the others to their knees with him. The time would come when someone would throw in the towel, but Rae could not be the first. In the meantime, he needed another source of income to cover the note at the bank and feed his family.

Leila, of course, was caught in the crossfire. Both Rae and Henry instinctively understood the dilemma and insulated her as best they could. Although Rae and Henry refused to enter each other's homes or to speak when they passed on the street for over two years, the feud had no impact on young Royce or Ken. Both were oblivious to the tensions that filled the atmosphere above their youthful heads. They simply trekked back and forth between both homes at will, while their mother walked a tightrope.

While Henry was a ruthless businessman who fully intended to drive his son-in-law into submission or bankruptcy, he was also a considerate father who would not expect his only daughter to align with him or be offended if she openly supported her husband. Henry was a family man with firm 19th-century values about a wife's role and duties. They transcended a daughter's loyalty to her parents. But Leila did not take sides, and that was also fine with Rae. He was not so foolish as to expect or require his wife to make such a choice.

The search for supplemental income lead Rae to contact the Trailmobile Company of Cincinnati, Ohio, about a dealership. The company manufactured a line of commercial, steel-framed trailers that were designed to be pulled in tandem behind the primitive automobiles and trucks of the day, thus doubling or tripling the capacity of a single flat-bed or boxed vehicle. The trailer was attached to the rear of the tow vehicle by a tongue. The bed, which could be staked on all four sides or left open, rolled on spoked wheels, which themselves rolled on steel ball bearings. The wheels were covered with hard rubber that was impervious to the widespread litter of horseshoe nails, and the front ones turned with the tongue.

The trailers not only saved time and increased capacity, but they cost just $375, about one-third the price of a single-bed truck.

Rae knew farmers. He was raised as one, sold them new and used machinery for several years, and served them for a decade while working for Henry. He also knew their needs and problems and spoke their language. Most farmers still used wagons and teams to deliver wheat to the mills and for other hauling chores. It was an agonizingly slow process. Many, of course, owned touring cars, tractors, or even small trucks, but none were suitable for hauling wheat, corn, livestock, or farm machinery. Rae believed there was an untapped market for the Trailmobile, and he got his dealership. Now all he had to do was sell them.

Youngsters Royce (left) and Ken were unaware of the 1916-1918 family feud.

Rae worked in his new lumberyard during regular business hours, selling only at a profit, however small. Let the others sell at a loss. After hours and on Sundays he hooked a trailer behind his auto and headed for the familiar back roads of Saline County, occasionally with one or both young sons beside him. Initially, sales were slow. It seemed no one wanted to be the first to take the plunge. Well, maybe it was time for a little advertising. Rae hooked a pair of loaded trailers to his car and sped off through the heart of Salina at something in excess of the 15 mile-an-hour speed limit. By prior arrangement, a policeman friend nabbed the lawbreaker while another friend who worked for one of Salina's two newspapers "happened by" on schedule to record the capture. The event was duly reported with photographs the following day.

But the lumber dealer didn't wait for the phone to ring. He took to the back roads again, this time with copies of the "embarrassing" news story that resulted in much thigh-slapping. The photo was impressive. One sure could pile the stuff high on those trailers, and 15 miles an hour was maybe five times faster than a team could pull a loaded wagon. Perhaps there was something to those trailers after all. Maybe one or two could be towed behind the Overland, Ford, or Dodge. That sure could save time; it was hard to argue with that Rae Rearwin. He made sense when it came to talking money.

A small truck and a single Trailmobile loaded with alfalfa. Rae is in the center.

The farmers of Saline County, if they had cash or credit, soon owned Trailmobiles and proudly found themselves on the cutting edge of agricultural transportation. As often as not, they also had Rae pile on some lumber or other building materials. It didn't seem right to have the new trailers de-

Rae is seated at the front of the loaded Trailmobile, *circa* 1920; others are unidentified.

livered empty, and the price of lumber now sure was cheap!

The Salina Trailmobile dealer also established a network of sub-dealers or agents in scattered parts of northern Kansas, and split his commission when the trailers were paid for and delivered. One trailer sold another, and more than 100 were sold in one 12-month period. Rae earned over $10,000 in commissions that year, as well as a diamond pin from the ecstatic manufacturer. Even more would be sold in the next year or so.

Salina farmer Freida Hepner replaced a dozen teams that ate hay year-round with three Trailmobiles. The Salina Alfalfa & Meal Company bought one. And George Stuart hauled his engraved monuments to the cemetery in a Trailmobile.[1] Even those who could not afford to purchase one were not left out. Rae bought four himself and entered the contract hauling business. During the harvest season, a driver would drop off a pair of empty trailers at one farm, return to town and pick up a second pair to leave at another, and then return to the first and haul the trailers loaded with wheat to a mill or elevator. The driver was so busy that Rae bought a second Ford Roadster and a three-quarter-ton truck. Everyone, it seemed, was happy, except five of Salina's six lumberyard owners.

Testimonials praising the Trailmobile and local dealer Rae Rearwin poured into the company's headquarters in Cincinnati. If it was noticed that Kansas farmers spelled as well as any schoolteacher, seemed to use similar phrases, and were all high on praise for their Salina dealer, the company didn't mind. The letters made good advertising copy:

> . . . with my Dodge touring car pulling a no. 60 Trailmobile purchased from R. A. Rearwin in Salina I can haul a net weight of 4,000 pounds quite easily running at a high rate of about fifteen to eighteen miles per hour.

Meanwhile, the Salina lumberyard cartel, until now held together mainly by Henry's influence and ill-will, was crumbling. The other owners found it more and more difficult to squeeze a living from their operations, and they didn't have the kind of resources that Henry had inherited from his father. With increasing frequency they told Henry they were pushing water uphill with a broom. It must have been an interesting session when they finally informed Henry in late 1918 that it was time to wave the white flag. He had gotten them into the pickle — for their own good, of course — but it was now time he bailed them out, also for their own good. If he didn't, they would. The Great War in Europe was over, and there was room enough for everyone. If there wasn't, maybe Henry should retire. After all, he was at that age.

Surrender by the Salina lumberyards didn't come too soon for Rae. The easiest Trailmobile sales had been made, the local market was nearly saturated, trucks were improving, and a few farmers figured out

Rae used a Trailmobile rather than a wagon and team to deliver building materials.

they could buy the components and make a comparable wagon of wood at about half the price.

Henry made the overture, and his son-in-law gracefully accepted. The feud ended without fanfare or recriminations, but Rae did not delude himself into believing that he was family. If he gloated in triumph, he did so inwardly with the knowledge that, like the war that had just ended, there were losses on both sides. Satisfaction was savored in silence. The look in Henry's eyes was confession enough that he had misjudged the dirt farmer's son from Lincoln.

Rae was invited to the monthly luncheons to talk about restoring the health of the Salina lumberyard industry. If the citizens of Saline County thereafter noticed a gradual but steady increase in the prices of lumber products, they took it in stride. It was, they were told, due to heavy postwar demand and unscrupulous wholesalers who were cashing in on the dawning of the decade that appropriately would be called "the Roaring Twenties."

Rae (standing) speaks with a customer towing a pair of Trailmobiles behind a Hudson, *circa* 1918.

## *Chapter 6*

# The Twenties Man

*THE '20s were good years for the Rae Rearwin family — indeed, for most of the country.*

*As the curtain rose on the decade, the postwar housing boom was still unspent and farmers were feeding Europe wheat and corn at record prices. The horse economy of the past millennium was surrendering to the motor carriage, and a man strangely named "Ruth" was hitting more home runs than entire teams. Fortunes were made overnight in oil and gas fields from Appalachia to Amarillo, and the stock market was making barons of beggars.[1] And even those who had never tippled when it was legal relished thwarting the purposes of the "Volstead Act," which had closed the nation's breweries and distilleries.*

*The lumber business in Salina was also "roaring." The owners of the six lumberyards could be seen on any given Sunday patrolling the city's new residential areas for basement excavations. Both Royce and Ken recall the rides in a seven-passenger Cadillac sedan. Rae and Henry sat in front, while Mother and Grandmother properly rode in back. The boys sat on jump seats that sprouted from the floorboards. It would still be many years before they learned that the outings were for more than ice cream and sodas.*

*For Rae Rearwin, however, there was never a time to stand pat. He built and opened a filling station adjacent to the lumberyard, remodeled and doubled the size*

This family portrait was used as the passport photo for a trip to Europe in 1926. Kenneth is on the left, Royce on the right.

The population of Salina was about 15,000 when this photograph of Santa Fe Avenue was taken in the early 1920s.

Salina Historical Society, Salina, KS

Rae erected this filling station on Elm Street adjacent to the lumberyard office in 1926.

of the lumberyard office, and entered the heating business, offering three grades of coal. The four Trailmobiles were sold and replaced with large International trucks that delivered coal, lumber, and an expanded line of building materials. Within a few years another lumber shed and a three-truck garage were added.

Rae was a born saver for a rainy day, and always would be. He quickly accumulated sufficient savings to keep his family afloat through a deluge of Biblical proportions. But idle time and money bordered on sin, and thus much of the savings, in the manner of its maker, went to work. Rae invested in Salina real estate that could be rented to earn its way and in vacant lots that promised a reasonable return when sold. Because the lumberyard property was leased, Rae also had his eye on part of the 300 block of North Santa Fe Avenue and the 300 block of North Fifth Street (one street east) as a backup site. He purchased several contiguous properties on both streets.

The Smoky Hill River occasionally flooded North Santa Fe Avenue.

Salina Historical Society, Salina, KS

Rae later built two commercial buildings on Santa Fe Avenue across from the lumberyard. The first, a one-story brick structure, was erected in 1924 at a cost of about $18,000. It was profitably leased to a Topeka grocery wholesaler, Lux Mercantile. The second, a three-story brick warehouse called the "UP" building because it abutted a Union Pacific rail siding, was built in 1926 at a depreciable cost of just over $31,000, exclusive of land. It was promptly leased to Goodyear Tire for five years. Both ultimately returned their cost several times over, and so-called "depreciation" meant cash flow.

Rae built this structure on North Santa Fe Avenue in 1924 and leased it to Lux Mercantile long before Mama baked cookies there in the 1960s when this photo was taken.

Rae also invested conservatively in the common stocks of the Western Star Mill, the Planters State Bank (where he would become a director), and well-managed companies that he was convinced would not fail and which had a respectable dividend history. No horseshoe or harness manufacturers, thank you. The petroleum industry was his favorite. It was indisputable that the automobile would become the primary source of personal transportation — it fed on gasoline only when used, not oats all year around.

This three-story structure was built by Rae in 1926 at 316-320 North Santa Fe Avenue and leased to the Goodyear Tire Company.

Oil gushers, it seemed, were sprouting in Oklahoma and Texas like sunflowers. Rae wanted a chance at the *real* fortunes being made there. Leila, however, would not hear of it. Young children needed roots, stability, and both parents. The family was not going to bounce around Oklahoma, Texas, or wherever like ping pong balls searching for "black gold." Didn't they already have enough of the green, folding kind?

Domesticity prevailed. Rae settled for expanding the Salina business. He obtained a jobbers' contract from the Marland Oil Company of Ponca City (which was subsequently absorbed by Continental Oil), and added a tank truck to deliver gasoline, kerosene, and fuel oil to farmers and local homeowners. Without distor-

The office of the R. A. Rearwin Lumber Company, *circa* 1926; from left to right: Mildred Johnson, Rae, office manager Ted Brotherson, and bookkeeper Leslie Keever.

The Western Star Mill shipped bulk flour to Eastern brokers and produced "White Elephant" flour.

tion, he could sheepishly claim that he was in "the oil business."

Chance also resulted in Rae getting into the flour milling business early in the decade. The Sudendorf brothers' Western Star Mill had been operating around the clock shipping flour to brokers for sale overseas. It was a rare night during the milling season when a train loaded with flour did not start from Salina for East Coast shipping docks. But milled flour did not enjoy a long shelf life in those days, and in 1922 a group of brokers saw the chance to make a killing on several loads the Western Star Mill had shipped on their order. The banks, which held payments in escrow, released the funds only when they were notified by the brokers of acceptance.

The scam in this case involved the brokers refusing to accept Western Star flour sitting dockside in railroad cars. The Sudendorfs had few options. Recalling it to Salina was out of the question. Moreover, brokers could seldom use flour that had not been scheduled for delivery weeks or months in advance, so it could not be resold. Finally, the railway demurrage charges were so high that they would ultimately exceed the value of the cargo.

Desperate, Edward and Henry turned to someone they believed could solve the problem. They offered Rae a salaried position as a Western Star vice president and a reasonable block of stock. He promptly went East, put up his own money to retain the fiercest lawyers he could find, and forced the brokers, who had hoped to buy the stalled flour for pennies on the dollar, to release the payment for the flour that was held by the bank. There was no coronation, but there was no doubt among the brothers Sudendorf, the Rearwins, and those in the know that Rae had assumed the role vacated by Herman's death.

Postwar Europe's hunger was satisfied by 1923 or so, and the bottom fell out of the breadbasket grain markets. Edward was unprepared for that inevitable event. The Western Star Mill lost over $50,000 in a single year and failed to pay dividends for two years on its common

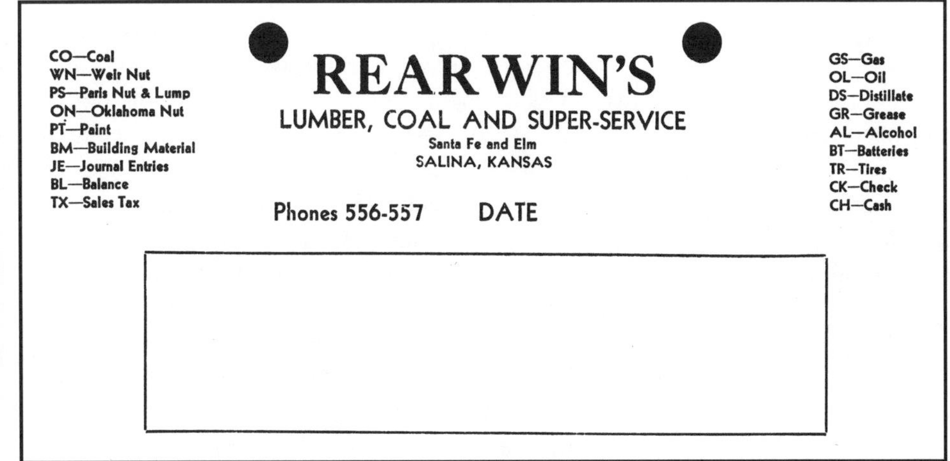

REARWIN'S

LUMBER, COAL AND SUPER-SERVICE

Santa Fe and Elm

SALINA, KANSAS

CO—Coal
WN—Weir Nut
PS—Paris Nut & Lump
ON—Oklahoma Nut
PT—Paint
BM—Building Material
JE—Journal Entries
BL—Balance
TX—Sales Tax

GS—Gas
OL—Oil
DS—Distillate
GR—Grease
AL—Alcohol
BT—Batteries
TR—Tires
CK—Check
CH—Cash

Phones 556-557 DATE

Henry and Carrie Sudendorf, Leila and Rae, and Kenneth and Royce, *circa* 1923.

stock, much of which was held by Salinans. Edward was not the most popular man at the Country Club, or in the barbershop either. He swallowed his pride and sought help from the mill's newest vice president, who served principally as a consultant.

Rae thrived on challenges as much as financial success. Applying business techniques that had somehow eluded Edward, Rae managed to turn the operation around and break even within a year while still profitably operating his own businesses.

In 1925, Rae convinced Edward and Henry that it was time they should sell their controlling stock. But who would buy it? There were already scores of mills on the brink of insolvency for sale across the Heartland. Rae Rearwin had sold a lot of things in his 47 years. A floundering flour mill, he reasoned, was no different from a used farm implement, a table, a trailer, a stick of lumber, or a drum of fuel oil. One simply needed to *find* the buyer, not wait for him to drop in out of the blue, and make the terms right. Perhaps, as he embarked on his newest challenge, he wondered why the obvious had not occurred to Edward.

Down Abilene way there was a "cracker-jack" flour broker named John Vanier — or so Rae had heard. If the rumors were true, why shouldn't John own his own mill? Rae invited Vanier to Salina to look at the Western Star Mill. Before he left, Vanier owned the controlling interest, which included Rae's stock, all of his father-in-law's, and a big chunk, but not all, of Edward's.

The terms of sale were not complex if one understood leveraged financing *and* trusted the buyer. Most of the mills on the market were family-owned and so deep in red ink that the owners needed the full purchase price at the time of sale. They could ill afford to sell a failing business on credit to someone they were convinced would likewise fail. Such reasoning, of course, was why most mills remained unsold.

The former farm implement salesman, however, had studied his prospect. Rae learned that Vanier had discovered the secret to selling flour when others couldn't, just as the former Beebe & Runyon furniture salesman had done. Instead of using outside commissioned salesmen, whose expenses increased prices and reduced profits, Vanier sold it himself over crackling telephone lines. It was simple; he could sell flour faster and cheaper than his competitors. Rae had confidence in that kind of businessman. Indeed, he faced one in the mirror every morning. He also knew that the majority owners of the Western Star, himself included, did not need the purchase money up front. They could sell on installments, which was necessary to make the deal viable for Vanier. Rae was convinced that Vanier was honest and would not go belly-up and leave them with notes useful only as fireplace kindling.

Rae continued to watch Vanier — not because he was concerned about payment, but because he suspected money could be made in his wake. Within a year, Rae advised Edward and Henry that they should start repurchasing all of the Western Star stock they could find, which wasn't hard to do. Local owners were unhappy and ready to sell. They had not received dividends for several years and the price of milling stocks, including the Western Star, had continued to fall. Rae bought heavily at prices well below what he had sold for. Edward bought sparingly. Henry again underestimated his son-in-law and stubbornly sat on the sidelines. Within a few years Vanier became one of the largest flour barons of the era, and Rae and Edward were handsomely rewarded. Indeed, the Western Star Mill paid dividends throughout the Great Depression.

But life was not an endless series of business

deals, even for Rae Rearwin. He was also a family man who somehow made time to take his wife and growing sons on vacation trips every year from 1920 through 1928. The first, in a Buick touring car, was to Colorado and Estes Park where, as in the airports and sports stadiums of the last decade of the century, the prices of food and beverage were severe: 25 cents for a cup of coffee that sold elsewhere for a nickel or was free with a two-bit sandwich. The itinerary also included Colorado Springs, Pikes Peak, and the gold and silver mines of Cripple Creek.

In 1922 the family trained to Chicago and to Detroit, where Rae took delivery of a new Cadillac. Ken, who was almost nine, remembers touring the factory and, in particular, hearing the horn testing. An installed horn that didn't have the distinctive Cadillac tone was immediately replaced. The trip continued by night steamer across Lake Erie, with the new automobile aboard, then to Niagara Falls and the Buffalo area, where the Salina Rearwins met for the first time the branches of the family tree that John and Elizabeth Rearwin had left behind some four decades earlier.

Royce, who by age 12 had earned a deserved reputation as a prankster, convinced his Buffalo cousins that Indians still roamed the Kansas prairie and that it was unlikely the family would get back to Salina without an arrow or two in the Cadillac's tires or radiator. The trip continued to Boston, New York City, Philadelphia, and Washington, D.C., and included an historical tour and handshakes all around during a meeting with President Warren G. Harding that had been arranged by an Army general Rae had met on the street.

The 1924 vacation included a ride across Canada from Winnipeg on the Canadian Pacific Railroad with stops in Lake Louise and Banff, as well as a tour of the Pacific Northwest, where the raging issue of the time was whether a certain snow-covered peak should be named "Mount Tacoma" or "Mount Rainier." The trip continued south through California and then east toward Kansas, with mule rides to the bottom of the Grand Canyon for all but Leila.

In 1926, the family toured Europe. En route they attended the Shriner's convention in Philadelphia and the opening of the nation's sesquicentennial celebration; they then sailed in June from New York on the SS *President Harding*. They visited France, Italy, Switzerland, Austria, Belgium, and, of course, Germany, by rail and motorcar. They would leave for home from England, the last stop on the ten-week odyssey.

Rae learned of a scheduled air service from Brussels to London and persuaded Leila that air travel was quite safe. Royce and Ken needed no convincing. Unfortunately, the flight was canceled because of bad weather. The men of the family were disappointed, but if Leila had known how rough the Channel crossing would be by ferry, she might have been more eager to fly. "The trip of a lifetime" was the last such adventure the family would make.

Rae was by now supporting his aging parents, who had retired to Lincoln from the land they had worked for nearly 40 years. He was also an active member of the local Kiwanis Club and the Salina Country Club, where he occasionally played golf with his sons or friends Bert Breon, Mel Shaible, and Chet Housel. In the fall and winter he hunted rabbit, duck, and quail with Royce and Ken, both of whom later competed as successful marksmen in college and in private gun clubs.

If there was a sour note for Rae during the decade, it had been ringing unnoticed since 1926. Even then, it had to be brought to his attention which, starting in 1928, had been increasingly focused on aircraft manufacturing. As teenagers, Royce and Ken took their turns working at the lumberyard and the filling station during their spare time. One day in 1929, 16-year-old Ken playfully ribbed Ted Brotherson, the lumberyard manager, asking how it was that Leslie Keever, a subordinate bookkeeper, could drive a new Oldsmobile when Brotherson drove an old Ford. Ken impertinently asked, "Don't you make more than Les?"

Brotherson assured the meddling teenager he did earn more, and suggested that Keever, an alderman who attended Brotherson's church, probably didn't pay as much on his mortgage. But Brotherson thought about the matter briefly and raised the subject with Rae. An accountant was called in to audit the books during the evenings. Within a few nights it was confirmed that someone had been stealing. Rae gathered four key employees, including Brotherson and Keever, in his office, and told them the thefts had been discovered and the guilty party should own up.

Keever asked everyone else to leave and, in the melodramatic style of the flickering motion pictures of the period, confessed. Keever actually dropped to his knees, wrapped his arms around his employer's legs, and through tearful sobs begged to be forgiven. He admitted to taking $12,000 since 1926, but said he could pay it back if Rae would forego criminal charges. Several days later he presented Rae with two checks totalling $12,000 that were promptly endorsed and deposited.

The full audit took several weeks. The embezzlement actually amounted to more than $25,000, including between $8,000 and $9,000 dollars over the prior 12 months. In the meantime, Keever transferred the title to the Oldsmobile and the deed to his home to his wife, hired a high-priced criminal lawyer from Hutchinson (who, no doubt, was paid up front), and prepared to avoid prison by suing Rae to get "his" $12,000 back.

During the criminal trial it was determined that two years earlier Keever had paid off his mortgage at Cravens Savings and Loan, where Rae was a director, after business hours with several thousand dollars in fives, tens, and twenties. Rae was justifiably upset with the loan officer who had not become suspicious of such payments by the $150-a-month bookkeeper. It also developed that Keever had invested several thousand dollars in Cities Service stock, one of the high-flyers of the period. It had doubled or tripled in value, and Keever had sold it at a substantial profit to repay the $12,000.

Keever testified that he had obtained the money to pay off his mortgage, buy the new Olds, and purchase the stock from his father, who, it turned out, was actually supported by Keever. He also testified that he had given Rae the checks not to repay stolen money, but to invest for him. Indeed, the back of the canceled checks produced at his trial had the words "For Fairfax Airport Stock" written just above Rae's endorsements. But the prosecutor produced several witnesses who testified that Rae had advised them against buying the stock as too speculative. More importantly, it was apparent with a magnifying glass that the lower portions of two letters (the second "f" in Fairfax and the "p" in Airport) crossed over and on top of Rae's endorsements, meaning the words were added *after* Rae had signed the checks.

Keever was sentenced to three years and served the full term. He also lost his civil action. But that didn't help Rae, who was still out more than $13,000. He rightfully blamed himself for being too trusting, failing to recognize and heed the signals, and neglecting to conduct periodic audits. But Rae had been fortunate. If the embezzlement had been discovered just a few months later, after the stock market crash in October, Keever would not have been able to repay a dime.

*Part Two*

# The Airplane Years: 1928-1942

The owner of Ken-Royce NC12579, built in 1933, is unidentified, but he apparently preferred a tailskid over a tailwheel for landing on sod fields.

*Chapter 7*

# The Aircraft Decision — The Ken-Royce Biplane

*LIKE ACORNS, little things lead to bigger ones. Rae's decision to enter aircraft manufacturing is clearly traceable to the family's 1926 European vacation. Before departing, he had instructed Ted Brotherson, his lumberyard manager, to place a lien against an apartment project if the materials bill was not paid by a certain date, but Brotherson failed to do so. A legal squabble followed, but the debtor had sold the property to an innocent purchaser protected by law. In satisfaction of the debt, Rae ended up owning a dilapidated house in Wichita that was in need of personal attention and repair.*

*Wichita is about 95 miles south of Salina on U.S. Route 81, and Rae disliked making the all-day round trip alone. Teenagers Royce and Ken took turns going along to do the driving in the summer of 1927. The Lindbergh flight, of course, had taken place only weeks before, and aviation was the primary topic of discussion. The sons pleaded to visit Wichita's several aircraft factories, and Rae himself was curious. On one occasion, he and his sons took their first flights in a Travel Air biplane.*

*While the trips were pleasant outings for the teenagers, Rae was a studious observer of the near-frenzied activity at the factories and the pilots pitching pennies as they waited for their aircraft. He visited the plants frequently, took repeated* tours as a prospective aircraft buyer, asked insightful questions, and made mental notes. It was fascinating, building a flying machine from spruce, steel tubing, cotton fabric, aluminum, thread, and glue.

Rae also saw waste and inefficiency that would have curled his hair if he had been in charge. He learned that the owners were not businessmen or engineers, but mostly pilots. Slowly he convinced himself that, as in the auto and oil industries, there was money to be made in aircraft manufacturing — particularly, he thought, by employing tried and true business practices. It mattered not that he was neither pilot nor engineer; those skills could be hired. He was a successful businessman, something that wasn't so easy to come by.

Discreet inquiries were made about buying into one or more of the Wichita firms, but none seemed to need fresh money. Indeed, Travel Air stock had shot from $50 to $200 in a year. What the firms really needed were skilled woodworkers, welders, and mechanics. That, too, was a good sign.

Rae Rearwin, *circa* 1928.

Just as there had been room for a sixth lumber dealer in Salina, Rae believed there was room in the sky for another aircraft, particularly a fast, well-built one. He still regretted letting the oil field opportunities in Oklahoma and Texas pass him by. Many investors had become incredibly wealthy, and he had been left behind. But not this time. His sons were older now, and airplanes could be built in Salina, perhaps in the old automotive garage he owned on Sante Fe Avenue across from the lumberyard.

Royce, the older son, was finishing his last year in high school. He had inherited his father's aptitude for things mechanical and was ecstatic with the decision. Indeed, he was planning to enroll in Kansas Wesleyan in the fall to become a mechanical engineer. Ken, at 15, was less enthusiastic, but certainly not uninterested. A Rearwin aircraft factory would increase his celebrity and stature among Salina's teenage feminine populace.

Leila, however, was not so pleased. She thought Rae should stick to what he knew — lumber, coal, gasoline, and fuel oil — and she said so. But Rae would not be swayed. Leila had had her way when he wanted to chase oil. Now it was his turn. Besides, Rae assured his wife, he would drop out in a year or two if the new business wasn't successful. While her husband set out to build airplanes, Leila consoled herself with the knowledge that at least the work could be done in Salina.

Rae decided that the airplane would be built in the garage across from the lumberyard, but a qualified engineer was needed. He had met Herb Rawdon, the assistant chief engineer at Travel Air, during his tours of the Wichita plants and was impressed by him. But Rawdon, involved in designing the Travel Air Model R Mystery Ship, was happy where he was and suggested another young engineer.

Fred Landgraf was born in Chicago on November 1, 1903, six weeks before the Wright Flyer flew at Kitty Hawk, North Carolina, for 12 seconds and 120 feet. He was raised in Colorado and earned a degree in mechanical engineering at Colorado State University before landing a job with the Alexander Eaglerock Airplane Company in Englewood in June 1926. Young Al Mooney had left Eaglerock to design the Montaque Monoplane in Marshall, Missouri, and Landgraf was assigned to drafting and stress analysis by Mac Short, an MIT graduate engineer from Salina. Short was acting as a contract consultant to Eaglerock president J. Don Alexander.

Mooney returned to Eaglerock in December, and he and Landgraf were independently assigned to adapt the airframe for the new Wright J5 engine. Landgraf's conversion was acceptable, but Mooney's was simpler and less expensive. Landgraf moved on to Travel Air in the spring of 1927 and was assigned to design drafting and performance analysis.

Rae outlined his plans to Landgraf. A week later, the young engineer presented Rae with preliminary drawings of three aircraft, including a pair of biplanes that faintly resembled the popular Eaglerock. One was a tandem-seater with a 90 hp engine, the other a three-place craft requiring an engine of 125 to 200 hp. The third was an enclosed

Left and below: A crew of nine built the Ken-Royce prototype in this vacant garage at 342 North Santa Fe Avenue. The building has since been razed and is now the site of an auto dealership. Identified employees include Salina helper Harold Penix at far left; coatless designer Fred Landgraf with right arm on wing; welder Smokey Nelson in background to left of Landgraf; young and tall draftsman Jack Clark; Bill Hauselman and wood worker Robert Carver in white shop coat and tie.

CODES:
ACME · BENTLEY'S
A.B.C. 6TH

CABLE ADDRESS:
"REARWIN"

Ken Royce

REARWIN AIRPLANES, INC.

FAIRFAX AIRPORT

KANSAS CITY,
KANSAS

USA

Rearwin used different stationery — letterhead — for replying to prospects about different aircraft.

two-place monoplane, with cantilever wings, in the 60 to 80 hp range.

Rae already knew what he wanted in an aircraft — a sleek, streamlined shape that was as fast as it looked — and it had to carry two passengers for barnstorming. Landgraf favored the monoplane because of the closed cabin and the aerodynamic advantages of a single wing and fewer struts. "Besides," he added, "everyone is building biplanes; there is less competition in monoplanes." The lumber dealer reportedly snapped, "Competition doesn't bother me; we'll build the biplane with three seats." Whether the decision was made that quickly or in response to what Rae perceived as a challenge is doubtful.

Only mothers-in-law and business partners have unerring foresight. In the spring of 1928, biplanes were still the overwhelming choice of sportsmen pilots and barnstormers. Indeed, Travel Air, Swallow, Waco, and American Eagle, among others, were selling the two-wingers in record numbers. In 1927, more than three biplanes were built for every monoplane. Although that ratio would shrink in 1928 to about 2.25 to 1 and again in 1929 to 1.5 to 1, such statistics were in the future. At the time, Rae's decision to build a biplane was not unreasonable.

Rae gave Landgraf a desk in the lumberyard office in May, and they went over design issues, staffing, materials, production costs, and timing. Workmen also prepared the vacant garage, while Rae took the family east on a month's "vacation" to visit as many aircraft factories as he could. They made inspection tours of the Nicholas-Beazley plant in Marshall, Missouri, the Curtiss-Robertson plant near St. Louis, one near Cincinnati, and the Waco facility in Troy, Ohio, before heading north.

In Dearborn, Michigan, Rae arranged a plane ride (Leila's first) in a Ford Trimotor for the entire family. Moving west, they stopped at the Velie Motors works in Moline, Illinois, where the new Monocoupe 70 was in production; at the Lincoln-Page plant in Lincoln, Nebraska; and at the Arrow Aircraft Company in nearby Havelock. Rae asked probing questions about manufacturing methods, engines, costs, and other details. He was not viewed as a competitor but simply as an inquisitive potential purchaser, so he generally got answers. By the time the Rearwins returned to Salina, the budding aircraft builder had a book full of notes and a head swimming with ideas. Landgraf had completed a good portion of the engineering analysis, the garage was ready, and Rae was itching to get underway.

The drafting and detail engineering was done by 20-year-old John J. "Jack" Clark, a numbers whiz recruited from Travel Air. Clark was born in Arkansas City (pronounced "R-Kansas City"), Kansas, in 1908, but was raised in Wichita. He completed all of the drafting, math, and physical science courses offered by his high school and majored in electrical engineering for a year at the University of Kansas before running out of money.

On the first Saturday in June 1927, the lanky youth strolled confidently into the old Travel Air office on Wichita's West Douglas Street searching for a summer job. Lindbergh had set the country ablaze with his trans-Atlantic solo flight only weeks earlier. If Clark was going to work, it *had* to be in aviation.

Walter Beech and recently hired chief engineer Horace Weihmiller, an MIT graduate with Army Air Corps engineering experience at McCook Field in Dayton, were alone in the office.

Young Clark swallowed hard. "I'm looking for a job in your engineering department," he blurted out.

"Oh?" Weihmiller responded. "Have any experience?"

"Well, no," Clark admitted. Then brightened, "I've just done a year at KU and I'm willing to learn."

Weihmiller turned to Beech. "I can't use him," he shrugged.

Beech, observing the youth's deflation, thought a moment, then spoke. "What would you do if you were in the engineering department and were told to sweep the floor?"

"Why, I'd sweep the floor!" Clark responded quickly.

Beech winked at Weihmiller. "Well, he seems pretty smart to me, Horace. I think maybe we should hire him." Turning to Clark, Beech added, "My car is over at Winton's garage. Get it and bring it over here. And report to work Monday."

Clark started not as a suit-and-tie engineer, but as a general laborer. No matter; he had slipped through the magic door. He spent the first several weeks packing, loading, and moving equipment to Travel Air's new plant on East Central, and then toiled as a fuselage assembler installing seats, controls, and instruments in monoplanes ordered by National Air Transport (NAT). A few months later he learned Weihmiller was hiring draftsmen for a new project, the Model 6000. He applied, was hired to draw prints of aileron fittings at $30 a week, and never returned to KU.

In the spring of 1928 Landgraf confided to Clark that he was leaving Travel Air to become the chief engineer for a new aircraft company in Salina. He asked Clark to join him as his assistant and chief draftsman. The pay would be $35 a week. But Clark was courting his future wife Ramona and preferred to stay put. Weihmiller, however, refused to match Landgraf's offer, and Clark quit.

By Wichita standards, the factory facilities in Salina were meager. Clark and Landgraf were cramped in the front office of the old garage. Little of the equipment and tools abundant at Travel Air were available. Thus, the new biplane would be virtually handcrafted, a fact the pair kept in mind during their detail design, layout, and drafting work.

Landgraf also recruited a cadre of skilled workers from Wichita and Salina, including Bill Hauselman, a foreign-educated engineer-draftsman who toiled as a production worker; Smokey Nelson, a welder from Travel Air; Harold Penix and Robert Carver, both woodworkers from Salina; and two or three others.

Rae was in the shop several times a day, frequently with teenage sons Royce and Ken. Clark describes Rae as "an excellent businessman who ran a tight ship," which included a policy of personally approving all purchases. Although such control presumably resulted in economy, it occasionally backfired. On one occasion, Rae rejected the purchase of a special chisel costing about three dollars. Undaunted, Hauselman made one himself at a labor cost several times the price of a new one. Rae never knew.

The work went more slowly than expected, but there were few snags in the production of the first aircraft. The detail design work was uncomplicated and readily fabricated. If anything slowed the project, according to Clark, it was Rae's acute inquisitiveness, suggestions, and tinkering. He not only needed to know what was being done, but how and why. Rejection of a Rearwin idea also required justification and a convincing explanation. If the workers thought the owner was impatient and officious, they failed to recall who paid their salaries.

### *The Ken-Royce Prototype*

The graceful and tapering fuselage that emerged from the factory was clearly reminiscent of the Eaglerocks on which Landgraf had worked. It was constructed of welded chromium-molybdenum (chrome-moly) and low carbon steel tubing. A 35-gallon fuel tank was fitted just ahead of the front cockpit, while a second 20-gallon tank was installed in the center section of the top wing.

The wings, which used the Rhode-St. Genese airfoil, were made by Bob Carver, a Salina native with Wichita aircraft experience, using only a hand saw, joiner, circle saw, and glue pot. Royce, waiting to enter Kansas Wesleyan in the fall, pitched in on the jigs and, under Carver's guidance, made all but the tip ribs. The spars, made from laminated spruce, were ordered finished from a production mill that specialized in aircraft parts. The ribs used routed basswood webs with spruce cap strips. The leading edges were made of birch plywood, the trailing edges were of duraluminum, and the tips were steel-

The unmodified vertical stabilizer, which currently hangs in Royce Rearwin's Santa Barbara home, establishes this as the Ken-Royce prototype.

This photo of the still uncertified Ken-Royce prototype was taken before the vertical stabilizer was modified; note the tailwheel.

tubed. All of the woodwork was coated with a varnish-like material called "Lionoil." The entire structure was then covered with cotton fabric and doped.

Shock-absorbing struts containing oil and water were used on the split-axle landing gear, and 30x5-inch wheels incorporated Bendix brakes. The tail feathers (empennage) were conventional steel tubing, and the horizontal stabilizer was adjustable in flight. Push-pull tubes actuated the elevator, and steel cable was used for rudder control. Frieze-type ailerons actuated by both torque tube and cable were on the upper wing only. Controls were in the rear, and bucket seats were used to hold either four-inch leather cushions or seat-pack parachutes.

The prototype, designated X-44E, was fitted with the new six-cylinder Curtiss Challenger power plant rated at 170 hp at 1,800 rpm, but it would actually produce somewhat more. Rae received the ninth engine made. The cylinders were staggered on a two-throw crankshaft, the equivalent of having two three-cylinder engines mounted back-to-back. The short-stroke, large-bore engine had minimal frontal area. Three cylinders were fed from each barrel of a double-barreled Stromberg carburetor, while dual ignition was provided by a pair of high-tension Scintilla magnetos with two spark plugs in each cylinder.

Because the engine alone cost \$3,000, a reasonable profit dictated a selling price of about \$8,000. The Travel Air 4000 and the Alexander Eaglerock used the same engine but sold for \$6,275 and \$6,096. Although neither could keep up with the X-44E, nearly \$2,000 was a lot to pay for the additional speed.

Clark and several production workers were laid off in late 1928 as the prototype "Ken-Royce," named by Leila after her sons, neared completion. Such layoffs were routine in the early years of aircraft manufacturing. Clark returned to Travel Air, but at \$35 a week. Meanwhile, Landgraf celebrated the Salina birth of a daughter.

By the time the prototype was finished in early January 1929, hard winter had settled in. The flying weather was poor, and the new, unpaved flying field, frozen and snow-covered one week and too muddy the next, was considered unsafe. Pending improve-

An artist's rendering of the original Ken-Royce biplane was used extensively in advertising literature.

Left: Rearwin test pilot George Halsey, *circa* 1929.

Right: The first aircraft built in Salina, Kansas, was displayed in an auto dealer's showroom while Rae waited for the Salina weather to improve. John J. Clark

ment, the unflown biplane, painted "Dianna Cream," "International Orange," and black was displayed by Salina auto dealer Bert Breon. Much of the citizenry stopped by the showroom to ogle the first aircraft ever built in Salina, and Breon presumably sold an extra DeSoto or Plymouth.

George Halsey, a World War I pilot, barnstormer, and instructor with more than 2,000 hours in the air, was hired to make the first flight. Halsey was from nearby Culver. He had heard about the plane and had visited "the plant" on several occasions, frequently offering sage suggestions and advice.

The first flight was scheduled for the afternoon of Sunday, February 24, 1929. The weather was rotten. The rolling pasture was soggy and muddied in parts. The ragged ceiling was far less than 1,000 feet, and visibility was under three miles. Halsey considered conditions marginally suitable but was concerned the weather would worsen. The *Salina Journal* reported the next day:

> While it had not been planned to make a flight unless weather conditions were favorable, R. A. Rearwin, owner of the plane, and the pilot were both anxious to make a test and it was decided to disregard the weather. Mr. Halsey took off from the field shortly after noon, in a mud that motor cars could not traverse and which stuck to the wheels of the plane. After a run to the

Ken, on wing, and Royce exit the biplane named for them after their first ride on March 2, 1929.

> graded portion that had been arranged for the take off, the plane took to the air beautifully, soaring up out of sight of the ground. Due to the fact that the clouds were low, Mr. Halsey did not make a high flight; but while up, circled and maneuvered around making several bank tests at an altitude of 100 feet above the ground. In an ordinary plane, such a test would have been dangerous, but the pilot's confidence in the behavior of the Ken-Royce was such that he took a chance. The plane landed very easily, Mr. Halsey stated, the shock being so minimized that he did not know he had touched the ground.

Ken has a different recollection. He claims that Halsey disappeared into the low ceiling and that many were concerned he would come falling out in a spin.[1] Halsey probably flew briefly in layers or drooping shrouds. While those below may have temporarily lost sight of the plane, it is unlikely that Halsey lost sight of the horizon. Rae was furious and chastised Halsey for taking what he considered were unnecessary risks. The pilot, however, was too elated with the flight and the performance of the new ship to be bothered by Rae's anger. It would pass.

The *Journal* article continued:

> There was a large crowd to witness yesterday's flight, in spite of the fact that it had been advertised to be in the afternoon. With the thought in mind of the weather conditions getting worse, the flight was made earlier than had been planned. As soon as the weather is better, a second and longer flight will be made, thus permitting persons who were disappointed Sunday because of being too late for the flight, to see the plane perform under much better conditions.
>
> R. A. Rearwin, owner of the plane, had planned to go up yesterday, but the shortness of the flight did not permit this.

The second flight took place six days later on Saturday, March 2, without public fanfare. Royce and Ken rode in the plane while Halsey speed-tested it back and forth across section lines south of Salina.[2] Another public demonstration was held the next day from a grass field about a mile east of the Salina Country Club. Rae and Leila rode in front.

The following week, while Landgraf was in Washington, D.C., meeting with L. V. Gerber, the government's chief engineer, about certification, Halsey and Rae flew to Wichita and then to Kansas City, Missouri. The plane was demonstrated at Richards Field, where Halsey had once worked, and across the river at the new Fairfax Airport. Rae also met with the aviation committee of the Kansas City, Kansas, Chamber of Commerce about a possible plant site.

## *Chapter 8*

# Kansas City, Here I Come

*FOUR MONTHS before the first flight, Rae had announced plans to exhibit the biplane in December at the International Aircraft Show in Chicago, expand the Salina factory, and start work on a closed cockpit monoplane. The* ***Salina Journal*** *reported on November 10th, 1928:*

> *The airplane factory is located at 342 North Santa Fe Avenue. The building in which it is housed is to be extended at once to the alley back of it, in order to allow for construction of several planes at the same time and accommodate the increased force of workmen at the factory, Mr. Rearwin announced today. As soon as the present biplane is completed, work will start on designs for a monoplane of just as exclusive of design. When both ships have been thoroughly tested and found correct as to design, the models will be accepted as final for the Rearwin factory and production will begin on a large scale, Mr. Rearwin states.*

*Finished aircraft would have to be disassembled, trucked to the new but unfinished airport east of town, and reassembled, but there were offsetting advantages.*

The lumberyard was virtually across the street. Keeping on top of both enterprises would be easier than if the factory was located elsewhere. The investment required to expand the garage would also be less than acquiring land and putting up a new factory building. The money saved could be used as working capital. The biplane, however, was not completed in time for the Chicago exhibition, and the automotive garage was never enlarged.

The *Journal* announcement had raised the eyebrows of Salina's flour mill owners and other businessmen. The mills dominated Salina's economy and politics. Several owners were either on the Chamber of Commerce or the City Council, or controlled others who were. The mills also employed much of the area's skilled labor force at wages about half of what Rae paid his aircraft workers. The owners had an interest in maintaining the existing wage structure and stood to lose many skilled workers to the fledgling aircraft builder.

Rae was summoned to an off-the-record meeting with a self-appointed committee of city fathers intent on maintaining the *status quo*. They wished Rae well with his new venture, but without ambiguity suggested that it would be in the community's best interests, as well as his own, should he decide to locate his factory elsewhere. The invitation must have reminded Rae of his struggle with the Salina lumberyard cartel a decade earlier.

Rae was a long-time Salina merchant and intended to continue as one. He was also a director of the Western Star Mill, the Planters State Bank, and Cravens Savings and Loan. While he was surely rankled by the ultimatum, he understood it and kept his cool. More likely than not, the proud and pragmatic businessman sought to defuse the situation by telling the committee he had already decided to build elsewhere but had delayed the announcement pending selection of a site.

Although Rae considered Wichita, Denver, Moline, St. Louis, Tulsa, Kansas City (Missouri), Colorado Springs, and Oklahoma City, among others, no decision had been reached before the first flight. The *Salina Journal*, apparently unaware that the factory would be relocated, published an editorial the next day:

> The successful testing of a Salina airplane is no ordinary event. Someday it may be so, and let us hope that will be the case. Today, it marks a new departure in the history of Salina, an entrance into a field that not only is growing but which bids fair soon to take the world by storm.
>
> • • •
>
> The first Salina built, Salina designed, Salina named airplane is no trivial affair.
>
> • • •
>
> R. A. Rearwin, builder, exhibited the faith that wins in the construction of the ship. That faith was backed by an expenditure of thousands of dollars. This faith, as well as its successful result, deserves the encouragement of the city. It is worthy of more than a passing tribute. It is something in which the city can afford to interest itself greatly.

Rae finally decided on Kansas City, Kansas, where the new privately owned Fairfax Airport was under development by the Woods Brothers Corporation. American Eagle Aircraft, which had sold over a hundred biplanes in 1928, and two flight schools were already located there. With the flair of a seasoned politician, Rae announced his decision, which the *Journal* reported on March 13, 1929:

> Mr. Rearwin is now making plans to move his airplane factory from Salina to Kansas City, having purchased two and one-half acres of ground at Fairfax airport, Kansas City, Kan., securing a location which he considers the best on that fairway, situated across from the administration building and adjacent to the main entrance. Only a few details remain to be settled in connection with that move. If those details adjust themselves satisfactorily, Mr. Rearwin said today, he will transfer his factory from Salina to that city.

Many Salinans wanted the factory to stay in town, if not for the economic advantages it might provide, then as a matter of civic pride. Many proudly recalled that Glenn L. Martin, the "Flying Dude," Mac Short of Stearman, and Tom Braniff were their own.[1] Martin, although born in Mackburg, Iowa, had graduated from Salina elementary and high schools, worked in a local bicycle shop, and studied business for a year or two at Kansas Wesleyan before moving West. He had built his own plane in California and

Aviation pioneer Glenn L. Martin, center, considered Salina home.
Salina Historical Society, Salina, KS

Below: Martin returned to Salina by train in 1911 as an "exhibition flier." Here he readies his bamboo and wire plane for the first aircraft flight in Salina.
Kansas Room, Salina Public Library, Salina, KS

taught himself to fly before returning "home" as a barnstormer to make the first aircraft flights in Salina on October 31 and November 1 and 2, 1911.[2]

Rae believed that there might be an unwelcome impact on the lumber and fuel businesses if the community considered the move simple abandonment. There was also a need to muffle grumblings that the Chamber of Commerce had not done enough to keep the new business in town and to squelch budding rumors that the firm had actually been asked to leave. Rae also wanted to assure those who had urged the departure that he harbored no resentment. They must have marveled at his public relations genius as they read the balance of the *Journal* story. It was more a Madison Avenue campaign than a news article:

> I have arranged for ground space there with the full intention of going to that city with my fac-

tory, Mr. Rearwin stated, although I deeply regret moving from Salina. All my interests are in this city and have been for years. I would greatly prefer to develop the airplane industry into which I have entered in this city, but the advantages offered by the larger city cannot be overlooked. I feel that Kansas City will be the greatest aviation center in this entire section of the country, outranking Wichita. Because of its transcontinental air routes it is the logical place for such development in the airplane industry, as it can easily draw purchasers, so that sales prospects are much greater.

As far as my inclination is concerned, I desire to remain in Salina with my factory, but I cannot afford to wait for the development of the aviation opportunities here. The launching of a corporation for airplane manufacture is easier in a city like Kansas City, where people are already acquainted with the industry and its financial aspects. I more than appreciate the cooperation offered me here by the Chamber of Commerce which proffered everything within reason but the greater advantages of the larger center of trade outweighed those which Salina is able to offer at present, with her airport just being started. The location of the airport in this city, incidentally, I consider as good as any I have seen and as suitable to development. I believe Salina has an opportunity to get into the game right.

Ironically, everything reported was accurate. Except for the family's local ties, Kansas City was a far better choice in every respect for aircraft manufacturing than Salina. Rae must have reflected many times that despite their motives, the city fathers had actually done him a favor. The story continued:

Because the pioneer work in this form of airplane development is already done in Kansas City, launching a company of that size is easier there than it would be in Salina, Mr. Rearwin feels. Much interest has been shown in the Ken-Royce by men already in the airplane industry there. Another influencing factor lies in the fact that the Curtiss company now has a plant in Kansas City, is to conduct a flying school there and develop a sales organization of its own, all of which means the drawing of more purchasers. Since the Rearwin company uses the Curtiss motor that proves another feature of the contemplated Kansas City factory.

Mr. Rearwin will not dispose of any of his business interests in Salina, he states emphatically, intending to be here part of the time to look after his affairs, since the trip back and forth by air is only one hour and forty minutes. The family will continue to reside here for the present at least.

After a minor mishap, Martin made the first aircraft flight from Salina in the fall of 1911.
Kansas Room, Salina Public Library, Salina, KS

Leila was not pleased by the Kansas City decision. "For the present at least" meant that she would be expected to move there when Kenneth finished high school in two years. The move would indeed be more difficult for her than for Rae or her sons. She had lived in Salina all of her 47 years, enjoyed the comfort of being two doors from her aging parents, and was entrenched in Salina social circles and clubs.

Fairfax was located on marshy bottom land looped on two sides by the shifting Missouri River. The land grant rail-

The hangar and clubhouse at Sweeney Air-Port in the late 1920s. Identifiable aircraft visible include an Arrow Sport Pursuit, three Curtiss Jennys, a Travel Air, a Standard, and a Swallow. Wyandotte County Museum, Bonner Springs, KS

The Woods Brothers — Mark, George (standing), and Frank — owned the Arrow Sport Aircraft Company of Havelock, Nebraska, and built and developed Fairfax Airport at Kansas City, Kansas, in 1928-1930 as a privately owned stock company. The Woods Family

road property was owned by the Kansas City Industrial Land Company, a Union Pacific subsidiary, and had been the site of an air meet sponsored by the American Legion in 1921. One of the participants, E. J. Sweeney, considered the site suitable for a flying school and had leased it in 1923. Two years later, business was so good that he built a hangar that would hold six planes and a pilot's clubhouse. Students and pilots took off and landed in whatever direction the pasture was mowed, and by late 1928 about 1,200 pilots, many from other states and countries, had been trained at "Sweeney Air-Port."

In 1928, the Woods Brothers Corporation, consisting of Mark, George, and Frank, acquired about 1,000 acres of the 1,700-acre tract from the Union Pacific subsidiary, bought Sweeney out of his lease, and established "Fairfax Airport, Inc." The brothers were hooked on aviation. They owned Arrow Aircraft, Inc. of Havelock, Nebraska, which built the Arrow Sport line of biplanes, and believed that Kansas City, because of its central location, would soon become "the Air Hub of the Nation" for the emerging airline industry.

Through the sale of stock the Woods brothers intended to build the country's finest privately owned airport. It would include a dominant and luxurious passenger terminal, complete with "fine dining" facilities, a reflecting pool and fountains, and lush landscaping consisting of acres of flowering gardens, trees, and shrubs. Field facilities would include three fully lighted asphalt runways, one of them 7,000 feet long; beacons and flood lights; a control tower; a field-length tarmac; and three separate fueling locations. The boundary would also be flanked by flying

Fairfax Airport had been operating for several months before the formal dedication on August 3-4, 1929.

Wyandotte County Museum, Bonner Springs, Kansas

This photo of Fairfax Airport was taken during the dedication ceremony, but before completion of the main terminal. Note the autos parked along the adjoining roadways.

Wyandotte County Museum, Bonner Springs, KS

The Fairfax Terminal with the landscaped entrance.

The field side of Fairfax Terminal.

The waiting room of the Fairfax Terminal.

The first Rearwin factory in Kansas City was in the north (left) one-third of the Massey-Harris building, which was itself about a half-mile from Fairfax. Mercury Aircraft occupied the site briefly after Rearwin operations were moved.

By the mid-1930s the double sales hangar was used for private plane storage, the Eddie Fisher Flying School, and for Ben Gregory's Ford Trimotor.

Right: The American Eagle factory at Fairfax was built in 1928 after Ed Porterfield sold a 48 percent interest in his firm to A. A. Durant.

**Fly With Ben**

Enjoy a Ride Today Over Both Kansas Citys

FORD TRI-MOTOR TRANSPORT PLANE

*Extra Special Today Only*

**$1.50**

CHILDREN $1.00

BEN GREGORY, FAIRFAX AIRPORT

An advertisement for public rides at Fairfax.

Antique Airplane Association, Blakesburg, IA

schools, manufacturers, and other aviation-related businesses. Finally, the Union Pacific subsidiary planned to develop the remainder of the area into a commercial and industrial park, but a natural gas discovery on the site intervened. The grandiose scheme to build Fairfax Airport attracted more than 2,800 shareholders who were publicly reminded barely a year later to pick up their dividend checks — the only ones they would receive.

When Rae announced his intentions to settle at Fairfax in March 1929, American Eagle, headed by Ed Porterfield, Seitz Flying Service, and Porterfield Flying Service (then a division of Universal Flying Service managed by Truman Giles with about 150 student pilots enrolled) were already operating at the field. The Curtiss Flying Service, Universal Aviation, Southwest Air Fast Express (a.k.a. "SAFE-WAY Airlines"), and Beacon Airways were also scheduled to open within a short time. Nor was it long before Fairfax was the choice of the infant airlines. National Air Transport landed there when the primary field on the east side of the river was too muddy, found it to its liking, and for a while made Fairfax a regular stop. Taxi, charter, and airmail services soon followed. Fairfax also became "home" for barnstormers Tex LaGrone and Ben Gregory. Dr. John Brock, Kansas City's "flying doctor," who flew an airplane daily for ten consecutive years, was also based there.[3]

In early April 1929, George Halsey flew the Ken-Royce to an aircraft exhibition in Detroit. Rae and Fred Landgraf followed, making stops en route to inspect and evaluate manufacturing methods at other factories. On their return the *Salina Journal* reported:

> Ten men are employed in the Rearwin factory in this city now, and all arrangements are being made to take most of that crew to the Kansas City factory, the owner announced today.

Dr. John Brock with his Siemens-Halske-powered Waco and Hupmobile, April 4, 1930. Kansas City Museum, Kansas City, MO

Ben ("Fly With Ben") Gregory, *circa* 1926. Kansas City Museum, Kansas City, MO

George Halsey, who has been pilot of the plane since its first tests in the air, has been permanently employed as pilot and he too will go to Kansas City with the Salina manufacturer.

Machinery which will do in one day the work which required three weeks on the Ken-Royce machine, entirely built by hand, has been ordered, a fuselage being welded in one day by the process of machinery to be installed in the Rearwin factory. Fred Landgraf, engineer who designed the first Rearwin plane, visited the leading factories of the east on the trip to Detroit and return, gathering ideas from all of them. Those ideas will be combined and woven into the equipment of the Kansas City factory which Mr. Rearwin is now having designed by I. L. Zerbe, Salina architect. Development of the Kansas City fairway where the factory is to be located is being pushed rapidly ahead, the Salina man found on his visit there this week.

An announcement in a Kansas City newspaper also reported that Rearwin Airplanes had opened an office in the old Kansas City Can Company plant, known as the Massey-Harris building, on April 15th, pending the completion of a new 100- by 300-foot plant that would be built at the northwest corner of Fairfax and Funston Roads. Meanwhile, the Salina equipment and a few employees were on the road.

The 1929 ground-breaking for the new Curtiss-Wright facility at Fairfax was accomplished with a plow towed by a Curtiss-Wright biplane.
Wyandotte County Museum, Bonner Springs, KS

Left: An architect's rendering of the factory Rae planned to build on two-plus acres at Fairfax.
Wyandotte County Museum, Bonner Springs, KS

Below: Rae Rearwin, second row center, was on the Fairfax Airport management board. Tex LaGrone is at lower right.
Wyandotte County Museum, Bonner Springs, KS

Fairfax Airport, *circa* 1931, with the Missouri River in the background. The first Rearwin plant was one-half mile beyond the arrow in the lower right corner. (1) Inland Sport and (2) Rearwin factories in the A. R. Jones Building; (3) Airport Terminal and Administration building; (4) Saunders Fly It Yourself System; (5) Eddie Fisher Flying School; (6) Ben Gregory hangar; (7) former Sweeney Air-Port clubhouse and hangar used by the new Porterfield Flying School; (8) Universal Air Service, subsequently occupied by Rearwin in 1936; (9) Naval Reserve hangar; (10) Curtiss-Wright sales hangar; (11) American Eagle plant built in 1928; (12) site of proposed Rearwin factory that was never built.
Wyandotte County Museum, Bonner Springs, KS

## Chapter 9

# Fencing with Foxes — Rearwin Airplanes, Inc.

*THE KEN-ROYCE prototype was in the air, but the cash register had yet to ring. Establishing the new factory at Fairfax Airport would require a substantial investment. According to the* ***Journal*** *article, about $300,000 would be needed for a site and building, fixtures and equipment, and working capital to build the first ten planes, planned in two clusters of five. Although Rae was ready to invest another two or three years' income in the venture, outside capital was needed. That meant borrowing heavily, taking in a partner or two, or incorporating and selling stock.*

*Although Rae's net worth and track record as a successful businessman would have supported institutional financing, substantial borrowing was out of the question. It wasn't that he hadn't borrowed before or lacked faith in the financial future of aviation. He had borrowed heavily to start the lumberyard business, and his investment of cash and time in the Ken-Royce biplane was testament to his confidence in aviation's future. But while the prototype was drawing raves, the self-made businessman was not so foolhardy as to collateralize most of his personal wealth at age 50. He had worked too hard and too long to go back to step one. He was also cognizant of the frailties and pitfalls of partnerships, not the least of which was shared control.*

AVIATION SHARES CORPORATION
SPECIALISTS IN AVIATION SECURITIES
610 ELLICOTT SQUARE
BUFFALO, N. Y.

you control without causing any undue comment."

The 10,000 shares of Class A stock were to be marketed at $25 a share net to the corporation giving Rae, as Hoy noted, "a total value of $125,000 for your five thousand shares." The Class A shares were to be sold as follows: 4,000 at $25 net to four directors (excluding Rae) and 6,000 as a prior market syndicate sold to the Kansas City area public at the same price.

The decision, as they say, was a "no-brainer." The safest move was to spread the risk widely and hold the reins tightly: incorporate. Following the Lindbergh flight, the stock market had digested promising new aviation issues, and speculative trading could result in profits for those who played that game. Also, less than two years earlier Rae had been rebuffed when he had sought to invest in Travel Air, Swallow, and other firms.

Whether by accident or design, Rae met E. W. Hoy and O. J. Todd of Buffalo, New York, at the Detroit exhibition. Both were principles in Aviation Shares Corporation, an underwriting firm with a letterhead proclaiming they were "Specialists In Aviation Securities." Rae outlined his financing needs and planted a few seeds about developing a cabin ship and a mail plane once the Ken-Royce was in production. Rae met the pair again at the Presidents Hotel in Kansas City, Missouri, on Saturday, April 13, 1929, and opened his books, such as they were.

Hoy wrote Rae from Buffalo two days later outlining a tentative financing plan that included the sale of stock to a pair of preorganization syndicates and temporary incorporation in Kansas, followed by reincorporation in Delaware. The plan was designed to initially raise a minimum of $250,000 and, as needed, another $500,000 after the Delaware corporation was formed and swallowed the Kansas one.

The plan called for 30,000 shares of Class A no par common stock and 10,000 shares of Class B no par voting stock. Rae, as founder, would "receive liberal value for all assets conveyed to the corporation." That, Hoy's letter explained, meant 5,000 shares of the Class A stock and *all* of the Class B stock in exchange for Rae transferring the rights to the Ken-Royce and all tangible assets to the new corporation. Only 10,000 of the remaining Class A shares would be sold, leaving Rae with 60 percent of the 25,000 shares outstanding. Hoy wrote, "This is done to give

The initial sale was to be completed within six months. At that time, a new Delaware corporation would be formed consisting of 250,000 shares of no par common stock. It would succeed the Kansas corporation with a five-to-one stock split, giving Rae 75,000 shares and the directors and investors 50,000. The remaining 125,000 shares would be held in reserve for future financing.

Hoy's two-page letter was sprinkled with vague phrases such as:

> There is much to be said on this. Really much more than can be outlined in a letter. . . . It is really hard to cover all of this in a letter . . . this outline and letter is submitted to you in confidence.

Translated, such phrases meant, "We cannot, and dare not, put everything in writing."

The deal was too good to be true, a fact that did not escape Rae. The proposal placed no monetary value on the 10,000 shares of Class B voting stock Rae was to receive. Additionally, both classes of stock were eligible for dividends on an equal footing. In sum, Rae would actually receive 15,000 shares of stock for the Ken-Royce assets. Looking at it another way, if the assets Rae was to convey to the new corporation were worth $125,000 (and even that was doubtful), he would receive 15,000 shares of stock and all corporate voting rights at an average price of only $8.33 a share. Liberal value, indeed!

Hoy had fatally misjudged the tall Kansan. There was no way Rae would permit the New York underwriters to buffalo his potential directors and the Kansas City area public by selling them stock for $25 that he would receive for one-third that amount. Rae had earned a deserved reputation as a frugal but honest businessman. He was not about to "pull one over" on his Kansas City business associates or the area's investors, not to mention risking legal problems.

Rae mentally wrote off Aviation Shares Corporation, but figured the firm could be used to his advantage. Hoy's April 15 letter had stated, "the preorganization subscription agreement was practically complete and ready for use." If Rae could get his hands on a copy, it would not only be instructive but save time in starting over with another underwriter.

Rae told Hoy the proposal was too top-heavy. He also expressed concern about the unit price of the shares and the Fairfax Airport stock issue that was to be marketed shortly in the Kansas City area. It could jeopardize the proposed offering to the directors and Kansas City public. He doubted the local community could absorb both new issues at the same time.

Hoy swallowed the bait and wired Rae at his home in Salina on Saturday, April 20:

> By starting syndicate sales plan Monday April Twenty Ninth we would be firmly enough entrenched within thirty days so that announcement of Airport issue would not be particularly harmful as (our) initial syndicate sales effort permits of elastic corporate structure to follow STOP. Unless we could swing into immediate action we are not interested STOP. We would like to meet you in Chicago Wednesday morning for final discussion. Please wire answer.

The proposed meeting in Chicago never took place. Instead, Hoy met Rae in Kansas City, Missouri, on April 27 and presented a five-page "Agreement" that he mistakenly believed the Salina lumber dealer would sign on the spot. But Rae had no intention of doing business with Aviation Shares. If they would scam his potential directors and the Kansas City public, even for his benefit, how could he be sure they wouldn't rip him off, too?

Rae never saw the "practically completed" agreement referred to in Hoy's letter. However, the revised document presented under the telegram's "now or never" ploy reflected the changes Rae had sought. First, a Kansas corporation would be capitalized with 50,000 shares of no par common stock, with half outstanding. There would be only one class. The proposed offering price and selling costs were to be established not by fiat, but approved by the securities commissions of the states in which the stock would be sold. If either Rae or Aviation Shares Corporation was not satisfied with the proposed offering price, they could walk away from the deal.

Secondly, Rae would receive 5,000 shares for his investment in the Ken-Royce and another 5,000 shares and $62,500 cash from the corporation when he completed the factory building on the Fairfax property and transferred both to the corporation. Subject to regulatory approval, Aviation Shares was to market the other 15,000 shares: 4,000 were to be sold to four directors at $20 net to the corporation ($80,000); 8,500 were to be sold at $24 net in the Kansas City area ($204,000); and the final 2,500 would be offered at $25 per share ($62,500).

At first blush it appears that Rae, owning only 10,000 of the 25,000 outstanding shares, could lose control, but that was not so. It was no coincidence that the cash he would receive upon completion of the factory building ($62,500) equalled the net price of the last block of 2,500 shares to be sold. Rae would purchase those shares and at least one other on the open market if and when the second block of 8,500 shares was fully subscribed. Thus, he would hold more than half of the 25,000 shares outstanding.

The deal was now fair. The average net price of the shares offered to the four directors and the public would be $22.92. Using that figure, Rae would receive a total of $291,700 in stock and cash for his land, the new building and equipment, and the Ken-Royce assets. Nary a dime was earmarked for his prior efforts. Moreover, Rae would pay $25 a share plus commissions for the final block of 2,500 shares if he purchased them.

Hoy's revised proposal also contained an irritating provision that would permit the "banker" (Aviation Shares Corporation) to use a plane and pilot when both were not in service for corporate business. To bust the deal, Rae rejected use of the plane, boiled the proposal down to three pages, and added a hold harmless clause. Hoy left town without Rae's signature and without suspecting he had been outfoxed.

With a financing degree from "ASC" (Aviation Shares Corporation, Buffalo campus), Rae launched a search for a local underwriter he could trust. He was steered to the C. J. "Hat" Haterius Investment Company of Missouri.

Using the proposed agreement unwittingly furnished by E. W. Hoy, Rae drew up the first draft, which was later fine-tuned by Haterius. The final agreement was executed on May 22, 1929. Rae would establish a Delaware corporation with 150,000 shares of no par common stock, and would qualify and license the new corporation to offer securities for sale in both Kansas and Missouri. He would also transfer the rights to the Ken-Royce and all other related assets to the corporation, including the factory site and the new building when complete, and receive a total of 40,000 shares of stock and $87,500 in cash.

Haterius, the "banker," would have an option on 55,000 shares at $5 per share for six months, which were to be resold to the public, and Rae agreed to advance Haterius $1,500 in selling expenses. To maintain control, Rae reserved a three-year option on 39,000 of the remaining 55,000 shares of unissued treasury stock, also at $5 net. Thus, if and when all the stock was sold, Rae would own 79,900 shares, or 53.3 percent.

This deal was also fair. Rae had purchased the two and one-half acre Kansas City tract bordering the airport south of the American Eagle factory. With construction complete, the total land-plant-machinery investment was calculated at $200,000. The 40,000 shares of stock he would receive at $5 each equated to $200,000, so the $87,500 cash essentially was for the rights to the Ken-Royce and related equipment. Whether or not the new corporation and the stock "went South," there would be no finger-pointing or charges of manipulation.

The stock market, however, had trembled. On April 17 one firm's stock had dropped 71 points, Wright Aero's dropped 31, and the call money interest rate — the amount charged on margin balances (stocks purchased on credit) — had rocketed to 17 percent. The ticker was 40 minutes late, and the date was labeled "the worst day in market history." A Utah Senator demanded an investigation of what he called "price pirouetting" and a ban on margin sales, but was silenced when the market rebounded. The smart money, however, was cautious about new issues and began holding, if not imperceptibly liquidating. Haterius was skeptical that the proposed issue could be fully sold. It might also be that he had an alternative financing plan in mind from the start.

Before the stock was qualified for public sale, Haterius brought together Rae and Albert R. Jones, president of the A. R. Jones Oil and Operating Company of Kansas City, Missouri. The Northwestern University graduate had more than a passing interest in aviation and earning a dollar. Jones had made a fortune in the Kansas, Texas, and Oklahoma oil fields. According to rumor, he could heat his Tudor mansion on Kansas City's fashionable Mission Drive all winter with dollar bills instead of coal and never let the temperature drop below 70 degrees. He paid $66,000 for an unsigned oil painting in 1923, was an avid collector of George Innes's landscapes, and owned much of Padre Island in the Gulf of Mexico off the Texas shoreline. He was also one of the five principals in Fairfax-based Beacon Airways, which had a new building under construction.

Albert R. "Bert" Jones, *circa* 1952. *The Kansas City Star*

Jones, who preferred to be called "Bert," was a native of Virginia, Illinois. He was born there in 1875 and, after attending Northwestern, was educated as a lawyer at Illinois Wesleyan University in Bloomington. However, a childhood interest in geology got in the way of the law. During a 1902 trip to Independence, Kansas, while awaiting the results of the bar examination (which he passed), Jones explored the contents of an abandoned oil well filled with salt water and commissioned a drilling test. Forty barrels a day was enough to start Independence on its way to becoming a boom town. But that was only the beginning. Jones later happened on a promising three-mile-long geological formation in Greenwood County that became famous as the "Golden Lane." He leased 9,000 acres. By 1918 he owned the Kansas City Oil Refining Company, the Manhattan Oil Company, and hundreds of service stations in the Midwest operating as the Independent Oil Company. Two years later he struck natural gas near Amarillo, Texas.

With Haterius's consent and his retention of the $1,500 advance as a finder's fee, the public stock sale was abandoned in favor of a closed corporation to be equally owned by Rae and the A. R. Jones Oil and Operating Company. The gentlemanly page-and-a-half "Memorandum of Agreement" was signed on July 29, 1929. The document reflected the parties' mutual trust, not by what it said, but by what it did not. Each party was to receive 45,000 shares of the new Delaware corporation known as "Rearwin Airplanes, Inc.," with the remaining 60,000 shares to be issued as the parties might agree. The stock was priced at $2 a share. Rae put up all rights and interest in the Ken-Royce, including tangible assets other than the airport land, while Jones put $45,000 up front and agreed to pay the other half in installments as needed. In effect, Rae entered into a partnership with a heavyweight who could pin him to the financial mat if he was so inclined — which Jones wasn't.

Rearwin Airplanes, Inc. now had $45,000 of working capital in the bank and another $45,000 in notes payable on demand from the rock-solid A. R. Jones Oil and Operating Company. That was sufficient to produce the first group of five biplanes and gather in the cash for the next five.

NUMBER 3

SHARES 4,500

REARWIN AIRPLANES, Inc.

10,000 SHARES

WITHOUT NOMINAL OR PAR VALUE

This Certifies that R. A. REARWIN is the owner of FOUR THOUSAND FIVE HUNDRED Shares of the Capital Stock of REARWIN AIRPLANES, INC. transferable only on the books of this Corporation in person or by Attorney upon surrender of this Certificate properly endorsed.

In Witness Whereof, the said Corporation has caused this Certificate to be signed by its duly authorized officers and its Corporate Seal to be hereunto affixed this 1st day of SEPTEMBER A.D. 1930.

SECRETARY PRESIDENT

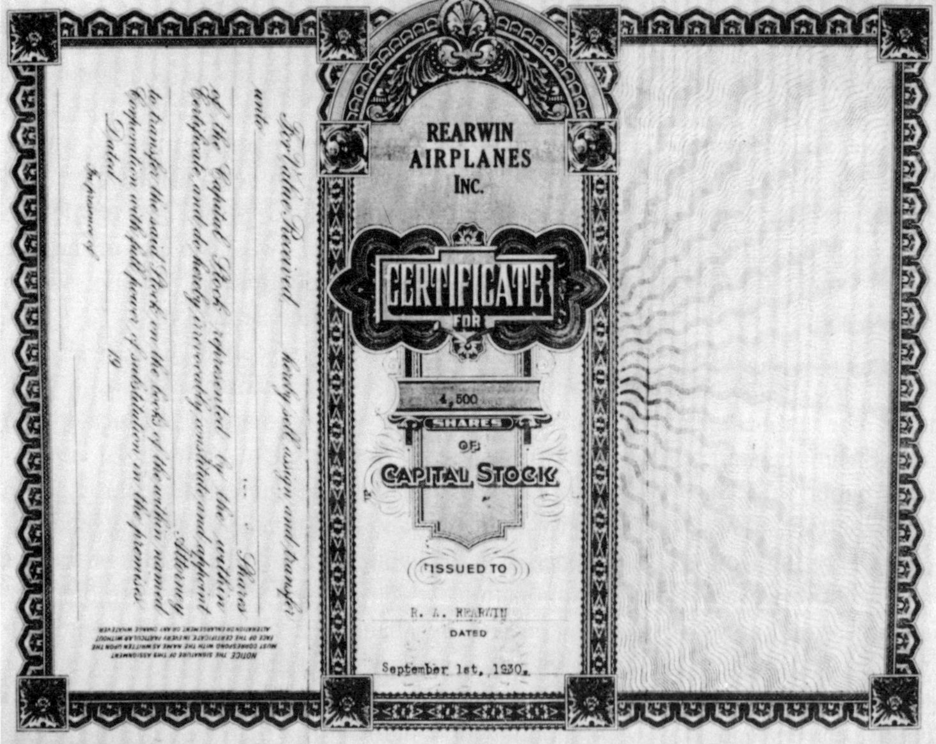

For Value Received ___ hereby sell assign and transfer unto ___ Shares of the Capital Stock represented by the within Certificate and do hereby irrevocably constitute and appoint ___ Attorney to transfer the said Stock on the books of the within named Corporation with full power of substitution in the premises.

Dated ___ 19__

In presence of

REARWIN AIRPLANES INC.

CERTIFICATE FOR 4,500 SHARES OF CAPITAL STOCK

ISSUED TO R. A. REARWIN

DATED September 1st, 1930.

Stock certificate number 3 is dated September 1, 1930. It was issued after a "reverse" stock split.

The parties also agreed

on a handshake that Rae would work without salary until profits were realized and would have full control in operating the company. True to his word, Jones never meddled. However, he did suggest an accurate set of financial statements for income tax purposes. He sent C. W. Trapp, one of his accountants, to Fairfax to update the bookkeeping system with cost accounting procedures and the periodic issuance of profit and loss statements and balance sheets.

Rae most certainly was elated. The Ken-Royce was setting records, Rearwin Airplanes, Inc. had a Fairfax address, two Curtiss Challenger models were now in the air, and government certification was just around the corner. Had he been so inclined, Rae might have thumbed his nose at the upstanding businessmen of Salina who had suggested he leave so that they could keep a lid on the wages of the skilled workers who kept their mills running. But he wasn't.

*Chapter 10*

# The All-Kansas Air Tour, 1929

*WHILE Rearwin Airplanes, Inc. was being set in motion, the second "All-Kansas Air Tour," a flight to 16 Kansas cities, was also in the planning stage, scheduled to start from Wichita's East Central Airport on Monday, June 3, 1929, and end with an "air extravaganza" at the formal opening of Wichita's new municipal airport on June 15. The purpose of the tour, as proclaimed by Arch Merriam, governor of the Kansas chapter of the National Aeronautics Association, was "to promote airmindedness the length and breadth of the State." If it also afforded manufacturers a chance to display and publicize their flying wares, so be it. Front-page press was better than a paid advertisement any day, and the sleek Ken-Royce was ready to be tested against all comers.*

*By Sunday, June 2, most of the 35 entries, including a covey of Travel Airs, Swallows, and American Eagles, were gathered at the old Wichita airport ready for Monday's late-morning departure to the starting point at Pratt. The planes were divided into three classes: A, under 100 hp; B, under 200; and C, 200 and over. The Tour included "onto" or "city-to-city" races in each class and a 20-mile race over a 4-mile triangular course at each city. Stunting, balloon-bursting, spot-landing, and bomb-dropping contests, as well as parachuting and passenger hopping, were optional.*

THE WICHITA SUNDAY BEACON

WICHITA, KANSAS, SUNDAY, JUNE 2, 1929

ALL KANSAS AIR TOUR NUMBER

This front-page drawing hyped the Second All-Kansas Air Tour of 1929.
*The Wichita Beacon*

Rae saw little sense in having pilot George Halsey stay overnight in Wichita, particularly since there was time to fly from Fairfax in the morning. It was a fortuitous decision. One of the fiercest storms in a generation rolled through Wichita Sunday evening, and destroyed many of the aircraft assembled there for the start of the Tour. The trimotored *Stanolin II*, the Tour flagship, was dragged several hundred yards from its mooring, shearing the gear and one wing. Merriam's Swallow and hangar were also destroyed, and the beacon tower at East Central was downed. Eight new aircraft over at Swallow Field were also heavily damaged.

The Tour Committee met overnight to assess the damage and decide whether the Tour should go on and, if so, how. Twenty of the original entries were still available, so it was decided to cancel the first two days (eliminating stops at Pratt and Hutchinson), and start the tour on Wednesday from Dodge City.

The fog in Dodge City was like pea soup. Several of the 14 pilots who made it for the official start reported flying in at less than 200 feet. The other six turned back and would join the Tour at Garden City, the next stop. The ceiling, however, lifted, and the fog went wherever fog goes. The Tour started on time with the first "onto" race to Garden City. Bill Ong won the Class A race, while Halsey and the Ken-Royce won the Class B event. Both also won their 20-mile lap races and hopped passengers while other pilots cavorted in the spot-landing, stunt, and balloon contests. More than 6,000 people turned out for the event.

Halsey rang up another "onto" win at Colby, but Ong was beaten by a Swallow flown by Ross Jackson. Halsey also bested a Lincoln-Page and a Travel Air in the 20-mile closed-course race before the Tour moved on. The stop at Hays was skipped because of weather, but the Tour was able to land at Ellsworth, where race officials Luke Christopher and Arch Merriam again made speeches extolling Kansas aviation and, in particular, the National Aeronautics Association. Halsey once again won the Class B "city-to-city" race, beating Ken Field in a Travel Air and Ed Ockander's Lincoln-Page. But there was more at stake than races. The local paper reported:

> Barnstorming is worth while in this part of the state. All fliers are doing a good business and hundreds of persons who never have had a chance to take an air ride are keeping the planes in the air. At Colby, it was estimated the fliers cleared $2,000.

On Saturday, June 8, the Tour raced to Concordia for the morning's ritual and then on to Washington where it was greeted by another 2,500 people. It was the site of the only mishap. A pilot and reporter for *The Wichita Beacon* who were following the Tour were slightly injured while landing. A crosswind caught their Spartan as the pilot unsuccessfully sought to avoid a collision with a Skelly Oil fuel truck parked at the edge of the runway.

Halsey and Ong again won the "onto" and lap sprints in their respective classes. Halsey also en-

George Halsey, of Culver, Kansas, test flew the Ken-Royce prototype. This "all smiles" photo was taken in June 1929 during a stop on the All-Kansas Air Tour.

tered the 170 hp Ken-Royce in the Class C race for planes with engines of over 200 hp and finished second! He also finished first in the spot-landing contest, open to all pilots, missing the mark by only *four feet*, and won first place in the balloon-bursting contest. Halsey was having fun and it was another proud day for the Ken-Royce's owner.

A crowd of almost 12,000 met the fliers at Topeka upon their Sunday morning arrival from Washington. Halsey again won the Class B "onto" race and flew in the Class C sprint, finishing third against the over 200 hp craft. He also finished third in the spot-landing, balloon-bursting, and bombing contests. It was now clear the new Ken-Royce was the best of the field. It had yet to lose an "onto" heat or a lap race in its class.

It was more of the same as the tour headed for Fairfax, familiar territory for Halsey and the Ken-Royce. Ong, however, who had been the major winner in the Class A division, was forced down at Lawrence with engine trouble. Bert Thomas won the Class A race to Fairfax in a Curtiss Robin, while Halsey again placed first in the B event.

The race moved next to Fort Scott, Pittsburg, and Emporia, with Halsey again picking up firsts in the "onto" races. At Fort Scott he won both the Class B and Class C triangular sprints and the spot-landing and balloon-breaking contests. Before a crowd of 5,000 at Emporia, he won three more contests, and the local press called it "the biggest aviation event in the history of Emporia."

The final day included the last "city-to-city" heat to Wichita's new municipal airport and the air show and racing events planned for the "grand opening." Lady Mary Heath, the famed English pilot, was present. So were Air Corps squadrons from Marshall Field at Fort Riley, Kansas, and Richards Field in Kansas City, Missouri. More than 15,000 spectators showed up on a workday Wednesday, including Walter Beech from Travel Air; Clyde Cessna, who had his own company; Mac Short of Stearman; McGinnis Moore of Swallow; and, of course, a trio of Fairfax upstarts, Arthur Hardgrave of Inland Sport, Ed Porterfield, and Rae Rearwin.

Halsey and the Ken-Royce had dominated the Tour, and the former barnstormer wasn't about to

Rae maintained a hangar at the new Salina Municipal Airport until the late 1930s.

relax on the final day in front of the Tour's largest attendance. Ong was out of the Class A events. The "onto" Class A race was won by Bert Thomas in a Curtiss Robin. Mae Haizlip, the only woman pilot on the Tour, finished third in a Spartan.

The Ken-Royce, of course, won the Class B "onto" race, but Halsey wasn't done. He won the Class B closed-course race (now open to all planes of less than 200 hp) by about 30 seconds over a Travel Air flown by Lady Mary Heath. He also entered the Class C event and finished third behind a Knoll KN-1 piloted by Russell Dick and a Thomas Morse pursuit flown by an Air Corps pilot. Halsey and the Ken-Royce then finished first in the spot-landing contest, second in the balloon-bursting contest, and second in bomb-dropping, again just ahead of Lady Heath.

It was a great week for Halsey and the Ken-Royce. Tour Chairman Arch Merriam summed up:

> The performance of the Ken-Royce airplane was unsurpassed, winning first money in every event in which it was entered. Some in its class were powered by the J-5 Whirlwind motor capable of developing 225 horse power. The Ken-Royce, powered with a 170 horse power Curtiss Challenger was the talk of the entire tour. Without question of doubt in my mind, it is the best craft I ever saw.
>
> . . . On the tour it won first place in every event of Class B, representing ships of 225 horse power. It took second place in many of the Class C events, representing ships of 475 horse power. George Halsey piloted the Ken-Royce and won fifty-one places during the six days in which he participated in the Tour. This meritorious performance was all the more interesting because of the fact that this ship is the first one built by the Rearwin Company.

While Halsey's skill and experience played no small role in capturing a lion's share of the $10,000 prize money and trophies awarded that evening at the Hotel Lassen banquet, there was no doubting that the Salina-born Ken-Royce could cut the air with the best Wichita had to offer.[1] Rae was now wedded to the aircraft manufacturing business, as is said, "for better or for worse." Halsey and X-44E promptly

George Halsey (left, with the Class B trophy) and Rae Rearwin (second from left) at the Hotel Lassen banquet following the Kansas Air Tour. Bill Ong is on the far right.

headed for another air race in Memphis, where they placed first in the only event the plane was eligible to enter. The Ken-Royce also placed first in its division at the Petroleum Convention Air Races held in Tulsa. Meanwhile, Leila agreed to come to Kansas City with her maid, but only for the summer. Rae rented a furnished home for his family and moved out of his temporary residence, the Kansas City Athletic Club.

## *Chapter 11*

# The "Powder Puff" Debacle

*RUTH NICHOLS, a society debutante from Rye, New York, learned to fly in 1921. She was a well-known aviatrix in early August 1929 when she contacted Rae to borrow a Ken-Royce biplane to compete in the first all-women's cross-country air race. The event, promptly dubbed "The Powder Puff Derby" by humorist Will Rogers, would start from Santa Monica on August 18 and, after about 2,200 wandering miles and 15 stops, end in front of the grandstand at the National Air Races in Cleveland on August 26.*

*There were fewer than 100 licensed female pilots in the country, and Nichols was one of only seven who held the coveted transport rating.[1] She had set several records and was nearing the end of a six-month, nationwide tour to promote "Aviation Country Clubs." As a result of the tour, she became the first woman to take off and land in all 48 states, and was recognized as one of aviation's most dedicated evangelists.*

*Nichols' own Curtiss Fledgling was not only tired from the tour, but it was also basically a trainer that even in top form could not match the pace of other entries. It was, as she said, "an unbeatable platform from which to watch the scenery below, especially if you were not in a hurry." It had a top speed of about 104 miles per hour and cruised at less than 90.*

Ruth Nichols beside the Ken-Royce (No. 8) prior to the start of the race from Clover Field, Santa Monica, on August 18, 1929.

The Curtiss Motor Company was anxious to have a Challenger engine in the Derby and agreed to financially sponsor Nichols and the Ken-Royce prototype. But time was short. Nichols's tour would stop in St. Louis in a few days, so it was agreed Nichols would pick up the biplane on Sunday, August 11.[2] She would then head for the starting line in Santa Monica. As it turned out, the trip West was more harrowing than the race.

Compared to the plodding Fledgling, the plane, now designated R-44E, was a joy for Nichols to fly. However, as she descended several miles east of

The Ken-Royce prototype can be seen in the upper left of this famous photograph taken at the start of the first Transcontinental Air Race for Women in 1929. Willis M. Allen, Jr., Allen Airways

Amelia Earhart in a Lockheed Vega waits for the starter's flag. Willis M. Allen, Jr., Allen Airways

Wichita, the Challenger engine suddenly quit at about 300 feet. Out of time, altitude, and options, Nichols side-slipped the silent biplane toward a small fenced field. Fortunately, she was too fast on her final approach. The plane floated over a pair of trenches she had not seen, touched down, and rolled through two barbed wire fences with Nichols standing on the brakes, expecting to nose over. It didn't happen.

Hitting a ditch normally would have resulted in disaster, but the plane was hardly damaged — just a couple of tears on the bottom of one wing. Nichols pulled away the clinging wire and discovered the fuel tank was empty. A mechanic was summoned from Wichita to fill the tank and repair the torn fabric on the wing, an overnight job. In the morning, the plane was pushed to the next field where a portion of a fence was removed for takeoff. Before departing, however, the mechanic pointed out to Nichols the second fuel tank, which was full. She had not known it was there! (Unless Rae read Nichols's autobiography, he never knew that she had "run out of fuel.")

Two days later, after Nichols landed in El Paso, oil was discovered sloshing on the cockpit floor and back to the tail. Prolonged full-throttle operation needed to outrun bad weather on the way to El Paso had caused a rigid oil line to vibrate excessively and break. Again, it took all night for a mechanic to install a new line, weld several small cracks in the tank itself, and clean up the mess. Nichols left early Wednesday morning under clear skies, full of confidence that she would reach Los Angeles late in the afternoon and have a few days to "tweak" the Ken-Royce and rest.

She stopped for fuel in Phoenix, skipped lunch, and hurriedly took off behind a trimotored transport with the idea of trailing it to Los Angeles. However, she fell behind at cruising speed, and so advanced the throttle until the biplane indicated 145 mph. Even then, the transport slowly pulled away. She pushed the throttle to the wall but dropped still farther back. Moreover, after 90 minutes of bucking headwinds, thunderstorms loomed ahead. She would have to detour around them, which meant another fuel stop.

The stop, however, came sooner than expected, and it was not for fuel. The oil pressure gauge suddenly read zero. Without lubrication the pistons would "freeze," perhaps in seconds. Like it or not, Nichols would soon meet the Arizona desert. This time, however, she had more than 4,000 feet of altitude, and glided toward a wide valley that offered her a chance of walking away unscathed. But she saw no signs of civilization.

Florence "Pancho" Barnes flew a Travel Air in the first "Powder Puff Derby," but didn't finish the race. Willis M. Allen, Jr., Allen Airways

At 1,000 feet a cabin appeared in the distance, but seconds later the idling engine quit, frozen solid. There was nothing to do but set the "glider" down and avoid as much sagebrush as possible. Nichols mushed the plane to the ground at its 35 mph stalling speed and miraculously kept it upright, again barely scratching a wing. However, the engine was shot, the prop unmovable. (Nichols had no idea she was near Flat Top Mountain in the Harquahalla Range northeast of Salome. The spot was only 80 miles north of Wellton, where her friend Marvel Crossen would die a few days later on the second day of the race.)

Nichols gathered up her emergency supplies, which included water, a three-day stock of food, a pistol, matches, and a flashlight, and headed in the general direction of the cabin. It was deserted. A second cabin that appeared on the horizon was also vacant, but from there she saw a dirt road and yet another dwelling. It was occupied by a lone woman who spoke no English, and there were no telephone wires in sight. There was no way to let anyone know she was safe. Finally, Nichols heard the clamor of an automobile. The four occupants made room for her, and an hour or so later deposited her at a railroad station where a Los Angeles-bound train was due at 11:00 p.m. It appeared that the race, which was to begin Sunday, would start without her.

The Wall Street broker's daughter started scheming and sent off a telegram to her sponsor, the Curtiss Company. If she could still make the race, would they install a new engine? The train had barely rolled to a stop in Los Angeles when Nichols headed for the Curtiss Flying Service at Glendale's Grand Central Air Terminal. She begged, pleaded, and cajoled the station manager to find a Ford Trimotor and fly a new Challenger engine to the desert. He reluctantly agreed, but it was nearly 4:00 a.m. on Friday before a plane was located and equipped as a flying maintenance facility. The sun was well up when the biplane was spotted from the air, but the Ford pilot could not land closer than a mile away. The mechanics, who would have to lug the engine and other equipment to Nichols's plane, coaxed him to try taxiing. Dodging sagebrush, cactus, and gullies, and by throttling first one engine and then another, he finally nosed up to the forlorn Ken-Royce.

The mechanics worked all day and into the night, using a block and tackle suspended from the Ford's center-mounted motor to switch engines. They also installed rubber connections on the oil line to minimize vibration and hung a new oil tank, which had to be fitted to the existing Ken-Royce mount, in sponge rubber. The job was finished shortly before noon on Saturday, and the planes took off from the nearest stretch of land reasonably free of sagebrush. One of the mechanics, a brave soul, rode with Nichols to Clover Field in Santa Monica. They arrived less than

This photo of the Ken-Royce was taken by the Thaden family sometime during the race. The mountains in the background suggest San Bernardino, the first stop. William M. Allen, Jr., Allen Airways

In the Arizona desert, Curtiss mechanics used the center engine of the Ford Trimotor to hoist a new Challenger engine in place on R-44E while Ruth Nichols, the unidentified pilot (with tie), and local residents watched. NASM, Smithsonian Institution, Washington, D.C., 2B-20062

Ruth Nichols sits on the wing while Curtiss mechanics install a new Challenger engine on R-44E.
NASM, Smithsonian Institution, Washington, D.C., 2B-20073

The Travel Air flown by Louise Thaden in the 1929 Powder Puff Air Derby has been rebuilt and is now owned by Willis M. Allen, Jr., El Cajon, California.
Bill Wright

Below: Louise Thaden won the first Transcontinental Air Race for Women in 1929.
Willis M. Allen, Jr., Allen Airways

half an hour before the registration deadline, and there was no time for anything but sleep.

After all Nichols had been through, the race itself was anticlimactic. The new engine, of course, was not broken in, so she began with a handicap. She started out at 1,600 rpm and advanced the throttle 50 revolutions a day. By the time the "Powder Puff" fliers reached Texas, the retarded Challenger was humming with little vibration. Nichols had flown through this country on several occasions and was able to cut a few corners. She was in third place when the group reached Abilene. In Wichita, she had four seconds on Amelia Earhart, who was still fourth. By the time the racers reached Columbus, Ohio, where only the last half of the runway was useable because of construction work, Nichols had stretched

R-44E, crumpled on the runway at Columbus, Ohio. Ruth Nichols escaped injury.

Below: Amelia Earhart, Ruth Nichols, and Louise Thaden, *circa* 1935, were charter members of the all-women's "99s" established in 1929.
Willis M. Allen, Jr., Allen Airways

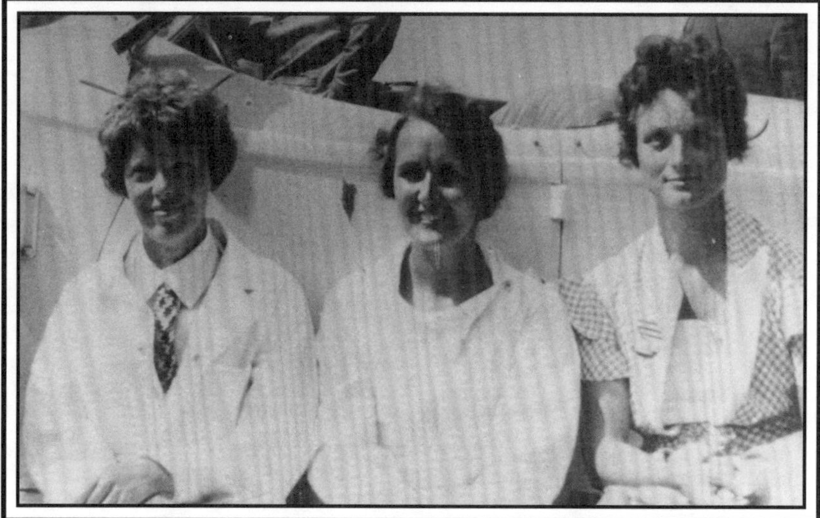

her lead over Earhart and her Lockheed Vega to one minute and 52 seconds.

Columbus was the last overnight stop. Barring disaster, Louise Thaden and Gladys O'Donnell had locks on first and second places. The only duel over the final 120 miles would be between Nichols and Earhart — for third place and $875. Blanche Noyes was far back in fifth.

Earhart, of course, was hoping to somehow pick up two minutes; Nichols had other plans. The new Challenger engine was now a broken-in veteran of nearly 25 hours of operation. To keep Earhart at bay, Nichols decided to increase the power output by changing the pitch of the prop and advancing the throttle. The work was done overnight so that she could test the plane in the morning before the 1:00 p.m. departure.

In her 1957 autobiography, *Wings For Life*, Nichols reported that the motor "had never run better, smooth as butter, just the right revs and no slippage" as she turned to land:

> Heading into the wind, I ruddered toward the center of the runway, since the rest of the field was being graded and was too soft to land on. Out of the corner of my eyes I saw a tractor at the right edge of the landing strip, and just as the wheels were about to touch the ground a side current of air caught the plane and carried it to the runway's edge. The wing struck the tractor and my racer did a double cartwheel, finally landing on its back, leaving me hanging by the seatbelt upside down in the wreckage.

Louise Thaden witnessed the accident, which she described in an interview for *Aviation Quarterly* published in 1974:

> I noticed a large steamroller parked alongside the edge of the active runway's unusable segment, near the beginning of the useable portion.
>
> Idly I watched Ruth Nichols' Ken-Royce on close final approach, undoubtedly coming in from a test flight. It seems to be drifting slight-

ly as it skims over the segment of the unusable runway. Before my unbelieving eyes, pieces of airplane are flying through the air, the explosive sound of impact not yet heard. The Rearwin somersaults, coming to rest up-side-down on the ploughed ground. Transfixed, I watched

**The Rearwin "Ken-Royce" Wins National Air Derby**

**Victory in the National Derby from Miami to Cleveland definitely establishes the Rearwin Ken-Royce as the fastest biplane in America of its power. Previously the Ken-Royce won 55 firsts in the Class "B" Kansas Air Tour races for motors up to 200 h. p. Powered by a 170 h. p. Curtiss-Challenger motor it was a close second in Class "C" races for motors up to 420 h. p. The Rearwin Ken-Royce is the nation's outstanding 3-place biplane, not only because of its speed, but also for its beauty, quick take-off, fast rate of climb, easy controllability and slow landing speed. For details and specifications, write,**

REARWIN AIRPLANES, Inc.
**900 Land Bank Bldg. Kansas City, Mo.**

This ad appeared in the *Kansas Citian* dated September 29, 1929.

her crawl from under the wreckage. Cars race toward her.

Miraculously, Ruth is unhurt. I share with her the bitter flow of inward tears, her agony of heartbreak.

Nichols's anguish was matched by that of the plane's owner who heard the news while sitting in the grandstand at the Cleveland finish line. But Rae Rearwin was not one to lament long over the unalterable past. While Earhart finished third, he was pondering how to turn defeat into victory. After all, hadn't the sleek Ken-Royce prototype, with only 170 untamed horses up front, beaten Earhart and two other ships powered by the larger 220 hp Wright J5 Whirlwind engine to Columbus? It was, of course, small consolation for the loss of third place — in truth, none at all. Nonetheless, Rae had the carcass of R-44E ingloriously shipped back to Kansas City by rail and rebuilt.

Tuesday, August 27, was a better day. George Halsey, piloting the second biplane (NC591H), won the Class B division of the men's Miami to Cleveland race for planes of less than 275 hp in 12 hours, 42 minutes, and 4 seconds, winning $1,200. Two days later he finished fifth in a 10-lap sprint

Rae failed to sign his participant's pass for the 1929 National Air Races in Cleveland.

against 11 other entries and won another $75. As was customary, pilot and owner split the prize money. Later the same day, Rae entered Nichols in a 100-mile Cleveland to Pittsburgh race for women using NC591H. He knew she needed to "get back on the horse." She finished fifth behind four planes with engines of 200 hp or more.

Nichols's oil line problems at El Paso and in Arizona had resulted from vibration caused by the even-cylindered Challenger engine at or near full throttle. Indeed, the Curtiss Aeroplane and Motor Company acknowledged the problem while promoting an improved version in 1931:

> The first models of the Challenger, involving a new principle by which a radial engine operated with an even number of cylinders, were rough in operation and developed vibration. While the engine was adversely criticized, deservedly, it proved so reliable and so rugged that the engineering staff redoubled its efforts to improve the Challenger to a satisfactory degree.

The belated admission, of course, was too little, too late. Although, a third Ken-Royce, NC592H, SN103, was built with the Challenger engine, Rae decided to switch to the new Continental A-70 engine rated at 165 hp, which cost somewhat less.

Two months later, on Tuesday, October 29, 1929, the stock market took a dive.[3] According to legend, investors and brokers alike joined it from bridges and windows of varying heights. By December 31, Bert Jones had reduced his stock debt by more than half, but Rearwin Airplanes, Inc. had sustained a six-month operating loss of over $21,000. The only income since August 1 was $637.50, half of the prize money George Halsey had won at Cleveland. But neither Rae nor Jones were quitters. Both were savvy businessman. By aggressive promotion, tightening of the corporate belt, and the application of conservative practices, the new firm would turn the corner in 1930. Few, however, had ever experienced the widespread economic chaos to which the exhausted Roaring Twenties submitted.

*Chapter 12*

# More Races, Tours, and Disappointment

*BEACON AIRWAYS, which sold aircraft from a tent pending completion of its new building at Fairfax Airport, had folded in the summer of 1929, even before "Black Tuesday." Bert Jones took over the construction project, completed it as the "A. R. Jones Building," and leased half to Inland Sport, the builder of an open-cockpit, parasol-type monoplane with side-by-side seating. Bill Ong, a local pilot who had worked as a Beacon salesman, was referred to Rae as a replacement for George Halsey, who left to become the Fairfax manager for Midland Air Express. Ong would serve as both test pilot and salesman. Jones also suggested, and Rae agreed, that Rearwin Airplanes, Inc. should rent the other half of his new building.*

*Ong spin tested the new Continental prototype, SN104 (NC400V), at full gross weight from 5,000 feet over Fairfax. Unexpectedly, it failed to recover, and Ong used up 4,000 feet before sorting matters out. When he did, however, he was staring through his windscreen at a Fokker transport preparing to land. The Fokker pilot reported Ong for "stunting" in the airport area, and he was suspended for ten days. If Rae was unhappy with the suspension, Ong made up for it later during the "International Air Races and Pilot's Reunion," a ten-day event sponsored by Fairfax Airport, and Jack B. Story later successfully flew the plane at the Omaha*

Approved
8/20/29 Phelps

Form R-6

Application No.
A10917

No. Assigned
R-591-H

DEPARTMENT OF COMMERCE
AERONAUTICS BRANCH

Restricted NR-591 H

**APPLICATION FOR LICENSE FOR RACING, EXPERIMENTAL, OR OTHER SPECIAL CLASS AIRPLANES**

To The Secretary of Commerce:

Application in duplicate is hereby made for Racing (Experimental, racing, special) Airplane license.

1. Name Rearwin Airplanes Incorporated (Print or type)
2. Permanent address Fairfax Airport (Street) Kansas City (Post Office)
   Kansas (State) Wyandotte (County) Fairfax ~~xxxxxx~~ 3552 (Telephone)
3. Is owner individual, partnership, or corporation? Corporation
   *a.* If an individual, is he or she a bona fide citizen of the United States?
   *b.* If partnership, names and citizenship of each partner
   *c.* If a corporation, names of president, directors, and managing officers, and citizenship of each
   R.A.Rearwin, Pres: C.W.Trapp, Sce. & Treas.
   All American Citizens
   Also give per cent of voting interest in the corporation which is controlled by citizens of the United States 100%
4. List any other EXPERIMENTALLY LICENSED airplanes owned by applicant:
   R-44-E
5. Does the airplane now display any license or identification number issued by the Department of Commerce? If so, what is it? R-591-H
6. Is the airplane registered under the laws of any foreign country? no
7. Is the airplane registered under the laws of any State? no ? Name State Give State No.
8. Is the airplane to be flown by licensed pilots exclusively? Yes
9. Check (√) purpose for which airplane will be used.
   (*a*) Experimental ( ) (*b*) Racing ( X ) (*c*) Endurance ( ) (*d*) Long Distance ( )
   (*e*) Other—describe

Note.—Application will be submitted to the Secretary of Commerce, Washington, D. C., in duplicate, the original of which must be notarized.
Unless all questions are answered, it will be necessary to return the application.
A fee is not required.
In the event owner's address is changed, this office should be immediately notified.

11—0598

The Department of Commerce record indicates the second Ken-Royce biplane (SN102) was registered in the "Restricted Class" for racing in August 1929 prior to sale.

"Air Circus" in November. Ong also took it to the St. Louis Air Exposition in December 1929, which was held in an arena-amphitheater across the street from Forest Park.

Bill Ong at Fairfax, September 1929, shortly before he went to work at Rearwin Airplanes, Inc. Kansas City Museum, Kansas City, MO

In January 1930 Rae told Ong to take the prototype to the Miami Air Races being held later in the month. Ong took along mechanic Fred Baxter, who had also worked at Beacon and had just been laid off by American Eagle. Baxter was a bear of a man who had the strength to pull the often-balky Challenger past three compression points to get it started without losing his fingers. He would also be needed to handle any mechanical problems.

The pair left Fairfax for Louisville, but foul weather forced a detour to Indianapolis, where Baxter rewelded a vibration-induced crack in the engine mount. They also spent three days in Louisville, waiting in vain for the weather to clear. Impatiently, Ong decided to test a reported 1,200-foot ceiling over the 1,100-foot ridges to the south. It was a bad decision; within an hour the ground was pushing the pair into the overcast, and Ong was snaking between crests trying to slither through. Suddenly, his windscreen and goggles were coated with ice.

Not knowing where they were and catching only fleeting glances of forested hills, Ong scribbled Baxter a note telling him to get ready. Ong was going to take the plane up high enough to bail out. Baxter shook his head violently, turned in his seat, and flung his coat open. He was not wearing the chute that Ong had borrowed for him. It was buried under baggage and Baxter's massive tool kit. There would be no bailing out for either of them — Baxter was not a pilot.

Nearly three hours into the flight, Ong caught a glimpse of a paved road that he was able to follow to

The A. R. Jones Building at Fairfax housed Inland Aircraft on the right and Rearwin Airplanes on the left. Rearwin later took over the entire building.

NC400V was the first of the Ken-Royce biplanes powered by the Continental A-70 engine rated at 165 hp.

a flat, fenced quarter-section of land that he knew would be precisely 1,320 feet long. There was a dirt road about eight feet below the level of the field at the up-wind end. "No problem," as Ong would say, "the Ken-Royce could stop on a dime and give back a nickel in change." But Ong's approach was long and fast. Just as when Nichols thought she had run out of fuel near Wichita, the biplane floated while the field unwound behind it. Moreover, the plane rolled forever on the wet grass and stopped only upon impact with the fence posts just above the dirt road. The left strut was bent and the lower left spar was cracked by the collision, a small price to pay for their safety.

Baxter assured Ong that he could repair the plane and they could still make Miami. A few cars showed up, and Baxter negotiated for a flatbed truck and a crew to remove the wings. Ong finally asked where they were. The answer: Dale, Indiana. That was about 70 miles *west* of Louisville, and they had been headed southeast for Miami!

With the wings off, four men got under the tail to heave the aft end of the fuselage onto the truck bed. As they lifted, the fuselage rolled forward the last few feet and over the eight-foot embankment. No one had chocked the wheels. The propeller, as luck would have it, had stopped vertically and was now badly damaged. There would be no racing in Miami. The plane left Evansville two days later in a railroad boxcar headed for Kansas City. Ong and Baxter rode in a Pullman.

In early May 1930, still looking for sales, and encouraged by interest in the plane at St. Louis, Rae sent the Continental-powered Ken-Royce prototype (NC400V) to the Detroit Air Show. Although Ong demonstrated the plane's short takeoff and landing performance and outran the biplanes hosting the more powerful J5 Wright engines, the show failed to produce any sales.

Meanwhile, the Continental Model 2000Co was certified on April 16, 1930 (ATC No. 314), and Fred Landgraf was laid off. However, he landed on his feet as the project engineer for the Curtiss-Wright Sportsman A-14-D Series certified in August 1931.

Jack B. Story won first place in the Pony Express Race held during the Third Annual Pikes Peak Air Meet, August 9-10, 1930.

Ong left the Rearwin corporation in late May to join rival Inland Aviation as a vice president, salesman, and test pilot.[1] Before departing, however, he sold the twice-rebuilt Challenger prototype (now NC44E) for $4,000 to a Sioux Indian from Pawhuska, Oklahoma, named Standing Bear.[2] The Sioux had recently married Mary Strike Axe, an Osage. She had received a full share of a government settlement made for land that later became an oil field, and bought the biplane for her new husband. According to Ong, Standing Bear, true to his name, would stand in the cockpit on final approach, hold the stick in his fingertips, and sit down at the last second to make a landing. Whether he stood for visibility, in honor of his name, or because he was given to the bottle is anyone's guess.

*Pikes Peak or Bust*

The Third Annual Pikes Peak Air Meet was held in Colorado Springs on the weekend of August 9-10, 1930. A new event, a race to the top of Pikes Peak, was scheduled, so Rae sent Jack B. Story west in the Continental A-70 prototype, NC400V. With Ong long gone, Rae had hired Story, a radio announcer from Kansas City. He had been taught to fly by Slonnie Sloniger, an early barnstormer and DH-4 mail pilot with Robertson Airlines, who later became *the* senior pilot for American Airlines. Story, who also flew for National Air Transport (a predecessor of United Airlines) and had once bailed out of a Travel Air, took along Penny Rogers, one of half a dozen women pilots in the Kansas City area.

More than 45 planes from 20 states showed up for the meet, which included pylon races, a free-for-all "Pony Express" race, balloon-bursting contests, and a record-shattering parachute drop from 30,000 feet by local jumper Jimmie Donahue. As usual, the aircraft were divided into three horsepower classes, with the Ken-Royce in the 100 to 225 hp division.

With over 12,000 people in attendance on Saturday, Story was determined to make a credible showing in the Ken-Royce against the local Eaglerocks, the new Cessna monoplanes, and the Travel Airs. He finished third in the 25-mile pylon race behind a pair of 225 hp Wright Whirlwind-powered Cessna monoplanes piloted by C. P. Kysar and Cessna chief pilot Jack Bridges.

Story and the Ken-Royce then won the Class C heat of the "Pony Express" race, a five-lap event that required the pilot to land in front of the judges' stand on each pass. Story also finished fourth in the balloon-bursting contest, while Rogers, flying her first race in the Ken-Royce, finished second in a 15-mile pylon race.

Weather delayed until Monday the three-class race to the top of Pikes Peak, more than 8,000 feet above Colorado Springs, and the record-setting parachute jump. Donahue did his thing from a Wasp-powered Ryan Brougham, but from 28,000 feet. He lost consciousness during the drop when his oxygen tank malfunctioned, but survived and set his record.

Left: The inscription reads: Third Annual Pikes Peak Air Meet Colorado Springs Municipal Airport, August 1930, 38 Mile Race Over Pikes Peak, Altitude 14,109 Feet: Motors 170 Horsepower and Less Won By Rearwin Ken-Royce.

Story won the 30-mile Class C race around the summit of Pikes Peak with a time of 25 minutes and 41 seconds, just 4 minutes behind the Class B winner. All things considered, Pikes Peak was hardly a "bust" for the Ken-Royce or its owner.

*The National Air Races*

The 1930 National Air Races were held in Chicago from August 23 to September 1, and the Ken-Royce (NC400V) was present. Rae had no illusions about winning any big money, and he was not disappointed. He was more interested in sales. Story finished third in Event No. 18, a 5-lap, 25-mile race for open cockpit planes with engine displacements of less than 650 cubic inches, winning $240. If there was a bitter pill, it was finishing behind a pair of open cockpit Warner-powered Inland Sport monoplanes, with first place and $600 going to Bill Ong, who averaged 129.8 mph. The Ken-Royce finished at 123.8 mph. If Rae recalled what Landgraf had said two years earlier about monoplanes being faster because of fewer wings, struts, and wires, he didn't say anything.

A few days later, C. B. Allen won Event No. 42, another 5-lap, 25-mile race for open cockpit planes with a displacement of less than 650 cubic inches. Allen was the aviation editor of the *New York World* and a pilot in the Army Air Corps Reserve. A year earlier he had stirred up a controversy with a series of articles about the quality of the aircraft furnished to Reservists at Milwaukee's Mitchell Field. He beat Western movie star Hoot Gibson for the Sportsman's Trophy offered by the Chicago Athletic Association by less than one mile per hour. Gibson flew an Axelson-powered Swallow, and a Lambert-powered Monocoupe flown by C. B. Burmood finished third.

A year later, Roy Hill flew a Challenger-powered Ken-Royce in the Atlantic Wing of the Cord Cup Race (from Miami to Cleveland), finishing 22nd and taking home $100.

*The Ford Reliability Tour*

The 1930 Ford Reliability Tour was a continuation of the National Air Tours started by the Ford Motor Company in 1925 to demonstrate the increasing dependability of aircraft. Ford, as the builder of the Tri-

The Inland Sport model R-400 was a two-place parasol built in the other half of the A. R. Jones Building. The firm went bankrupt in 1931 and less than 30 such aircraft were built. Kansas City, MO, Public Library motor transport, had an obvious interest in promoting public confidence in aviation. The two-week tour, open to all manufacturers, was heavily covered by a still-aviation-frantic press, and a good showing could result in sales.

The Salina lumberyard dealer entered the Ken-Royce. He had no expectation of beating the Wacos from Weaver Aircraft Co., which had won the race two years running, but if an American Eagle was going to be in it, and one piloted by the company's flight-school instructor Larry Ruch was entered, Rae wanted a Ken-Royce out in front for the whole 4,813-mile course across the United States and Canada.

Grumbling about the rules being changed to favor the Trimotors had upset the Waco people back East. Rumor had it they were designing an even faster plane to win again and keep permanent possession of the Edsel B. Ford Reliability Trophy. None of that concerned Rae. His entry would be off the shelf.

The 1930 Tour started as usual from Dearborn, Michigan, on September 11, wound its way west to Davenport, Iowa, north and then west across Canada to Edmonton, south to Denver, then east through Kansas to Cincinnati, and finally north to Dearborn on September 27. The 16-day odyssey included 30 scheduled stops. The official entries were lead by a "pathfinder" advance plane flown by Frank Hawks and several other craft carrying the press and tour officials. Other aircraft, including a Fleet One, a Kari Keen Coupe, and an Aeronca C-2 unofficially joined the Tour for a segment or two.

Porterfield flight school instructor Larry Ruch test flew the American Eagle A-1 on April 1, 1926, and piloted American Eagle's entry in the 1930 Ford Reliability Tour.
Kansas City Museum, Kansas City, MO

Story finished 11th out of the 18 entries that completed the trip — not exactly what Rae had in mind. Even so, there were a few positives that could be accentuated. First, the Ken-Royce had performed flawlessly with the Continental A-70 engine. Second, on speed alone, the 165 hp plane had averaged 119.3 miles per hour over the run, the ninth fastest. Moreover, all eight with faster times were powered by engines rated at 240 hp or more. Indeed, the winning Ford Trimotor put out 1,020 hp but averaged only 12.6 miles an hour faster than the Ken-Royce.

The 1930 Ford Reliability Tour covered this meandering 4,813-mile route.

If there was solace for Rae, it was that the Ken-Royce completed the grueling tour and had averaged 17.9 mph faster than Ed Porterfield's American Eagle, even though both were powered by the same Continental engine. That said something about the design of the Ken-Royce. At least Rae would have bragging rights back at Fairfax.

*Duped in Dallas*

In July 1931, Jean LaRene took delivery of the third Ken-Royce biplane (NC592H, SN103) for the Dallas School of Aviation located at Love Field where she worked as a secretary and flight instructor for owner William F. Long.[3] LaRene was born and raised in Olathe, Kansas. She started flying before 20 and obtained a transport rating on October 1, 1929, while working at the Commandair factory in Little Rock, Arkansas. She was the eighth woman to do so. In January 1930, she went to work for American Eagle at Fairfax testing and delivering new aircraft.[4] She also placed third in the 1930 Women's National Air Race in an American Eagle Phaeton.

LaRene flew Bill Long's Ken-Royce in both the 1931 and 1932 Women's Air Derbies but didn't place in either event. In the 1932 race she was forced down in wilderness north of Abilene,

The Ford Reliability Tour stopped at Fairfax. Wyandotte County Museum, Bonner Springs, KS

The 1929 Kinner-powered American Eagle Model A-129, nicknamed the "Anteater," was no match for the Ken-Royce.
Kansas Aviation Museum, Wichita, KS

Texas, but without damage to the plane. Like Nichols's experience two years earlier, LaRene walked some 7 miles before coming to a house, and was then driven another 11 miles to town. Two years later she and Henrietta Summer attempted to break the then-existing light plane endurance record of 239 hours, but after 8 days (198 hours) they were forced down by a balking engine.

Jack B. Story, above, piloted NC400V to eleventh place in the 1930 Ford Reliability Tour.
Antique Airplane Association, Blakesburg, IA

LaRene subsequently married former airmail pilot Lou Foote and managed their fixed-based operations and flight schools at Dallas and Grand Prairie. She also barnstormed throughout the state on weekends, and joined her close friends Jessie and Jimmie Woods when their "Flying Aces Air Circus" was in the area.

At various times, LaRene owned three Ken-Royce biplanes. She purchased NC400V from Booth-Henning, Inc.

Jean LaRene married Lou Foote, an early airmail pilot, who owned a fixed-based operation and flight school on the north side of Dallas's Love Field when this 1935 picture was taken.

From left, the second and fifth planes are two of the three Ken-Royce biplanes owned by Jean LaRene.
Roger Freeman

NC12531, owned by Jean LaRene, was destroyed with 13 other aircraft in a disastrous hangar fire in 1942. The inscription on the photo, presumably written by the hapless pilot, reads: "Best Ever. Very slow inverted flying. Shorty Burwell." (He could have added "and low.")
Roger Freeman

Jean LaRene and NC592H. The lettering on the fin reads "Dallas School of Aviation."
Roger Freeman

(Dallas) in June 1937; NC12531 from G. L. Rutherford in May 1938; and NC592H, SN103 from Berton Holly of Seagraves, Texas, on September 26, 1940. NC12531 was destroyed in a disastrous hangar fire with 13 other civilian planes on September 27, 1942. The fate of NC400V is not known.

LaRene wrote of NC592H:

> I have a Ken-Royce with a Challenger motor that I fly all the time. It is fast — and I use it for racing, etc. It has pants on the wheels, cowlings over the motor, and for racing we close in the front cockpit. It's a beautiful plane — cream and orange and black.
>
> I take passengers on cross-country trips and every Sunday carry passengers on local hops, as we always have a huge crowd at Love Field Sunday — and the people of Dallas are very air-minded.

The original sale of NC592H to the Dallas School of Aviation for $4,500 with one-third down had been a bitter pill for Rae. The plane was sold with a written agreement that the balance would be paid in 12 monthly installments. Rae was skeptical of such deals in 1931, so he carefully hired a Dallas law firm to draw up a chattel mortgage. However, not one payment was ever made.

Rae was jolted when he notified the Dallas law firm to foreclose and repossess the plane. The lawyer who had taken Rae's money to prepare the lien quoted an exorbitant fee and told him he was foolish if he paid it because "judges here in Texas still haven't forgotten the Civil War." The message was

Advertising on the fuselage of Jean LaRene's Challenger-powered Ken-Royce reads, "Miss Dallas, Greetings from the Adolphus, Dallas' Finest Hotel."

Roger Freeman

Below: Jack B. Story also piloted NC400V at the Pikes Peak Air Meet and the National Air Races in 1930.

clear — there was little chance of collecting what was owed or getting the plane back. There is no evidence LaRene was in on the scam; Texas, apparently, had its own brand of justice.

*Ken-Royce Production*

The Ken-Royce was one of the premier biplanes of its day. Unfortunately, it was a victim of the Great Depression and only seven were built — each with consecutive serial numbers starting with 101. The first three (NC44E, NC591H, and NC592H) were mated with the 170 hp Curtiss Challenger engine; the final four were built with the Continental A-70. Thrcc of the last four (NC400V, NC12531, and

Royce believes this is a photograph of the seventh biplane built and that it was mistakenly given an "N" number (and the wrong one) before shipment to Honduras with a pair of Sportsters in 1937.

This Ken-Royce biplane bears the same "N" number as the "Honduras" plane shown above, but paint scheme, wheels, and tires are different.

36-17011-8500-527-N.Y.
36-17015-8500-529-Cal.
36-17017-8500-530-Ind.
37-17041-8500-531-La.
37-20
37-17042-9000-532-Colo.
37-17075-7000-536-Ohio
37-18023-7000-538-N.C.
37-18024-7000-539-Ind.
37-18007-9000-540-R.I.
37-17099-8500-541-Tex.
37-17048-8500-542-Cal.

Error on listing of Rearwin aircraft typed by government clerk in 1940 seems to confirm a Model 2000 biplane was built in 1937.
Antique Airplane Association, Blakesburg, IA

NC400V was sold in 1931 to Dewey M. Knox, above, an oilman from Graham, Texas. Dodson Goss and Royce Rearwin flew the plane to Texas, and Goss stayed on several weeks to teach Knox and his wife how to fly it.
The Dewey M. Knox Family

Below: NC591H was registered in San Juan, Puerto Rico, from 1931 to 1936. Sadly, it was destroyed in a mid-air collision with a Curtiss Fledgling (NC486K) over Jamaica Bay, Long Island, New York, on October 4, 1936. Three lives were lost, including new owner Max Stearns and his passenger.
Antique Airplane Association, Blakesburg, IA

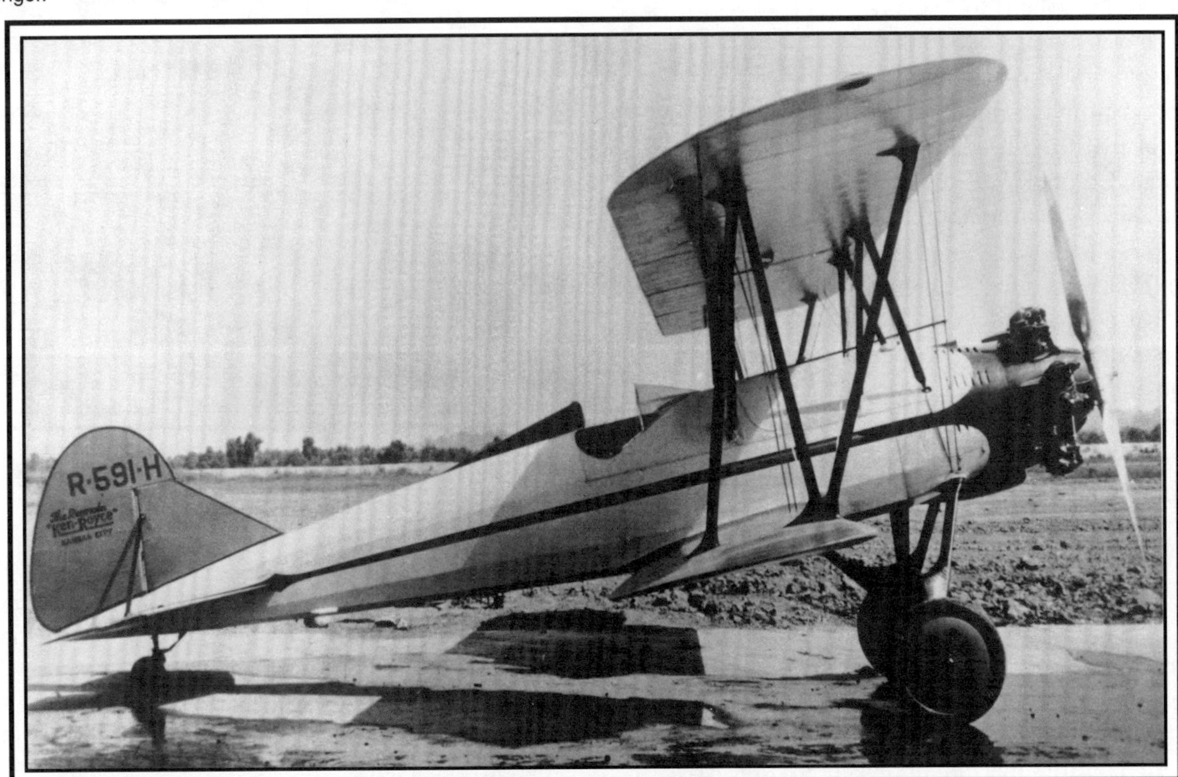

NC12531 was the fifth of the Ken-Royce biplanes. Note the wheel mods, cowling ring, and temporary racing number.
Antique Airplane Association, Blakesburg, IA

NC12579) are well documented and photographed; the elusive seventh (SN107) is not. According to both Royce and Ken, SN107's fuselage was tied to rafters in the plant for several years. It was finally built, along with a pair of Sportsters, for a 1937 order from the Honduras Air Corps, at that time headed by an American, Colonel W. C. Brooks. Indeed, a 1937 testimonial reads:

> The Rearwins are used daily for instruction, and I certainly do not know anything to beat them at this high altitude in any respect as trainers. Besides, they are very good for cross-country and small fields.
>
> Colonel W. C. Brooks
> Honduras Air Corps

The remains of NC592H. The plane was sold to the Dallas School of Aviation and was subsequently owned for many years by Jean LaRene. The current Texas owner vows it will fly again.
Roger Freeman

Although Brooks failed to specifically mention the Ken-Royce by name, a listing of Rearwin aircraft typed by the Civil Aviation Authority (CAA) in 1940 seems to confirm that an unregistered Ken-Royce Model 2000 was built in 1937. In the middle of the 1937 listings, the clerk typed the digits "37-20" and then struck them over with *X*s. It is not unreasonable to believe that the typist had come across the 1937 Model 2000. However, because it was exported and not registered with an *N* number, the entry was apparently deleted.

THIS LICENSE MUST BE PROMINENTLY DISPLAYED IN THE AIRCRAFT

UNITED STATES OF AMERICA
DEPARTMENT OF COMMERCE
AERONAUTICS BRANCH

THIS AIRCRAFT MAY BE FLOWN ONLY BY U. S. LICENSED PILOTS

**LICENSE AUTHORIZATION**

Commercial Aircraft License No. NC12579 Serial No. 106
Model Ken Royce 2000-CO A. T. C. 314
Two (Maximum passengers less crew) Engine Continental A-70

Weight empty as equipped 1447 lbs. Gross weight 2359 lbs.
(See equipment reverse side) (Not to be exceeded)

Maximum pay load is 370 lbs. with fuel of 55 gals.

Maximum pay load is 370 lbs. with full fuel tanks 55 gals.
Cargo spaces: Location and capacity Back of pilot 30 lbs.

THIS CERTIFIES, that the aircraft described above has been inspected and approved for the type of license indicated. This constitutes a temporary license and, unless sooner suspended or revoked, cancels upon receipt of annual license or expires July 17-34

Owner Rearwin Airplanes, Inc
Address Fairfax Airport, Kansas City, Kansas

Leonard Juden
(Department of Commerce Inspector)

Sold to / Sold by / Date of sale

NOTE.—All provisions of the Air Commerce Regulations are made a part of the terms hereof as though written herein.

Form AB-50 11—11034 (OVER)

The License Authorization for NC12579 suggests that the sixth Ken-Royce was built in 1933.
Roger Freeman

R

THIS CERTIFICATE MUST BE PROMINENTLY DISPLAYED IN THE AIRCRAFT

UNITED STATES OF AMERICA
DEPARTMENT OF COMMERCE
ADMINISTRATOR OF CIVIL AERONAUTICS

THIS AIRCRAFT MAY BE FLOWN ONLY BY U. S. CERTIFICATED PILOTS

**REGISTRATION-AIRWORTHINESS CERTIFICATE**

COMMERCIAL IDENTIFICATION MARK NC592H Serial No. 103
Passengers (less crew) TWO Engine CHALLENGER R-600 185 HP
Model REARWIN 2000-C 3 POLB A. T. C. 232

Weight empty as equipped 1505 lb. Gross weight 2380 lb.
(See equipment reverse side) (Not to be exceeded)

Maximum pay load is 355 lb. with fuel of 53 gal.
Maximum pay load is 345 lb. with full fuel tanks 55 gal.
Cargo spaces: Location and capacity—

1 REAR OF PILOT 15 LBS

THIS CERTIFIES, that the aircraft described above is a civil aircraft of the United States of America and has been found to be in condition for safe operation.
REGISTERED OWNER: JEAN LA RENE FOOTE GRAND PRAIRIE AIRPORT GRAND PRAIRIE TEXAS

Unless sooner suspended or revoked, this certificate expires MAY 15 1941
BY DIRECTION OF THE ADMINISTRATOR:

Chief, Certificate Section.

Sold to / Sold by / Date of sale

ANY ALTERATION OF THIS CERTIFICATE IS PUNISHABLE BY A FINE OF NOT EXCEEDING $1,000 OR IMPRISONMENT NOT EXCEEDING 3 YEARS, OR BOTH (OVER)

Form ACA-8—Rev. 7-10-40 2-30 16—16255

The Airworthiness Certificate for NC592H.
Roger Freeman

In June 1935, Royce delivered the sixth biplane (NC12579) to a Cumberland, Maryland, cash purchaser, a former British World War I pilot. While there, Royce had his closest call in an aircraft. The owner, like a kid with a new toy, was anxious to try the plane and asked Royce if he wanted to go along. Figuring he meant a short hop around the patch, Royce climbed in front and neglected to buckle his seat belt.

He was enjoying the lush mountain scenery from about 4,000 feet when, without warning, the pilot firewalled the throttle, dove at a steep angle, and then

The speed ring around the Continental A-70 added "sex appeal" and, presumably, a few mph, but note the tailskid.

The late Cleo Robinson beside his four-fifths scale Ken-Royce biplane. Robert W. Taylor pulled up into a loop. The sudden push-over separated Royce from his seat and left him flailing for something to hold on to. Seat and buttocks separated again at the top while Royce clutched the longerons inside the cockpit like a vise. He finally got his seatbelt secured, and was then able to enjoy a full routine of World War I air maneuvers.

Although it is completely inoperable and will hopefully be restored someday, the remains of the biplane owned by Jean LaRene is the only Ken-Royce known to exist. However, Bob Taylor, President of the Antique Airplane Association headquartered in Blakesburg, Iowa, owns a four-fifths replica (NX400KR) that was built in the 1960s by the late Cleo Robinson of Phillipsburg, Kansas. Cleo called it the "Robinson Mere-Merit." The plane has been restored over a ten-year period by Jeff Claypool, C. C. "Ace" Cannon, Willard Talley, and Brent Taylor, and is engined with a 125 hp Warner overhauled by Harold Lossner.

# The OUTSTANDING "BUY" in Airplanes Today!

## Ken Royce

**By REARWIN**

INTENSIVE VALUE marks Rearwin Ken-Royce apart as the irresistible buy among planes in its class of fineness and brilliant record.

Unchallenged in more than 100 performance tests, a wide appreciation and insistent demand was quick to follow. Advanced production methods were scaled up to the task. And now Rearwin Ken-Royce offers its unmatchable qualities at a taking price to the buyer who sharpens his pencil fine.

**PRICES REDUCED**
**$1250.00**

Rearwin Ken-Royce announces a price reduction of $1250 from former list.

Powered with Curtiss Challenger 170 H. P. or Continental 165 H. P. motor (other motors optional).

Rearwin Ken-Royce quality remains the same, with additional improvements developed by our engineering staff for 1930 models.

The Ken-Royce comes to you fully equipped including Steel Propeller, Brakes, Fire Extinguisher, Cockpit Cover, Navigation Lights, Instruments, Etc.

Fast and powerful in flight, yet with every safety feature, including slow landing speed—you owe it to yourself to investigate the Rearwin Ken-Royce at this remarkable price before buying an airplane.

*Write for detailed information, specifications, performance record, prices, etc.*

**DEALERS**

Let us prove the possibilities open to you in handling this remarkable airplane. Our Dealer Franchise is exceedingly attractive. Write or wire.

## REARWIN AIRPLANES, Inc.

FAIRFAX AIRPORT KANSAS CITY, KANSAS

# Chapter 13

# Ken-Royce and Then "Junior"

*THE GREAT DEPRESSION quickly smothered the growth of general aviation. Existing inventories could not be sold at a profit. Fifty manufacturers closed their doors in 1930, and student pilot applications were down by ten percent. Despite the gloom, there were brave entrepreneurs who were not ready to surrender. Interest in aviation had not died overnight, they reasoned, it was simply that those interested could no longer afford or justify the luxury. Aviation had to adjust, to make itself affordable with smaller, less expensive aircraft.*

*The Cincinnati-based Aeronautical Corporation of America (Aeronca) found itself at the front of the trend in 1930. The firm debuted the single-place C-2, based on Jean A. Roche's 1925 Roche-Dohse flivver, at the St. Louis Air Show in February 1930. It only carried one person on 26 horses and cruised at just 60 mph, but the somewhat comical-appearing machine, alternately labeled "The Flying Bathtub" and "Ruptured Duck," was well received at just $1,555.*

*Fairfax-based American Eagle, then still headed by Ed Porterfield, was one of the first to follow Aeronca's lead. The American Eaglet, originally powered by the two-cylinder Cleone engine and then by the Szekely SR-3-L, was test-flown in the summer of 1930 by American Eagle pilots B. Ralph Hall and Larry Ruch. It received a "Group 2 Approval"[1] on November 18, 1930, making it the only aircraft*

Rearwin sales manager Hart Bowman watches as the logo is painted on a new Rearwin Junior in 1932. Rae is at the far left. The object hanging from the ceiling is the fuselage of a Ken-Royce.

ever certified to carry two passengers on just 30 hp. Young designer Douglas Webber, with Noel Hockaday as his assistant, had done well developing the unconventional aircraft, but had missed the targeted $1,000 selling price by about $500. Rumor had it that Spartan, Curtiss-Wright, and other builders also had small, inexpensive planes on the drawing boards, if not already in the air being tested.

In January 1931, Rae saw an advertisement in an aviation trade journal. Webber, who had been cut loose from American Eagle when the Eaglet design was frozen, was advertising a new light plane design for sale. The package deal included full drawings, engineering and production data, and Webber's services as chief engineer through testing and government certification. He predicted the plane would sell for $1,500, about the same as the Eaglet.

Why Webber failed to just walk down the Fairfax ramp and drop the package on Rae's desk is a mystery. Most likely, he was seeking the highest bidder or had hoped to escape Porterfield's wrath. The plane, although beefed-up and improved, was strikingly similar to the Eaglet, but that didn't bother Rae. Rearwin Airplanes, Inc. needed a quick entry into the low-price market, and if Webber's design was better, flew faster, and would sell for about the same, that was the way to go.

Rae bought the design and Webber's engineering services for $1,500 and, at Webber's request, hired Hockaday as his assistant. Hockaday was a talented draftsman and hands-on welder. He had worked with Stan Wallace on the Touroplane before the Chicago firm was swallowed by American Eagle and both moved to Kansas City.

The new plane rolled out of the Rearwin factory in record time and, although Royce and Ken were Rae's only sons, it was promptly christened "Junior." The prototype Model 3000, like the Eaglet, was a conventional-geared parasol monoplane with a "chrome-moly" 1025 steel-tube fuselage and wooden wings with plywood leading edges. The wing was built in two halves with laminated spruce spars and spruce and birch plywood truss-type ribs. The center

This photo of E. E. "Ed" Porterfield, Jr., was taken in 1925, the same year he learned to fly, opened a flying school, and started the company that became American Eagle Aircraft Corporation.
Kansas City Museum, Kansas City, MO

The American Eagle Eaglet was originally engined with the 25 hp Cleone, but was underpowered.

Young Doug Webber in 1935. Webber designed both the look-alike American Eaglet and the Rearwin Junior. Parks Air College, East St. Louis, IL

section was mounted above the fuselage on steel struts. Twin struts were attached to the lower longerons and the outer wings, but without the cross-members that impeded cockpit access by pilots wearing parachutes. A cut-out in the trailing edge of the wing over the rear seat assisted entry.

The landing gear had a 72-inch tread that employed rubber compression rings to absorb shock, and Goodyear 16x7:4 air wheels without brakes were standard equipment. The elongated fuselage sat two in tandem, with plastic windscreens for both. The seats were welded, so that adjustments for pilot size were made with cushions. Both cockpits had controls, and the horizontal trim tab could be adjusted during flight from either seat. The prototype, X-507Y, SN201, was powered by a Szekely SR-3-0 radial engine rated at 45 hp.

The Junior was test-flown in April 1931 by B. Ralph Hall, who had been laid off by American Eagle, and certified (ATC No. 434) on July 9, 1931, less than six months after Rae purchased the design and Webber's services. By then Porterfield had been relegated to sales manager for the recently merged American Eagle-Lincoln Aircraft Company. Still, it is unlikely that he was pleased with the new Fairfax entry or its similarities to the Eaglet. But there were differences even a casual eye could note. The Junior

The Wing Department of Rearwin Airplanes, Inc. during the "Junior era," 1932.

was 5 inches longer, boasted a wing span 20 inches wider, and sat on main gear spread 18 inches farther apart.

As Rae planned, the Junior was also farther removed from the lightweight "flivver" class. The empty weight of the prototype was 100 pounds heavier than the Eaglet, and it could carry a larger payload and fly higher, faster, and farther. Rae's modifications and improvements to the design, including a small, 15-pound capacity baggage compartment absent on the Eaglet, resulted in an initial base price of $1,795, about $300 off target. Since the Szekely itself cost $625, there was little room for profit. Even the flivver market was limited.

Above: The Junior prototype Model 3000 (X507Y) was powered by the Szekely SR-3-0 engine rated at 45 hp.

Left: The tandem-seated Junior was flown from the front.

The second Junior off the line (NC508Y) was originally powered with the ill-fated Poyer engine and then with the Aeromarine AR-3, shown above.

FAIRFAX FACTS

Published by Fairfax Airports, Inc., operators of Fairfax Airport, Kansas City; Atchison Airport, Atchison; Weston Field, Weston; Parkville Port, Parkvill[e]
Office address, Second Floor, Fairfax Building, Kansas City, Mo.

Vol. 2 OCTOBER, 1931 No. 1

The masthead of the monthly in-house Fairfax Airport newsletter.

Wyandotte County Museum, Bonner Springs, KS

Late in 1930, A. R. Jones had asked Rae to provide some space in the factory for Guy Poyer, a business acquaintance who was developing a new three-cylinder radial aircraft engine. Jones was financing the project and said that Poyer believed it would produce 40 hp. Rae, of course, agreed, and Poyer and Russell Carter, also formerly with American Eagle, moved in and busied themselves in an unused corner.

The first two Juniors were finished and test-flown in time for the National Aircraft Show held at Detroit in April 1931. The first Junior, X-507Y, was outfitted with the 45 hp Szekely with overhead valves; the second, X-508Y, with Poyer's still-experimental 40 hp engine. Rearwin test pilot Ralph Hall flew the craft powered by Poyer's engine. Bill Ong, released by struggling Inland Sport, flew the other. The May issue of *Fairfax Facts*, a monthly airport newsletter, reported:

> . . . the Poyer motor was flown the entire distance to and from Detroit without servicing, with the exception of gas and oil. It used only 2-1/2 gallons of gas per hour.

The newsletter "Facts" were wrong, no doubt a result of Poyer "PR." The truth was that the engine had

The basic no-frills Junior (NC11092) owned and flown for several years by Marion McClure. David A. Warren

The Rearwin Flying School opened its doors in 1931. Flight instructor Ken McNeal is pictured above. Antique Airplane Association, Blakesburg, IA

vibrated so badly that several motor mount welds cracked en route. Thus, the Poyer plane was restricted to display, while the Szekely-powered Model 3000 was used for demonstrations. Poyer claimed the welds had been bad, but those acquainted with Rearwin welder Smokey Nelson knew better. Nevertheless, the matter was hushed up, at least publicly.

Poyer went back to the drawing board, and later that summer took the engine to Washington, D.C., for calibration tests. On his return he reported that it had actually developed over 45 hp and had run at full throttle for more than 23 hours without malfunction, except for a broken valve!

In July, a Junior powered with the still-experimental Poyer 3-40 and carrying two people flew the 240 miles between St. Louis and Kansas City in 3 hours and 3 minutes (about 80 mph) at a cost of just over one cent a mile. A Heath Parasol, also pulled by the Poyer engine, set altitude records for light aircraft twice that summer, first at Niles, Michigan (17,907 feet), and then at Chicago (19,050 feet).

Meanwhile, Hall and a lady friend were forced down in a Junior when a Poyer surrendered in flight. Rae wasn't convinced that the engine was sufficiently powerful or reliable, so the Junior prototype was certified with the Szekely, while experiments began with the Aeromarine AR-3 rated at 50 hp. Rae was also interested in setting records, but with Rearwins. Poyer, who had developed his engine in the Rearwin plant, had not endeared himself by putting his engine on a Heath to set his records. Rae had previously announced that a Junior would try for the same record. Poyer may have sought Jones's intervention, but there is no evidence that he interceded, and the Poyer project faded.

In June 1931, with Juniors coming off the line, Rae and Jones decided to establish a flying school. As a subsidiary corporation of Rearwin Airplanes, Inc., it would produce income from unsold Juniors, and keep the test pilots busy earning their way. Hall, new sales director Hart Bowman, Ken McNeal, and Paul O'Neal, who held transport license number 3104, would serve as instructors, and the school would be headed by Harry V. Clyborne.

Royce was still in college at the University of Kansas in 1931 but worked at the factory during the summer as purchasing manager. He was soloed by Ralph Hall and was the first from the new school to qualify for a private license (No. 22084) on September 12, 1931. The school initially charged five dollars an hour "wet" (including fuel), and eight to ten dollars with an instructor. An *Aero Digest* ad from the time reads:

> The Rearwin Flying School offers expert flight training in brand new Juniors at the low rate of only $10 an hour dual. Experienced transport pilots who are experienced also in student instruction take a personal interest in your progress. Their individual attention is part of the course.

Later advertisements announced a solo course for a flat $75 and a private pilot's license for just $175. Barnstormer Ben ("FLY WITH BEN") Gregory, based at Fairfax, jokingly complained to the Fairfax management board about the busy new school in late 1931: "Any time I want to take off with my Stinson I have to look around, there is always a Rearwin either coming in or taking off."

In the fall, Royce started flying Rae to Salina on

# EXPERT FLIGHT TRAINING

*in brand new "Juniors"*

# AT $10 AN HOUR

•

THE Rearwin Flying School offers expert flight training in brand new "Juniors" at the low rate of only $10 an hour dual. Experienced transport pilots who are experienced also in student instruction take a personal interest in your progress. Their individual attention is part of the course.

The Rearwin "Junior," because of its slow landing speed, inherent stability, cockpit arrangement for normal-tone conversation during flight, is an ideal training plane. We have been soloing students in this plane after as little as 3½ to 4 hours of dual training.

An advantage of the Rearwin Flying School which not many schools can offer is the affiliation with the Rearwin manufacturing activities. In the Rearwin plant the student is able to watch aircraft construction from the blue print stage through the final test hop. Write for further details today.

•

THOROUGHBRED — *The Rearwin* **JUNIOR** — OF THE LIGHT PLANE CLASS

# WATCH WHERE REARWIN "JUNIOR" GOES IN 1932

THE Rearwin "Junior" made its bow to the aircraft market early in 1931, in the face of stiff competition. Its popularity among flying schools and private fliers has grown rapidly in a comparatively short time. ¶ Backed by the personnel and organization which produced the performing "Ken-Royce" and supported by the policy that the basis of sound competition is quality and not price—the "Junior" was destined at the very start to occupy a prominent place in the light plane field. ¶ The Rearwin "Junior" has an adjustable stabilizer which can be operated from either seat, dual controls, sufficient gas capacity for cross country flying without frequent landings for refueling, wide landing gear with air wheels and shock absorbers, center section which lends itself to a winter enclosure, front and rear individual windshields, large roomy seats and plenty of leg room for large individuals in the six foot class. The beautiful new 1932 Rearwin "Junior" models are ready for delivery with the Szekely SR-3-0 45 h.p. or the Aeromarine AR-3 50 h.p. engine. In the very near future a detachable winter enclosure will be available as optional equipment. ¶ We are proud of the progress which our conscientious efforts have given to the Rearwin "Junior" during 1931. Watch where it goes in 1932—you will not be satisfied with owning anything less than a "Junior" if you are thinking of buying a training or sport plane.

## REARWIN AIRPLANES, Incorporated

FAIRFAX AIRPORT KANSAS CITY KANSAS

**$1795.00 with 45 H.P. Engine**
**A.T.C. No. 434**

**DEALERS:** If you have faith in the aviation market for 1932 we should like to explain the *Rearwin Protected Franchise* to you. Your written or wired inquiry will receive prompt and detailed acknowledgment.

weekends, a breezy two-hour flight in the open-cockpit Junior. As the temperature dropped, it wasn't hard for Royce to convince his chilled-to-the-bone passenger to develop a detachable, clear plastic canopy made of Pyrolean that enclosed both occupants. Webber went to work and designed two versions, one weighing 14 pounds and the other 28. Both were offered as options for about $100.

It was a slow news day in late October 1931 when Rae, a group of friends, and a reporter waited in Salina for Royce to arrive from Fairfax with a new Junior. Royce, who had barely two months on his license, overshot the first approach, but settled in nicely on the second. Rae, slightly embarrassed, teased Royce about his distance-judging ability and, as noted in the next day's paper, the 21-year old retorted, "Dad, I didn't do so bad. Jimmy Doolittle overshot Fairfax!"

At about the same time, Webber installed the new but still-uncertified Aeromarine AR-3 engine in the Junior (NC508Y, SN202) that had formerly hosted the Poyer. The engine was designed well and could develop 40 hp at 2,050 rpm, or 50 hp with dual ignition at 2,150 revolutions. The mating of the three-cylinder Aeromarine with the Junior was type-certificated on March 25, 1932 (ATC No. 469), and the plane was designated the Model 4000. However, only eight were built. The Aeromarine Company was under-capitalized and built engines only on order. The AR-3 engine weighed only 140 pounds, and at $560, cost $65 less than the Szekely, but delivery took up to six weeks, enough time for an anxious prospect to change his mind and buy something else — perhaps an Eaglet.[2]

Rearwin sales director Hart Bowman reported in the June 1931 issue of *Fairfax Facts* that the company had made deliveries to several dealers, including Boss-Fisher Air Service in Pekin, Illinois, Tarkington Aviation in Indianapolis, and Phipps Aviation Corporation in New York. Another Junior was sold in July to a Mrs. Florence Williams of Oakland, California. She took delivery at the Fairfax plant and promptly announced that she was the new West Coast dealer for Rearwin aircraft.

August was a banner month, with eight Junior sales reported by *Fairfax Facts*. Two more were sold by the end of 1931. One was purchased by Paul Dooley and based at Fairfax, while Bowman and Ralph Hall delivered the other to Fayetteville, North Carolina, after being forced down for several days at Newport, Tennessee, because of the season's first snowstorm. However, a CAA directive prohibited the Szekely SR-3-45 from being installed in new aircraft after December 31, 1932, so Rae cast about for a new engine, briefly considering the 3-cylinder Jacobs L-3 of 55 hp.

The problem with the Szekely was simple — unreliability. On one occasion, Bowman, with a Trans

The Pyrolean cockpit cost extra, but provided protection from the cold without impairing visibility.

Opposite page: The advertisement in December 1931 issue of *Aero Digest* promoted both the new Junior and the Rearwin Flying School.

Antique Airplane Association, Blakesburg, IA

A Rearwin Junior powered with the 45 hp Szekely SR3-0 engine.

World Airlines draftsman as a passenger, lost a prop at about 800 feet and less than a mile from Fairfax. He put the spindly craft down safely near an oil pumping station. Inspection revealed that the crankcase had separated and both the shaft and prop had exited the plane holding hands. Sometimes an entire cylinder head blew off. Whether it was Royce's idea or a borrowed one, he convinced Rae that the cylinder heads should be strapped in place with three-eighths-inch cable and turnbuckled.

But the Szekely also had its fans. One was Marion McClure of Bloomington, Illinois, who owned and flew a 45 hp Junior 3000 for several years:

> Before hand propping, the Zerk fittings on the rocker arm shafts were each lubricated with the small grease gun always carried. The push rods were given a shot of Marvel Mystery Oil and the clearance of each rod was then checked with a feeler gauge. It started easily. With a top RPM of 1750, one always felt the firing of each cylinder. My Szeke only missed one beat, but all three cylinders fired the next time around. I never lost the thrill of being behind that engine.

Rearwin was the first to try the new Szekely SR-3-55 engine rated at 50 hp. The upgraded power

The lettering on the fuselage of NC14423 reads, "U.S. Aero Units Inc., New York, Kansas City, Los Angeles." The aircraft is a Junior Model 4000 with an Aeromarine 50 hp engine.
Antique Airplane Asssociation, Blakesburg, IA

Elva Tarkington, a cousin of famous author Booth Tarkington, sold several Juniors from his fixed based operation in Indianapolis.

Below: A Rearwin Junior with two aboard plows through the Kansas skies, *circa* 1932.

plant had a higher compression ratio than the earlier models and operated at greater rpm. The third and last of the Junior series, the Model 3100 was certified (ATC No. 481) with the new Szekely engine on May 6, 1932. However, only two were built before Szekely, another victim of the Depression, closed its doors. One of the two Juniors was a previously built Model 3000 (NC11059) that was retrofitted. The other was NC12513, SN219.

Some experiences with the Szekely were Rearwin-personal. One Sunday afternoon, Royce was flying Rae to Fairfax from a weekend in Salina when a cylinder quit over the Flint Hills, a scenic and rugged open range area west of Topeka. Royce set the Junior down safely in a pasture to investigate. A cap on the end of a rocker arm was missing.

A local blacksmith had nothing that would work, but Royce thought that a new cap could be drilled from a section of a three-eighths-inch bolt. The next question was how much metal to leave on the bolt; Royce guessed at one-sixteenth- to three-thirty-seconds-inch, and was able to squeeze the new cap on and turn the engine over. It worked fine, and father and son were back at Fairfax by nightfall. Rae took another look at his eldest son that day. So what if he overshot Salina; Doolittle *had* overshot Fairfax, in

September during the Bendix race from Los Angeles to Cleveland.

Rae was not a pilot, but he had heard enough about accidents to insist that both sons be spin-trained before soloing. Ken O'Neal wouldn't teach spins, so the task fell to others, including Rearwin instructor Paul Dooley. Rae's insistence saved their lives. In late 1933, Ken traveled from college in Evanston, Illinois, to Kansas City, where he met Royce. The pair would fly a Junior to Salina for the Christmas holidays. Royce had just had some wisdom teeth pulled, so he slumped down in back to sleep. Ken, who had earned his pilot's license in 1932, dumped their bags in the luggage compartment and flew from the front. Climbing out from Fairfax at about 1,600 feet, Ken was suddenly watching the ground whirling to the right. He understood what was happening — an accidental spin — a center of gravity problem — that, with adrenaline flowing, took barely two turns to recover.

Rearwin test pilot Jack Le Claire (left) and Rae with a Junior in 1934.

Jack LeClaire

"Crash," pictured above in this photo taken at the Des Moines airport in 1934, was actually the owner of N12513, C. L. Wilson, who worked at Lunken Airport, Cincinnati, for many years as an FAA inspector.

Antique Airplane Association, Blakesburg, IA

Above: The last-known Junior still hangs in the late Oscar Cooke's farm implement museum "Oscar's Dreamland," in Billings, Montana.
Oscar Cooke Family

Right: The Junior prototype was crumpled when the Szekely quit on takeoff from West Liberty, Kentucky, in 1933. Owner Oscar Cooke surveys the damage.
William E. Miller Collection

The G-force of the pull-up woke Royce, who growled, "What the hell was that?"

"Nothing, Royce, go back to sleep."

Just 23 Juniors were built. One was sold to the Skoda Munitions Works in Czechoslovakia, the first of many Rearwin exports that would follow. The only known remaining example was owned by the late Oscar Cooke. Cooke had bought the Junior prototype (NC507Y) and learned to fly in it in 1932 from Bill Miller, then an instructor for Emporia Flying Service. Cooke cracked up the plane taking off from West Liberty, Kentucky, in 1933, and traded it in on an OX5 Curtiss Robin. Years later he purchased NC11092, SN218 from Marion McClure. It sported a Szekely Model SR3-O engine up front and was redesignated as N507Y. As late as 1996 it was on display at "Oscar's Dreamland," an early farm implement and steam-engine museum established by Cooke in Billings, Montana.

## *Chapter 14*

# Fingers in the Dike

*DESPITE THE stock market crash, there was optimism that the hard times would be short-lived. But as the early months of 1930 unfolded with widespread unemployment and escalating business failures, fragile hope was replaced by reality. The aircraft industry was particularly vulnerable and especially hard hit.*

*Between 1929 and 1934, the number of aircraft manufacturers decreased by almost two-thirds — from 132 to just 48. American Eagle, Butler, Inland Sport, Swallow, and others were gone. The same economic plague devastated engine manufacturing. Of 21 firms in 1929, only 10 were left by 1933. The Depression had an even greater impact on the number of civil aircraft produced. There were 6,193 civil aircraft built in 1929, but only 1,324 at the low point in 1933 — a reduction of more than 78 percent! Of those, 406 (about 30 percent) were exported.*

*Financial records indicate that the infant Rearwin firm sold only one Ken-Royce in 1930, the prototype sold to Standing Bear, at a loss of about $2,000. Overhead, including factory expenses, employee wages, pilots' salaries, and advertising, had resulted in a year-end operating deficit of $31,799 — a sizeable sum in 1930.*

*The outlook for 1931 was even bleaker. The chances of selling Ken-Royce biplanes in quantity, despite a deserved reputation for speed and quality, were re-*

mote. Closing the doors was not an option for Rae, and his determination not to do so had resulted in the Junior. However, even the sale of 14 Juniors and a pair of biplanes in 1931 failed to plug the dike. They had cost a total of $39,428 in direct labor and materials to build, and when the traditional overhead expenses were tallied on December 31, the firm had lost another $22,855. Net worth had decreased even further. If building aircraft was a determined and valiant endeavor, it was also a sure way to go broke.

Rae had loaned the firm $9,200 of his own funds in 1931 to develop and market the Junior and get the Flying School off the ground. Wing-builder Kelsey Chaney and a few others even agreed to work on a contract or piece-rate basis, and whatever raw materials were not needed were resold for cash. Rae, of course, did not draw a salary, but lived on investments and Salina income, which was also suffering. To outsiders, however, the firm appeared to be weathering the storm, but it was only an illusion that Rae worked hard to maintain.

While 1932 was better, there was still no profit. The year's operating loss was cut to $1,087 on gross sales of $13,681. The Flying School was busy and showed a profit, but the struggling firm was out of cash. The handwriting was on the wall; things had to change.

A. R. Jones, who had literally lost millions of dollars in "the Crash," was also strapped for cash. He had sold much of his art collection, still owed $27,000 for his stock, and the Rearwin firm's account receivables were ten times greater than payables. No one, it seemed, had cash. The corporation's capital account had shrunk to just over $130,000. More than half of that consisted of the intangible paper rights to the Ken-Royce. Jones was not about to come up with more money for the floundering aircraft venture, even if he had it. Besides the art collection, he had lost his investments in Beacon Airways and the Poyer engine. Enough was enough.

Yet, doggedly, Rae still believed in the long-term future of aviation and, in the short run, felt that a market existed for a fast, two-place enclosed monoplane — the one Doug Webber and he had recently talked about. It could plug the dike. But although Rae still had personal resources and income from the lumberyard, rental property, and stocks, and was willing to take more risks, he was not about to pour more cash into the near-moribund corporation alone.

Rae met with Jones in March 1933 and reported that Rearwin Airplanes, Inc. lacked the capital to continue building the Junior or to design and develop new aircraft. If that wasn't enough, the firm owed Rae more in loans than it was worth if Jones did not pay his stock debt. It was not news to Jones. As Chairman of the Board, he had signed the notes held by Rae. The only issue was what to do. Rae had several proposals.

First, they could keep the firm alive for now, selling the existing inventory of finished aircraft and parts. Additional Juniors would be built only on order. The income from the Flying School would cover some of the overhead, a mechanic's school would be opened, and Rae would slash expenses even further. Secondly, if Jones wasn't interested in funding the development of new aircraft, such as the Speedster, the monoplane that Rae described, he wanted Jones's permission to go it alone as a sole proprietor. Finally, Rae sought use of the Rearwin factory, machinery, and equipment, all of which were

FORM NO. 196—CLASS K — Demaree Stationery Co., 905 Walnut St., Kansas City, Mo.

$1,000.00 — February 8th 1932

On Demand after date We promise to pay to R. A. REARWIN or order

ONE THOUSAND AND NO/100 Dollars

at FIDELITY NATIONAL BANK AND TRUST COMPANY, KANSAS CITY, MISSOURI

For value received, with interest thereon at Six (6) per cent per annum from date until paid.

REARWIN AIRPLANES, INC. BY Albert R. Jones, Chairman of Board

ATTEST: Secretary — BY R. A. Rearwin, President

No. Due On Demand — This Note is Secured by

One of several promissory notes signed by Albert R. Jones and Rae evidencing Rae's loans to struggling Rearwin Airplanes, Inc. in 1931-1932.

essentially idle, to develop and market the new aircraft designs.

Without a blink, Jones agreed. The A. R. Jones Building could not be rented anyway, and the machinery and equipment would be idle except to build pre-paid orders. Moreover, they currently had little or no resale value. Jones was also aware that Rae had spent almost four years running their firm and had never drawn a nickel for his efforts. On the contrary, by 1933 he had advanced the corporation nearly

The fully cowled Speedster with the inverted, inline Menasco C-4 engine. NASM, Smithsonian Institution, Washington, D.C. 7A-37541

The Speedster's narrow profile increased performance, but occupants were cramped. NASM, Smithsonian Institution, Washington, D.C., 1B-32382

$10,000, and it was unlikely the loans would ever be repaid.

The two Kansans entered into a half-page agreement dated March 23, 1933. "For services past and to be rendered in the future," Jones agreed to permit Rae to use the east half of the A. R. Jones Building, which was already occupied by their corporation, and the related machinery and equipment free of rent. He also granted Rae permission to design, build, and certify the Speedster and other aircraft for his own account. The rental agreement was cancelable in 30 days.

The new "Rearwin School of Aviation," headed by George M. Prescott, offered both classroom and hands-on experience in airframe assembly and maintenance and engine repair. The fact that student training also involved production work was a plus not only for the company, but for the piece-rate workers. A four-page brochure advertising the school stated in part:

> Students enrolled in the Rearwin School of Aviation receive actual experience building new government-approved airplanes as well as repairing and overhauling used airplanes and motors. Dormitory facilities are available for students. The Rearwin Dormitories are located on the second floor of the Rearwin Factory building — a modern building constructed of fireproof materials. Rates are very reasonable. Students will find living in the Rearwin Dormitory just like a Club — convenient at all times and a real money saver, as there is no streetcar or bus fare to pay each day. You are right at the factory and school for all instruction. Entertaining facilities are provided for students in the living room. Games are played for diversion and aviation subjects of mutual interest are discussed informally. Lifetime friendships are formed in the Rearwin Dormitory.

Above: Jack LeClaire had earned his wings in the Marine Corps Reserve before joining Rearwin as a draftsman/test pilot/flight instructor in 1934 for the "princely" sum of $25 a week. Jack LeClaire

Right: Rae Rearwin with Jack LeClaire in the cockpit of the Speedster prototype, *circa* 1935. Jack LeClaire

In June 1936, Rearwin moved to Hangar 5, once used by Universal Aviation Corp. Later, in early 1938, the company double-decked the rear two-thirds of the building and put the LeBlond (Ken-Royce) engine operation at the rear of the first floor. Planes were built on the mezzanine and assembled in the front one-third of the ground floor. The offices were also on the ground floor, in the front half of the building. The stock room was at the back of the ground floor. The engineers were in the front half of the second floor, and wings were built in the rear half.

Athough the school was not a financial "barn burner," every little bit helped to prop the doors open during the mid-1930s, and it kept Kelsey Chaney and a few other Rearwin employees out of the soup lines.

Over the next three years only five Juniors were sold, the last in 1936. Even Fairfax Airport went bankrupt in 1934 and was repossessed by the Union Pacific's real estate subsidiary. Rae, however, pared expenses to the bone,[1] personally handled all corporate business, and reduced the aggregate losses for 1934-1936 to just $230.56! At the same time, he developed the Speedster and Sportster models for his own new firm, Rearwin Aircraft Company, a sole proprietorship. To outsiders and employees alike, no change had occurred.

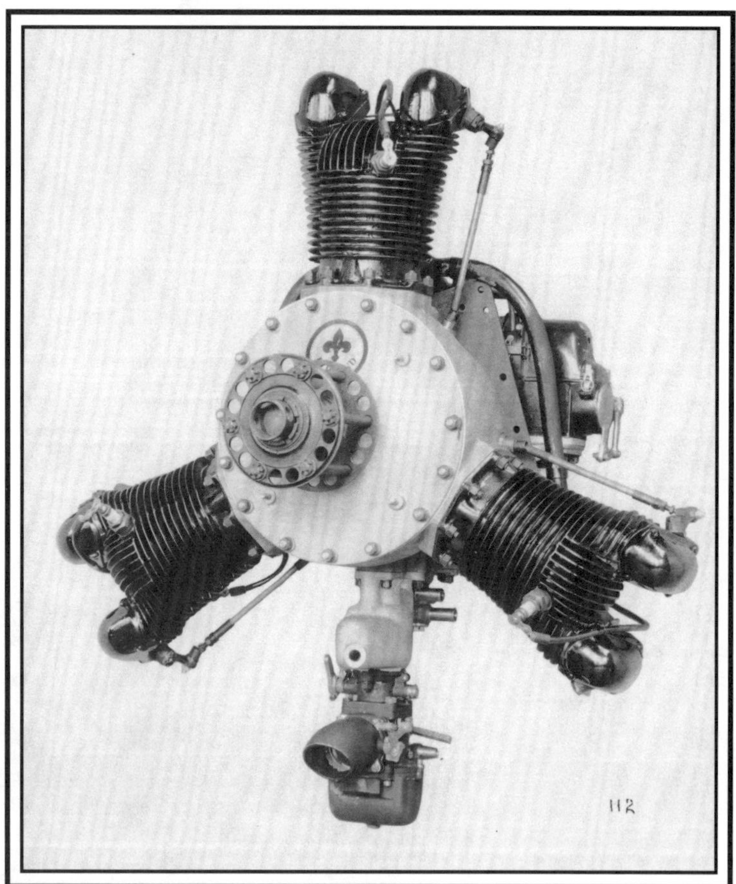


The three-cylinder LeBlond engine. Robert W. Rummel

# REARWIN AIRPLANES

FAIRFAX AIRPORT • KANSAS CITY, KANSAS • U. S. A. • Cable: REARWIN

## Chapter 15

# The Speedster Saga

*THE REARWIN SPEEDSTER was a sleek, highly streamlined two-place tandem aircraft that, when first designed in 1933 by Doug Webber, promised to be a real winner in the marketplace.*[1] *With trim frontal areas to maximize speed, good aerobatic handling, and attractive lines, it fit the swashbuckling, sport aviation era of the mid-1930s. However, like the Ken-Royce, it was never to realize its true market potential. Although the prototype 6000C, X12588 was off the ground in mid-1934, it would be more than three years before the slender, arrow-shaped craft was approved for production (ATC No. 637) in late 1937.*

*The prototype, powered with the four-cylinder inverted ACE Cirrus Hi-Drive MK3 inline engine of 95 hp, was first flown by Rearwin test pilot John B. "Jack" LeClaire on July 11, 1934. LeClaire, a Kansas City native, was a University of Kansas mechanical engineering graduate who had earned his wings as a Marine Corps Reserve pilot in 1931. He believed that although the Speedster fuselage was too narrow for pilot comfort, the ship was responsive and handled well. However, there was a major problem — spin recovery.*

*Federal rules in the 1930s required an aircraft to recover from a six-turn spin in not more than one-and-a-half turns, power and hands off. The plane also had to recover from a six-turn spin entered with controls crossed in not more than six*

Rae with the sleek Menasco-powered Speedster, *circa* 1937.

turns, again without power and hands off. In both instances the center of gravity had to be in the most critical, full aft position.

LeClaire, who also doubled as a Rearwin draftsman and flight instructor for $25 a week, once made 21 consecutive turns in the prototype with the controls neutralized, but it would not recover hands and power off. In his opinion, however, the plane was not at all dangerous. It responded immediately to full power and opposite control inputs, and it had no inclination toward flat spinning.

Rae brought aboard some new people to work on the spin problem. One was Henry Weeks, a 1931 MIT grad who had worked in the TWA engineering department and was president of Stevenson-Weeks Air Service, Inc. at Richards Field in Kansas City, Missouri. He was hired as a part-time chief engineer in 1935 when Doug Webber left in frustration to teach at Parks Air College in East St. Louis.[2] Weeks was born in San Antonio on April 8, 1906, and had earned a degree in physics from the University of Missouri in 1928.

A number of fixes were tried. Weeks enlarged the Speedster's rudder and stabilizer, sharpened the leading edges on the wings, altered the angle of incidence, and installed a larger fin. All of these modifications changed the original handling characteristics, much to LeClaire's displeasure. The solution eluded Weeks, LeClaire, and new test pilot William E. Miller, who replaced LeClaire when he left in late 1935 to join Trans World Airlines as an engineering draftsman and later as a distinguished line pilot.

Bill Miller was born in Chase County, Kansas, on May 30, 1913. He traded a motorcycle to instructor Wes Hague in exchange for flying lessons while still in high school at Cottonwood Falls and was licensed in 1931, the same year that he graduated. Bill "barnstormed" throughout Kansas and neighboring states as a youth in the early 1930s in a Halske-Siemans Waco, an OX5-powered Curtiss Robin, and an Eaglerock. He also used a Junior to instruct for the Emporia Flying Service before joining Rearwin as a test pilot and flight instructor in mid-1936.

Miller had the same frustrations with the stubborn Speedster as Weeks and LeClaire had. He recalled in 1960:

> It was redesigned, changed, altered and rechanged more times than I can remember . . . and I still regret that it was necessary to make a single change in it. I ran spin tests for hundreds of hours . . . and I recall no condition where the spin recovery characteristics were abnormal or dangerous where the airplane was not spun past two turns.

Royce repeatedly urged his father to throw in the towel on the project. The plane, although right at the time of conception in 1933, was outdated by 1936. The tandem cockpit was too narrow — the trend was toward comfort and side-by-side seating — and the speed advantage was lost. Moreover, the Cirrus engine had been discontinued in 1935, and a new power plant would have to be mated to the narrowly profiled airframe. Royce argued that the languishing product was draining time and money that could be better spent and, even if the spin-test problem was solved and a new engine found, the plane would never be a good seller. It would be better to lick small wounds now than bigger ones later.

The Speedster Model 6000C prototype with Cirrus engine was still uncertified in 1936.

William Henry Weeks.

Rae would not bend. He might have relented had he been a pilot, for he would have had a better understanding of what they wanted in a personal plane in 1935-1936. But Royce had talked his father out of learning to fly with arguments about what might happen to the business if Rae was involved in an accident. Rae accepted his older son's advice about learning to fly in his late 50s, but he rejected his pleas to scrap the Speedster project. As both sons would later say, "Dad never knew when he was licked." It was a matter of pride, if not just plain stubbornness. Indeed, the issue became so heated in 1936 that Royce suddenly found himself exiled to Salina to manage the lumber and fuel businesses, which by then were also struggling.

The search for a new engine was not difficult. Al Menasco was building a 4-cylinder, 125 hp inline inverted engine that had achieved recognition in racing circles. It almost seemed that Menasco had designed the engine with the Speedster in mind. Now, if the spin problem could be solved. . . .

That task fell to Robert W. Rummel, a 22-year-old native of Dakota, Illinois, who had headed West after high school and zipped through the Curtiss-Wright Technical Institute in Glendale, California, with honors. He had worked briefly on Howard Hughes's racer and on the Lockheed Electra Junior Model 12. He was en route to St. Louis for an interview with George Page of Curtiss-Wright, and along the way

Rearwin test pilot Bill Miller with the Cirrus-powered Speedster prototype, *circa* 1936. William E. Miller Family

Robert W. Rummel, *circa* 1939, as chief engineer of Rearwin Aircraft and Engines, Inc. Robert W. Rummel

Above and below: Most of the Speedsters built were engined with the 125 hp Menasco Pirate. Robert W. Rummel

# Around the Pylons

## *at 149.7 m.p.h.**

Jan. 1938 "Aero Digest"

● This is the record made by a 125 h.p. REARWIN Speedster at the Miami races.

The Speedster's rare combination of racing pace coupled with its safety, comfort, beauty and economy make it today's outstanding two-place airplane.

You'll thrill to the Speedster's climb of 1200 feet the first minute, 5000 feet in five minutes.

You'll be proud of the Speedster's .outstanding design and its beautiful hand-rubbed finish.

You'll enjoy the Speedster's comfortable sound-proofed cabin with harmonious upholstery, perfectly appointed instrument panel, adjustable front seat and 50 lbs. luggage allowance in two compartments including space for a large Gladstone bag.

You'll feel secure with the Speedster's exceptional visibility, ball-bearing controls throughout, 72" tread cantilever landing gear, 34 gallon fuel capacity in wing tanks, 550 mile cruising range.

You'll be surprised at what the Speedster, fastest two-place stock airplane in its horse-power class, will give you for only $4390.

And you can buy the REARWIN Speedster on our liberal time-payment plan . . . Write NOW for our new color folder giving complete specifications.

●

* Miami, Florida, Air Races. Event No. 2, December 3, 1937. Free for all, open or closed—549 cu. in. displacement or under—distance of 30 miles—6 laps around 5 mile closed course. Official AVERAGE speed for 125 h.p. Speedster was 149.7 m.p.h.

See Both At Chicago

Both the REARWIN Sportster and Speedster will be on display at the Chicago air show January 28 to February 6. Be sure to see them there!

**REARWIN AIRPLANES**

*Tenth Continuous Successful Year*

FAIRFAX AIRPORT . . . KANSAS CITY, KANSAS, U. S. A.

"REARWIN popularity is proof of REARWIN superiority"

stopped at the Beech plant in Wichita and, purely by chance, at the Rearwin factory in Kansas City.

Rummel was offered jobs by all three manufacturers, but Rae was the most persistent. Rummel accepted Rae's third offer and went to work at Rearwin in the fall of 1937. His first assignment was to certify the vexing Speedster. Miller handed Rummel a foot-high stack of spin test reports dating back to 1934, and then took him for his first "spin" — in fact, 17 turns from an altitude of 10,000 feet, with a full-power recovery at 1,000 feet.

Rummel digested the reports and went to work. The Speedster was first propped up in flight attitude to check control functions. They were, in the young engineer's words, "almost unbelievably heavy." That was promptly solved by installing ball and "oilite" bearings and adding rudder-centering springs. Rae wanted the plane tested immediately, but Rummel refused. There were other problems.

Next, Rummel redesigned and enlarged the vertical tail surface for improved effectiveness during spins. He also redesigned the slots in front of the ailerons to smooth the airflow so that the wing tips would be less inclined to stall at high angles of attack, and eliminated some of the excessive up-elevator travel Webber had initially designed into the aircraft. Miller test-flew the revised version and it quickly passed the hands-off spin test that had befuddled Rummel's predecessors.[3] Miller, however, was nonplussed. While the Speedster now met government standards, the certified version was not as fast or as maneuverable as the original.

The chief engineer at the time was not happy with young Rummel's quick success and sought to undercut him. He informed Rae that Rummel would have a particular job done in two or three days when he knew full well that it would take about a month. Rae, impatient and annoyed with the "delays," kept asking about the project. Rummel finally explained what was involved and how long the job would take. A short time later the chief engineer was "gone." His replacement didn't work out either, and Rummel was elevated to the job. He was still just 22! Rae was impressed by performance, not age.

Ken Rearwin had his only mishap in a Speedster in June 1935. Royce had flown the

*Powered with Menasco 125 hp and 150 hp motors*

**SKY-HIGH VALUE— DOWN-TO-EARTH PRICE!**

**NEVER before has so much been available at such low cost! Just look at some of the expensive features incorporated in the REARWIN SPEEDSTER — features every flier wants.**

Compare the Rearwin Speedster selling at only **$4390** With other planes of similar power. We're confident you'll agree the SPEEDSTER is "tops."

**Outstanding design and appearance . . . powerful motor . . . great speed . . . smooth rubbed finish . . . comfortable noiseless cabin with beautiful upholstery . . . perfectly appointed instrument panel . . . adjustable front seat . . . 50 lb. luggage allowance in two compartments with space for large Gladstone bag . . . exceptional visibility . . . ball bearing controls throughout . . . 34 gallons of fuel in wing tanks . . . 550 mile cruising range . . . specially designed feather soft cantilever landing gear with 72 inch tread. The REARWIN SPEEDSTER is the outstanding airplane in its price class in America! Send today for FREE color folder which gives complete details.**

**REARWIN AIRPLANES**

*Tenth Continuous Successful Year*

FAIRFAX AIRPORT . . . KANSAS CITY, KANSAS, U. S. A.

"REARWIN popularity is proof of REARWIN superiority"

Left: Ad from the December 1937 *Aero Digest.*

still-uncertified plane to Salina, where an airshow was in progress, despite the fact that portions of the sod field were extremely muddy. Ken taxied the plane from its hangar. Midway through the takeoff roll the aircraft suddenly stopped, went up on its nose, and flipped over. Mud had built up and jammed between the wheel pants and tires, braking the plane, if not on a dime, then on a half-dollar. Ken sustained severe embarrassment and a bloody nose. But a pair of farmers fared better; with a tractor and a team of horses they "cleaned up" by pulling scores of cars out of the mud for two dollars each.

The speedy prototype Model 6000C flew in the Miami airshow and races on December 3, 1937. The plane, piloted by Guy Ham, Jr., of New York's Troy Air Service, finished in the money twice — first in a 30-mile closed-course "free-for-all" at a speed of 149.70 mph. Veteran racers Rudy Kling and Frank Haines were killed on the first turn, apparently victims of high-speed stalls.[4] The other race was a handicapped event. Both races were won by the late Steve

**"From K. C. to CALIFORNIA at an AVERAGE SPEED of 130 MPH!"**

**● "All kinds of weather were encountered on this trip . . . turbulent air, snow, rain and a bad icing condition. The SPEEDSTER handled beautifully and was very easy to ride. In fact, the Speedster rode through the winds much better than other ships three times as heavy which I have flown.**

**"My cruising speed, 130 to 132½ miles per hour, was very outstanding, especially considering the above conditions.**

**"Another outstanding SPEEDSTER feature was its very excellent take-off performance. Take-offs at Denver (5300 feet), Albuquerque (5400 feet) and at Winslow (4900 feet) were made quickly and easily despite the high altitude and gusty conditions.**

**"All in all, the performance of the REARWIN SPEEDSTER is excellent." Signed,**

**D. W. Hoferer,**
**Hofco Pump, Ltd.,**
**Long Beach, Cal.**

**You, too, will agree with Mr. Hoferer after you have flown the REARWIN SPEEDSTER. Write or wire for complete details TODAY!**

***Be sure to investigate the 70 hp and 90 hp REARWIN SPORTSTER . . . the ideal airplane for student instruction and private use.***

**REARWIN AIRPLANES**

*Eleventh Continuous Successful Year*

FAIRFAX AIRPORT . . . KANSAS CITY, KANSAS, U. S. A.

"REARWIN popularity is proof of REARWIN superiority"

Rae and Ken, *circa* 1938. Note new wheel pants on the Speedster.

Left: Ad from the June 1938 *Aero Digest.*

Wittman in a specially built racer. The performance of the "off-the-shelf" Speedster evoked considerable interest and admiration, but no sales.

While in Miami, Rae teased the local press and the Chamber of Commerce about the possibility of moving the Rearwin factory to south Florida.[5] Accordingly, the Rearwin aircraft displayed at the show received more than their share of press coverage and attention. Following the Florida show, Ham also flew Rae to Havana where the plane was again put through its paces.[6]

Rae was not one to wait for a prospect to stumble in the door, so in mid-1938 he sent Ray Beebe on a national tour to exhibit and demonstrate the Speedster for dealers and at local airshows. Orders, however, failed to materialize in any significant number, even though the Model 6000C was priced at $3,295 and the 6000M at $4,390. Rae opened the export valve. Five of the 6000M series were sold overseas: three in South Africa (ZS-AIE, ZS-AMI, and ZS-AMJ), one in Argentina, and one in Costa Rica (TI-29). Despite rumors of more, only 11 Speedsters can be confirmed as built. As of 1996, there were still three registered with the FAA; one Model 6000C (NC16865, SN302) and a pair of Model 6000Ms (NC19412, SN308 and NC19415, SN309).[7]

By the time the Speedster's spin problem was solved in 1937, the promising market Rae had hoped for had all but vanished. Royce had been right. The Speedster was the wrong plane at the wrong time. It was the victim of an arbitrary spin-test rule that was subsequently rescinded, the failure to promptly solve the elusive problem, and the tick of the clock for almost four years.

## *Chapter 16*

# The Sportster Series

*WITH THE Speedster off the ground and being tested in the summer of 1934, Rae concluded that he needed a "bread-and-butter" aircraft. The logical progression, dictated by economics, was to redesign the Junior as a larger, enclosed-cabin monoplane using the recently developed LeBlond engine. In August 1934, with Doug Webber still trying to solve the Speedster spin problem, Rae contracted with Henry Weeks to get the new project rolling. Webber was to take over once the Speedster was certified, but things did not work out as planned. Webber resigned in 1935 with the Speedster still uncertified, leaving John Roche as the only draftsman on the payroll, and Weeks ended up as a part-time chief engineer working on both projects.*

*Instead of hiring a cadre of draftsmen and engineers, Weeks subcontracted much of the Sportster paperwork, including the detail design, to the Thompson Engineering Company, which operated the U.S. Aircraft Engineering School in Kansas City, Missouri. Ken Carter, a Thompson student who later became a top engineer on the Lockheed 1011, did the stress analysis. Weeks, however, retained overall design responsibility while still continuing to run his own business at Richards Field with partner Barton Stevenson.*

*The new Rearwin Sportster (X14443), motivated by the new LeBlond 5DE engine*

The cockpit of the basic Sportster.
NASM, Smithsonian Institution, Washington, D.C., 7A-37569

rated at 70 hp, was first flown by Jack LeClaire on April 30, 1935. Because of the Webber-Hockaday influence, the Sportsters bore a striking resemblance to the Porterfield Flyabout that had emerged only a few months earlier. It was certified on June 13, 1935, with ATC No. 574, just 33 days after Porterfield's new plane.

In early 1933, the manual arts students at Wyandotte High School in Kansas City, Kansas, decided to build an airplane under the guidance of shop instructor William House. With a local aviation club as a financial sponsor, House purchased a set of plans for the Pietenpol Aircamper then sold by *Popular Mechanics* magazine, but the "Piet" project never got started.

Guy Poyer, a former shop student of House's, offered to donate one of his engines to the project if the students would build a new plane designed by Noel Hockaday, who had worked with Webber at both American Eagle and Rearwin. House studied the design and agreed, but with one condition. The fuselage would have to be two and one-half inches narrower so it would fit through the shop's 30-inch-wide doors.

With Hockaday in the pilot's seat and the three-cylinder Poyer engine up front vibrating for all it was worth, the student-built "Wyandotte Pup" flew from Fairfax on May 4, 1934, under Ed Porterfield's watchful eyes. He had left American Eagle-Lincoln Aircraft after its bankruptcy in 1932 and, despite the raging Depression, was eager to get back in the aviation fray. He bought the plane and the rights to the Pup from the students and their sponsor, opened Porterfield Aircraft on the Missouri side of the river at 13th and Locust Streets, and lured Hockaday back on board with stock as his chief engineer.

Hockaday's first task was to replace the palsied Poyer. He experimented with the Aeromarine AR3-40, the Szekely 36, the Salmson 40, and the 5-cylinder Velie engine that produced 50 hp. The added power of these engines increased performance, but additional structural strength would be needed to accommodate any of them. Thus, the Pup was dismantled and reconstructed into a slightly larger and

*The Newly* **GOVERNMENT APPROVED PORTERFIELD FLYABOUT**

**ONE of America's most sensational and fastest-selling airplanes—made possible by Porterfield manufacturing experience and by Porterfield's skilled aircraft mechanics who helped him to become one of the industry's leaders during past years.**

IT IS TRULY THE AIRPLANE FOR:

**Sportsmen pilots . . . Student training . . . Solo students . . . Cross-country fliers . . . and those who wish to make more aeronautical dollars than can be made otherwise.**

**$1575**
(VELIE 65 H. P.)

**$1675**
(LeBLOND 70 H. P.)

**PORTERFIELD AIRCRAFT CORP., 1328 LOCUST ST., KANSAS CITY, MO.**

Antique Airplane Association, Blakesburg, IA

Similarities in the Porterfield Flyabout, left, and the Rearwin Sportster resulted from the Influence of designer Noel Hockaday.

stronger airframe, and the new 60 hp LeBlond was hung up front.

The revamped "Pup," renamed the Flyabout, received a "Group 2 Approval" on February 21, 1935, and was fully certified on May 9, 1935 (ATC No. 567). It was originally priced at $1,695 FOF — flyaway our factory — but by the end of 1935 the price was upped by $200 — still a bargain compared to the flivver-type Eaglet which had sold for $1,575 in

Flight instructor Bill Miller, left, and student-pilot Glenn Buffington, pose before a dual lesson in a Sportster, *circa* 1935.

1931. The Flyabout vaguely resembled the Eaglet, the Junior, and the new Rearwin Sportster because Hockaday had been deeply involved in all four designs. Despite rumors, there was no chicanery.

The Sportster clearly had more to offer than the Flyabout and, accordingly, was priced about $200 higher. In addition to more horsepower, it was slightly longer, taller, and heavier. It also had a larger wing area, V-shaped struts, and a three-piece angular windshield. It carried one-third more fuel (in wing tanks) and could fly 100 miles or so farther. If Ed Porterfield was unhappy with the look-alike appearance of the Sportster 7000, he could not be blamed. But the two planes simply shared a common design ancestry.

The similarities in the aircraft resulted in fierce competition between Rae and Porterfield, who were less than fond of each other. Rearwin test pilot and flight instructor Bill Miller recalled in 1961:

> Both Kansas City factories turned out competitive LeBlond powered models. At times sales were made as a result of the outcome of races between the two airplanes while the customer observed. Competition between these companies was always brisk, mostly clean — above all healthy. Neither bypassed an opportunity to beat the other out of a sale. The founders of both companies . . . were rugged individuals and shrewd businessmen — hence the strong competition between the Rearwin Sportsters and the performance and price-equal LeBlond powered Porterfields.

Face to face the pair were stiffly cordial, but out of earshot, they had unflattering nicknames for each other. Porterfield called Rae "The Green Man," a *non sequitur* apparently referring to a purplish complexion problem Rae developed briefly as the result of taking a medication called Argerol. For some equally obscure reason, Rae referred to Porterfield as the "Rin-Tin-Tin Man." Whether either was aware of the other's nickname is uncertain.

The Sportster Model 7000 was a no-frills, high-winged monoplane seating two in tandem that was aimed at flight schools, sportsmen pilots, and businessmen more interested in dependable transportation than luxury. It was agile but sturdily constructed, and had a range of nearly 500 miles. Although both cockpits had control sticks, all instruments were mounted on the front panel. The early units employed a fixed spring-leaf tailskid and Goodyear Airwheels without brakes, but steerable tailwheels and brakes were soon offered as options.

Rae and Ken with a Sportster, *circa* 1936.

Royce delivered the second unit to aircraft dealer Harvey Couch in Stamford, Connecticut, while Ken flew Rae and the new prototype to the Detroit Air Show in July. They stopped en route in St. Louis to demonstrate the plane for the Kratz Bros. Air Service and in Cincinnati to discuss the terms of an option on 100 LeBlond engines at $450 each. The Sportster was an immediate success. Several were sold at the show and prospects piled up, so father and son returned to Cincinnati and exercised the LeBlond option. While there, they sold the prototype and trained back to Kansas City.

At about the same time, Royce flew a Sportster to Philadelphia's Patco Field to demonstrate the new plane to Tony Little. He was a successful Monocoupe dealer, but needed a plane that was a little less squirrely for his relatively inexperienced student-pilots. Little (who actually topped six feet, three inches) considered the

Bill Miller in the cockpit of a Sportster, 1936.
William Miller Family

Sportster ideal, bought two, and sold several others in 1935-1936.[1]

While orders were being received from around the country and abroad, Ken and his wife took a Sportster on a seven-week sales-demo tour through Oklahoma, the Southwest, and California. The 22-year-old new salesman barely had 100 hours on his private ticket. The first sale was made to Dallas bus manufacturer Phil Hudson. He got the green light to buy from his wife only after she learned that Ken's wife Suzanne had flown from Kansas City without wearing a parachute. Embarrassingly, Ken had no order blanks for the deal so he sheepishly modified the manufacturer's sales form. Seven Sportsters fitted with the 70 and 85 hp LeBlond engines, including the demonstrator, were sold during the trip. Ken and his wife rode a train back to Kansas City. After being "trapped on top" — above the clouds — without instruments at 12,000 feet near Bakersfield, neither complained about viewing the scenery from the height of a Pullman car.

A Sportster on floats over the harbor in Rio De Janeiro, *circa* 1937.

The original Sportster Model 7000 was followed by two other versions, both offering increased horsepower and improved performance. The Model 8500 was a beefed-up 7000, the principal difference being the use of the recently approved LeBlond 5DF engine rated at 85 hp at 2,125 rpm. It weighed 85 pounds less than the 70 hp version, but cost $100 more. The standard Model 8500 was base priced at $2,370, but was outsold by the "Deluxe" edition which included, among other options, a Townsend speedring, spinner, wheel pants, navigation lights, and radio. It could also hold 31 pounds of baggage under the rear seat. The Model 8500 was type certified with ATC No. 591 on December 7, 1935, and was subsequently made available with either Edo pontoons or snow skis.[2] A *D* following the factory serial number meant it was a deluxe model.

The inscription on the photograph, taken in Brazil in 1936, reads: To Mr. Kenneth Rearwin, A very fond owner of one of your planes. I. J. Nargueria, Rio de Janeiro, Brazil.

The pontoon version was developed for George B. Cluett II, whose family controlled the company that made Arrow shirts. He was

The trophy reads: Greater Miami Airport Assoc. Trophy, Miami All American Air Maneuvers, 1936; Rearwin Airplanes, Inc., Kansas City, Kansas; Light Airplane Performance.

*Powered with LeBlond 70 h. p. and 90 h. p. and Warner 90 h. p. motors*

**MORE REARWINS SOLD in 1936 than ANY OTHER MAKE in same price range**

A few excellent territories for REARWIN AIRPLANES are still open. Make money and friends for yourself by selling REARWINS. Write or wire—TODAY—for further information.

REARWINS were FIRST in domestic sales in the $1800-$5000 bracket, according to production figures compiled and released by the Bureau of Air Commerce. These figures further reveal that

**REARWIN'S DOMESTIC SALES WERE 60% GREATER THAN OUR NEAREST COMPETITOR'S**

These Bureau of Air Commerce figures cover only domestic sales. Rearwin's 1936 export sales absorbed 26% of our entire 1936 output.

REARWIN AIRPLANES HAD TO BE GOOD to chalk up such a 1936 sales record. And THIS year they're even BETTER—with many improvements and with 1937 sales already three times as great as for the same period last year! Write for our new color folder giving full details, specifications, prices, terms. Write TODAY!

***Approved for FLOATS and SKIS***

**REARWIN AIRPLANES**

**Ninth Continuous Successful Year**

**Fairfax Airport, Kansas City, Kansas, U.S.A.**

**"REARWIN popularity is proof of REARWIN superiority"**

From *Aero Digest,* March 1937. Antique Airplane Association, Blakesburg, IA

Sue and Ken Rearwin at Albuquerque during their sales trip in the fall of 1935.

also the owner of Troy (New York) Air Service, which sold Sportsters and other aircraft in New York and New England. Cluett reasoned that the addition of floats would increase sales.[3] Guy Ham, Jr., who occasionally worked for Cluett, conducted the pontoon flight tests in May 1936. The first two spin trials went well, but the third, with the center of gravity full back, nearly resulted in disaster. The plane failed to recover hands off in the required two-and-one-half turns or with normal spin recovery inputs.

Ham was finally able to stop the spinning by rocking the stick with alternating bursts of power, but the plane was in an inverted, high-speed dive. The overbuilt aircraft stayed together as Ham pulled out just above the Flushing Bay. The problem was solved with an enlarged vertical tail.

The third version of the Sportster was the Model 9000 powered by various 90 hp engines. The first was pulled by the new five-cylinder Warner Scarab Jr. and was designated as either the Model 9000 or

Above: A Sportster without floats over the harbor in Rio de Janeiro, *circa* 1938.

**1936 REARWIN "Sportster"—Model 7000 A. T. C. 574**

## Geo. B. Cluett II
## Buys Two Rearwin "Sportsters"

MR. CLUETT, of the well-known family (Arrow Shirts and Collars), decided on two Rearwin "Sportsters" after carefully examining every detail of design, material and workmanship—he wanted the best for his money! Mr. Cluett will distribute Rearwin airplanes with headquarters at Troy, N. Y., and Boston.

*Other Rearwin Representatives:*

F. A. Jones,
121 Alexander St.,
Rochester, N. Y.
H. A. Little, Jr.
Pateo Flying Field,
Norristown, Pa.
Main Line Flying Service,
Paoli, Pa.
Bennett Air Service,
Central Jersey Airport,
Hightstown, N. J.
Cape Cod Seaplanes,
No. Falmouth, Mass.
I. D. Jackson,
c/o Sinclair Refining Co.,
Clarksburg, W. Va.
E. G. Ashbaugh,
Harrison City, Pa.
National Flying Schools, Inc.,
McKinley Airport,
Canton, O.
General Air Service, Inc.
4500 W. 83rd St.,
Chicago.
W. Harvey Couch,
c/o Allen Brothers, Inc.,
Stamford, Conn.
Interstate Aircraft Sales Corp.,
Word-Chamberlain Field,
Minneapolis, Minn.
Wm. H. Hinrichs,
Sioux Falls, S. D.
Key Brothers Flying Service,
Meridian, Miss.
Land O'Lakes Flying Service,
Bay City, Mich.
Airplane Sales Corp.,
St. Louis Municipal Airport.

*Also Fully Represented in S. W. and Far West.*

**REARWIN AIRPLANES**

*8th Successful Year*

**Fairfax Airport** **Kansas City, U. S. A.**

Left: George B. Cluett II, who sold various makes of aircraft, had no objection to Rae promoting his purchase of two Sportsters in a 1937 *Aero Digest* ad. Antique Airplane Association, Blakesburg, IA

Royce (left) and his wife, Jacqueline, are greeted in Florida, 1937, after their arrival in a Sportster.

Above: Edo floats were installed on the 85 hp Sportster at the College Point, Long Island, New York, factory in May 1936.

Left: Sportster NC15831 on Edo floats.

9000-W. A "Group 2 Approval" was issued on September 3, 1936, and the plane was fully certified on January 23, 1937, by ATC No. 624. It was formally unveiled at the Pacific Aircraft and Boat Show in Los Angeles on March 13, 1937, and two Deluxe models were sold at $3,500.[4] The Model 9000 was also available with the LeBlond or Ken-Royce 5DF 90 hp engines. The former was designated as the 9000-L; the latter as the 9000-KR.

Although the Sportster was geared toward pilots of modest means, it was also owned by many businessmen impressed by its simplicity and ruggedness. Juan Terry Trippe, the president of Pan American Airways, purchased a Warner-powered 9000 on floats (NC16433, SN419) for his own use.[5] For business reasons, Trippe refused to personally endorse the Sportster, but he had no objection to Rearwin advertising his ownership, which clearly influenced sales in Central and South America where Trippe was already regarded as a legend of sorts.

Snow skis were added to the Sportster during the winter of 1935-1936.

Below: Rearwin test pilots Bill Miller, left, and C. R. "Mac" McDonald, about to test a Sportster fitted with snow skis.

Other Sportster owners included Cluett, who bought a pair in 1936; Colonel J. H. Lapham, the former head of Texaco; "Flying Baritone" Robert Crawford; Arthur Collins, manufacturer of aircraft radios; Frank Findley, a mining industrialist from Johannesburg; and Antonio Seabra, a textile manufacturer from Rio de Janeiro. Paul Poberezny, who later founded the Experimental Aircraft Association (EAA), also owned one, and referred to the Sportster as "the Bonanza of its day." The U.S. Department of Agriculture's Bureau of Entomology and Plant Quarantine purchased a pair of 90 hp Sportsters that were

Mac McDonald and the Sportster Deluxe on snow skis, 1937.
Antique Airplane Association, Blakesburg, IA

Experimental Aircraft Association founder Paul Poberezny owned this 70 hp LeBlond Sportster.
Rearwin Club

Below: This Sportster on Edo floats was reportedly owned by Pan Am's Juan Trippe.
NASM, Smithsonian Institution, Washington, D.C., 1B-32386

Ken used a Sportster to fly an empty envelope from Kansas City's Fairfax Airport to his grandparents in Salina to celebrate National Air Mail Week in 1938.

*Powered with 70 h.p. and 90 h.p. LeBlond and 90 h.p. Warner motors*

## There MUST Be A Reason . . .

$54,000 worth of REARWIN'S were purchased during the first week in January.

### AND HERE IS THE REASON . . .

REARWIN builds the finest airplanes selling up to $3500.

The REARWIN Sportster definitely has the fastest take-off, quickest climb, highest ceiling and slowest landing of any airplane anywhere near its price. It has a 500 mile cruising range . . . hydraulic landing gear . . . 50 lb. luggage capacity with 50 lbs. additional allowance for extra equipment . . . 24 gallon fuel capacity in wing tanks . . . unexcelled visibility in all directions . . . comfortable cabin . . . superior finish . . . cruising speed of 100-110 miles per hour. You need pay only one-third down to own a REARWIN. Write or wire for our new folder giving COMPLETE details TODAY!

**IT HAPPENED AT MIAMI, FLORIDA**

REARWIN'S superior speed was further demonstrated at the recent Miami races where a stock REARWIN Sportster, during a 25 mile race, completely lapped the entry of our nearest competitor, crossing the finish line 5 MILES AHEAD!

**REARWIN AIRPLANES**

Ninth Continuous Successful Year

Fairfax Airport

Kansas City — Kansas, U.S.A.

*"REARWIN popularity is proof of REARWIN superiority"*

Advertisement from *Aero Digest*, February 1937.

Antique Airplane Association, Blakesburg, IA

Powered with LeBlond 70 hp and 90 hp and Warner 90 hp motors

## ROYAL SIAMESE AIR FORCE *chooses* REARWIN SPORTSTERS!

■ Rearwin Sportsters are now on a 10,000 mile journey to Siam to serve as trainers in the Royal Siamese Air Force. Rearwins were chosen after careful investigation for their rare combination of sturdiness, outstanding performance, and absolute dependability. Rearwin features which appeal to hundreds of pilots in the United States and in seventeen foreign countries include: cruise of 110 m.p.h., with over 20 miles per gallon economy . . . 500 mile range . . . 24 gallon fuel tanks in the wings . . . 72 inch tread hydraulic landing gear . . . 50 lbs. luggage allowance plus 50 lbs. additional allowance for extra equipment. And the Rearwin Sportster has by far the fastest take off, quickest climb, highest ceiling, and slowest landing of any plane in its horsepower class.

Whether school operator or private pilot, you too will want the popular Rearwin Sportster, the airplane which gives you *most* for your money. Write or wire now for complete details.

APPROVED FOR FLOATS AND SKIS

**The SPEEDSTER, too!** With smart streamlining, racing speed of 150 m.p.h., proved performance and unusual economy, the REARWIN SPEEDSTER is unquestionably the finest airplane in its price or horsepower class. Don't delay . . . investigate TODAY!

**REARWIN AIRPLANES**

*Eleventh Continuous Successful Year*

FAIRFAX AIRPORT . . . KANSAS CITY, KANSAS, U. S. A.

"REARWIN popularity is proof of REARWIN superiority"

Advertisement from *Aero Digest*, October 1938.

Antique Airplane Association, Blakesburg, IA

These crates, ready for shipping, contain three Sportsters: two for African Flying Services at Rand Airport, Germiston, South Africa, and one for Air Taxie Company, Cape Town. The black vertical line on the nearest crate identifies the center of gravity.

## The "FLYING BARITONE" Buys Another REARWIN SPORTSTER!

**Famous composer of official army air corps song, Robert Crawford, the "Flying Baritone," just purchased his SECOND Rearwin Sportster.**

**Crawford says, "My first REARWIN SPORTSTER carried me over 550 hours in 46 states including 10 coast to coast trips in good weather and bad. Always she came through beautifully and the KEN-ROYCE motor never missed a beat. In our REARWIN my wife and I can fly from Newark to Los Angeles for only $49.50. That's REAL ECONOMY! Congratulations REARWIN! You are making a grand airplane. I'm proud to fly my SECOND SPORTSTER!"**

**Crawford liked his first Sportster; he'll be thrilled with the many improvements in his second! Changes such as streamlined, one-piece windshield; smooth NACA cowling, full pressure baffling, increased cabin width, vertical instrument panel, increased speed and range and still greater economy.**

**Yet the price, fully equipped, is only $3295. Write for folder with details about the Sportster and the side-by-side CLOUDSTER 2 and 3 place models TODAY!**

**REARWIN AIRCRAFT & ENGINES, Inc., Kansas City, Kansas, U. S. A.**

Antique Airplane Association, Blakesburg, IA

A pair of Sportsters on the line in Cape Town, South Africa, *circa* 1938.

The Deluxe Sportster with speed ring and wheel pants was a handsome craft.

used for grasshopper control. Another, purchased by the Fish and Wildlife Service in 1937, was used by government biologists for surveys in connection with the Migratory Bird Treaty of 1918.

In an article published in the April 15, 1939, issue of *The Sportsman Pilot* magazine, Robert Crawford reported flying his Sportster from Newark to Los Angeles for a total of $49.50, including hangaring. Using wind-aloft reports and *no* oil, the LeBlond-powered craft averaged just 4½

Above: Deluxe Sportster NC15858 on floats. Antique Airplane Association, Blakesburg, IA

Left: Some Deluxe Sportsters included front and rear skylights. NASM, Smithsonian Institution, Washington, D.C., 95-9178

Bill Miller demonstrates the Sportster's takeoff ability from the Chicago Stockyards field in 1938.

Three Sportsters and a pair of Speedsters in the Rearwin plant, *circa* 1938. Wyandotte County Museum, Bonner Springs, KS

This Sportster, refitted with a horizontally opposed engine, is reputed to be one of the Swedish Sportsters built in 1939.
Antique Airplane Association, Blakesburg, IA

gallons of fuel an hour, with pump prices ranging from 18 to 28 cents. Crawford put over 900 hours on his Model 7000, including ten transcontinental trips for professional appearances. In 1939, his composition of the "Army Air Corps Song" won $5,000 in a contest sponsored by Bernarr McFadden, and Crawford used the prize money to buy a deluxe 90 hp model (NC25407).

The deluxe model was streamlined and redesigned in 1939 by Bob Rummel to increase sales when the Sportster's production life showed signs of waning. The modified NACA-type (National Advisory Committee for Aeronautics) engine cowling was faired tightly to the fuselage all around except for a small cooling air exit at the bottom. The closed cowl and a new one-piece windshield enhanced both appearance and efficiency. Pressure baffling also improved engine and accessory compartment cooling, while a hinged cowling made access to the engine compartment easier. All of these Rummel changes were made without adding to the plane's empty weight and, as anticipated, extended the Sportster's production run.

Approximately 261 Sportsters (SN 401 to 661) were sold between 1935 and 1941, when production was ended by World War II. Approximately 48 were exported. The first exports were a pair of 7000s that went to South Africa (ZS-AGV and ZS-AGW). Both were impressed into the South African Air Force during the war. They were followed by 11 others that were used as trainers. Sportsters were also exported to Argentina, Australia, the Congo, Brazil, Canada, Honduras, New Zealand, Norway, Peru, the Philippines, Rhodesia, Sweden, Thailand, and Uruguay.

The Argentine planes were a Model 8500 (SN522) powered by a LeBlond 5DF, and a 9000L (SN588) engine with the 90 hp LeBlond 5F. The sale of one of the nine Warner-powered Model 9000s to the A. B. Gotaverken Shipbuilding Company in Sweden in May

Ken Rearwin used a Sportster to fly the U.S. Mail in May 1938.

## NEW ZEALAND REARWINS

**MINISTRY of TRANSPORT**

AURORA HOUSE
62 THE TERRACE
WELLINGTON
NEW ZEALAND

PRIVATE BAG, WELLINGTON
TELEPHONE: 721 253
TELEX No.: NZ 31324

Civil Aviation Division

Dear Mr. Rearwin:

Thank you for your letter of 5 December 1986 regarding the number of Rearwin aircraft on the New Zealand Aircraft Register. I hope the following information is useful.

Rearwin aircraft currently on the aircraft register:

Rearwin 9000KR
Serial: 654D
Registration Marks: ZK-AKF
Registered Owner: Earlybird Flying Limited
Address: Newbury Line, Bunnythorpe,
Palmerston North.

Rearwin 9000KR
Serial: 656D
Registration Marks: ZK-AKA
Registered Owner: Mr. I.T. East
Address: 34 Ashleigh Crescent,
Miramar, Wellington.

Rearwin 9000L
Serial: 613D
Registration Marks: ZK-ALF
Registered Owner: J.P. Galpin
Address: Station Road, Pongakawa
RD 6, Te Puke.

I hope your visit early next year is a pleasant one.

Yours faithfully,
J. Moore
For Director of Civil Aviation

1937 formed the basis of a licensing or royalty agreement. A dozen or so were reportedly built between 1938 and 1943 as the Gotaverken GV-38, including SE-AHG, SE-AHY, SE-AHD, SE-AHU, and SE-AGB. The latter two are now in Swedish museums.

At least three Model 7000s were shipped to Puerto Rico. The first (NC16460, SN485) was sold to Felix J. Serralles of Ponce in 1936 and was last registered to him in 1939. The plane's corroded data plate was discovered on the remote French Caribbean island of Tintimar (a.k.a. "Flat Island") near St. Martin in the early 1980s. The obscure island, located about 200 miles east of Puerto Rico, was reportedly used as a refueling, maintenance, and "R&R" base for the German submarine fleet that patrolled the Western Atlantic and the Caribbean during World War II. The discovery raises interesting questions about why the Sportster was there and what happened to it. The other two shipped to Puerto Rico were NC16457, SN486 and NC18543, SN507. The latter was sold to the Insular Forest Service in 1937.

Records of the Civil Air Patrol indicate that the organization used at least eight Sportsters during World War II, including four in the Michigan Wing (NC15474, 15891, 16476, and 19411).

A pair of Warner-engine Sportster 9000s also went to war with the Army Air Corps as UC-102s. Both were built in 1938, acquired from their owners in November 1942, and equipped for service at Homestead Army Airfield, Florida. The first (NC20733, SN627) served at Nashville, Tennessee, and Sweetwater, Texas, before being released to the CAA in June 1943 after the installation of a new Ken-Royce engine. It was subsequently assigned to the Dallas Aviation School and Air College, and released to the Reconstruction Finance Corporation (RFC) at Tinker Field, Oklahoma, on September 11, 1944, with 919 hours on the airframe.

The other Sportster 9000 (NC41667, SN661) was assigned to the Morrison Field, Florida, Caribbean Wing until released to the CAA in August 1943. It was transferred to the RFC on November 23, 1944, after 327 hours of military service. There is no record of the disposition of either UC-102, and neither has shown up on the civil registry under their original *N* numbers.

Two of four Sportsters exported to New Zealand were impressed during World War II, and three of the four were still registered in 1995.[6] A 1938 model (VH-UYS, SN612D) was sold to the founder of Australia's Ansette Airlines and is now in a museum in Victoria. The Sportster prototype (NC14443, SN401) was purchased by Ken and donated to the Airpower Museum in Blakesburg, Iowa, and a 1937 Model 7000, donated by Oklahoma's Colonel Tom Thomas, is displayed in the aircraft museum at Liberal, Kansas.

*Chapter 17*

# Transitions

*BY THE END OF 1936, the operating losses of the essentially dormant Rearwin Airplanes, Inc. were cut to a mere $59.26 on income of about $2,000, which included the sale of the last Junior for $1,750. Meanwhile, thanks to the popular Sportster, Rae's own operation, Rearwin Aircraft Company, turned a pre-tax profit of over $18,000.*

*It was time to collapse the shell of Rearwin Airplanes, Inc. and move on. There was no inventory left. While the firm owned the rights to the Ken-Royce and Junior series, both were outmoded, and the paperwork and tooling were of little value. Also, A. R. Jones still owed the corporation over $8,500 for his stock, even though he had been receiving rent credits from Rae for the use of the A. R. Jones Building and equipment. The Rearwin corporation, however, still owed Rae over $9,500 for the loans made in 1931-1932 to develop and market the Junior. Assets included Jones's debt, a small amount of dubious accounts receivable, the capital stock of the Rearwin Flying Service, Inc. and about $4,000 worth of machinery, fixtures, and supplies, which were probably overvalued. In sum, the corporation owed Rae more than it was worth, and he was planning on moving his own firm to the larger quarters previously occupied by Universal Airlines, known as "Hangar 5."[1]*

*On April 1, 1937, Rae and A. R. Jones agreed to close the books on Rearwin Air-*

University of Kansas graduate Royce S. Rearwin, 1933.

planes, Inc. Neither had received a dime on their investments, and it was apparent they never would. It was agreed that Rae would assume all assets and liabilities and forgive Jones's debt. On April 9, 1937, resolutions were adopted transferring all assets and liabilities to Rae as an individual and liquidating the corporation. Rearwin Airplanes, Inc. was history. There was no obituary, and it is doubtful that Rae's employees or the public noticed any change at Fairfax. The Rearwin Aircraft Company continued as it had the day before. So did the Flying School.

The financial records that Jones's accountant had established in 1929 indicate that the firm, another victim of the Great Depression, had sustained a seven-year *operating* loss of over $77,000. Moreover, the capital investment had virtually disappeared. With Jones's indebtedness canceled, Rae received about $6,000 in tangible assets, but still had to pay off some $750 in liabilities. Rae, however, had new plans, since both sons had graduated from college — Royce from the University of Kansas in 1933, and Ken from Northwestern University in 1935.[2]

On April 27, 1937, Rae entered into a partnership agreement with Royce and Ken, granting each an undi-

Northwestern University graduate Kenneth A. Rearwin, 1935.

Rae (center) in Havana, 1937.

vided one-third interest in the Rearwin Aircraft Company, which included Rearwin Flying Service, Inc. The agreement provided that if and when the partnership or its successor companies were sold, the principals would share equally in the proceeds on the condition that the sons' shares would be put into separate trusts managed and controlled for their benefit by Rae during his lifetime. The partnership gift and trust arrangement were more than a father's generosity. Rae hoped it would ignite both his sons, but there was no mistaking who would call the shots. Rae could buy out his partners for one dollar. Thanks again to the Sportster, the new partnership turned a pre-tax profit of over $15,000 in 1937 on sales of $174,635, even after paying partnership salaries.[3]

Rae in Havana, 1937.

*The Apprenticeship Program*

By the end of 1935 the Aviation and Mechanics School had evolved into an apprenticeship program aimed primarily at local youths eager to find a way into aviation. Such trade-offs of unskilled labor for experience were common in the mid-1930s. The apprentices worked without pay, and were rotated through various production departments for seven or eight months. They were then considered employable, if not at Rearwin, then elsewhere.

Teenage brothers Bob and Paul Faris were typical of the apprentices who trained at the Rearwin plant in the late 1930s. Bob graduated from high school in Barnet, Vermont, at age 16 in 1938 and, like many youths, was determined to get a toehold in aviation. Even before graduation he had sent a $50 non-refundable deposit to the Lincoln Airplane and Flight School, Lincoln, Nebraska, to enroll in a mechanics course taught by E. J. Silas. That, however, was before relatives in Kansas City, with whom he and older brother Paul would live, informed them of the tuition-free Rearwin Apprenticeship Program.

Apprentices built ribs, ribs, and more ribs. The partial rib permitted installation of a fuel tank between the spars. Robert W. Rummel

The youngsters started right in building Sportster ribs for nine hours a day under the supervision of Jim Crane. Three weeks later Bob went to

Kelsey Chaney where he assembled and double-varnished wings. Paul subsequently returned home. Crane and Chaney both worked at piece rates and certainly welcomed the extra help. Rearwin apprentices also washed aircraft around Fairfax, mowed lawns, and sought "go-fer" jobs to earn spending money.

Bob considered the work "the greatest opportunity in the world." Along the way he worked for Tony Slobodnick (cable splicing), Wesley Pipes (assembly), Archie Turpin, Maurice Shay, and Orlo Redmond (machine and engine shop), and Troy Keys (welding). Faris would later say, "I thought I'd gone to heaven in late 1938 when the Minimum Wage Act went into effect and I started getting paid 25 cents an hour."

Bob Faris progressed to the purchasing department in the spring of 1939, but department head Charlie Hall didn't know what to do with him. Hall had him inventory and catalog all the Army/Navy (AN) and Naval Aircraft Factory standard parts, a seemingly useless task. Hall quit a few months later and Faris, who had just turned 17 and knew the parts and inventory system well, was given a raise and was appointed purchasing agent. Rae initially told him "what, how much, and when," but the youngster did

Rae told young apprentice Bob Faris, above, "We don't hire kids here," but relented when Faris produced a high school diploma and proof that he was 16 years old. Robert W. Faris

Rearwin wing-builder Kelsey Chaney installed the wing ribs built mostly by apprentices. Robert W. Rummel

Apprentices also propped aircraft for Flying School instructors, students, and Rearwin test pilots. Charles Nixon, above, "armstrongs" a Speedster. Charles W. Nixon

Charlie Nixon was another apprentice who worked his way into a permanent job by doing whatever had to be done. He worked for Wesley Pipes in Final Assembly for three years, and studied on his own for a mechanic's license. On one occasion, Nixon had disconnected the aileron cables on a Flying School Sportster when Pipes called him to another job. When he returned, he saw the plane rolling into position for takeoff. He made a desperate dash across the field and fortunately got the pilot's attention. Back on the tarmac, the pilot was furious. Nixon, just 18, didn't dare ask the "pilot-god" why he hadn't noticed that the nuts were missing during the mandatory "pre-flight inspection."

the pricing, ordering, and other functions. Faris described Rae as "sometimes moody," but added, "come to think about it, so was everyone in those days. I remember he lived at the Phillips Hotel and drove a big 1936 or '37 Auburn convertible that I seriously coveted."

In 1939, Faris, Slobodnick, Chuck Cerokey, and another employee convinced Ken to sell them the used Sportster that "Flying Baritone" Robert Crawford had traded in. They bought it "on time" for $600 and no interest. Faris then took dual — flying with two sets of cockpit controls — from Flight School instructors Bill Miller and "Mac" McDonald for $1 an hour, and put some 300 hours on the plane in just two years.

Faris would use "his" plane to forge a friendship with Troy Keys, the outwardly gruff master welder who, when he wasn't busy, was always tackling someone else's job. He was born in Harrison, Arkansas, in 1905, and was the epitome of the "jack-of-all-trades." Out of earshot he was referred to as "The Bull of the Woods." He was also an imposing figure to the unworldly 17-year-old, who interpreted Keys's "What are you doing here, kid?" as serious intimidation. One day "the kid" summoned the courage to invite Keys to go for "a ride in *my* plane." The "Bull" grunted, and the pair dashed off into the yonder. They became lasting friends until Keys's death in 1983.

On another occasion, Nixon and Tony Slobodnick installed snow skis on a Sportster for Bill Miller. Neither had done this task before, and too much slack was left in the cables that restricted the skis' up-down tilt. As Miller took off, the skis tilted to almost a vertical position, creating severe drag. Miller somehow managed to get the struggling craft around the pattern and down safely. All three learned a lesson that day, but nothing was said.[4] Despite such incidents, neither the Rearwin aircraft firms nor the Flight School ever lost a test pilot, instructor, or student.

Joel Firmin, another apprentice, left work early one day in 1940 to attend an important function in Kansas City. He thumbed a ride with a stranger who asked how he liked the apprenticeship program. The 19-year-old candidly replied, "Well, I took the job to become a machinist, but so far all I've done is break off risers in the foundry. It smells so bad and is so dusty that my hay fever is about to kill me, so I guess I'll have to quit."

Firmin was dropped off at his destination. At work the next morning, Archie Turpin told him that he had orders from Mr. Rearwin to "put that kid on a machine, right away!" That's when Firmin learned he'd been given a ride by "Pappy" Rearwin.

The five-cylinder LeBlond engine.

Robert W. Rummel

## *Chapter 18*

# Merry Christmas, from Uncle Sam

*IN MID-DECEMBER 1937, Ken took a call from Rich LeBlond, who wanted to speak to Rae about selling him the LeBlond Engine Company. Rich explained that the LeBlond Tool and Die Company, which owned the engine subsidiary, had made a mountain of money in 1937. Unless the cash was paid in dividends or sheltered with losses, the Internal Revenue Service would get the lion's share because of the so-called "excess profits tax." The LeBlonds needed to unload the engine company at a loss in order to keep the cash that would otherwise be paid in taxes. LeBlond thought that a deal had been made to sell to another party, but it had just fallen through. The company had to be sold by December 31. Was Rae interested?*

*Rae said there was no way, that he didn't have the kind of money the LeBlonds would need. Rich wouldn't take no for an answer or discuss terms over the phone. He urged Rae to get on a train or fly to Cincinnati and, if he didn't own the engine company when he left, the LeBlonds would pay his expenses. Rae went to Cincinnati, not for an expense-paid trip, but because he was convinced that Rich was serious. There could be advantages for a manufacturer to own an engine works, particularly one like LeBlond. They were used in Rae's planes and by several other companies, including Aeronca, Porterfield, Bellanca, and Culver.*

The Ken-Royce engine shop was a beehive of activity in 1938 when this photograph was taken. Former LeBlond employee Ralph Kripplin (with hat) is at the far right.

**REARWIN AIRPLANES**

***announces . . . .***

—the purchase of The Le Blond Aircraft Engine Corporation of Cincinnati, Ohio. Rearwin Airplanes will continue to build the well-known LeBlond 70 h.p. and 90 h.p. five cylinder radial air cooled engines which have proved themselves on the skyways of the world. In addition, REARWIN will build a 125 h.p. seven cylinder radial air cooled engine. This model has already been extensively tested by the LeBlond company and is now ready for Government A.T.C. tests.

Rearwin Airplanes will continue to supply engines to other aircraft manufacturers both in the United States and abroad. Until further announcement parts will continue to be handled through the Cincinnati office.

We pledge ourselves to maintain the same high standards of materials and workmanship under which LeBlond engines have always been manufactured.

**REARWIN AIRPLANES**

Ad from February 1938 *Aero Digest.*

The LeBlond radial engine was a refinement of the 5-cylinder Detroit Air Cat, an air-cooled power plant of 60 or 65 hp that was itself developed from the "Rickenbacker" engine named after the famed World War I ace. Both engines were designed by Glenn D. Angle of Detroit. The Air Cat was used briefly in the Driggs Coupe and Central States Monocoupe in 1928, but proved unsatisfactory. Angle and Rickenbacker then sold their interests to the LeBlond Tool and Die Company, which by 1937 had invested about $500,000 in developing the various engine models.

LeBlond offered the company, then book-valued in excess of $250,000, to Rae for about ten cents on the dollar — $25,000. It was an offer Rae could not refuse. Although virtually a gift, it was also a good deal for LeBlond. It was the tax man who would take the beating. Most of the so-called "loss" on the sale would be retrieved by LeBlond as tax savings. Tax accountants made a good living outsmarting tax writers.

The deal closed four days before Christmas, and included a provision saying that Rae could lease the existing factory building or, if he chose, move the equipment and inventory of shelf engines and parts. He could also use the LeBlond name for one year. The sale was publicly announced on January 9, 1938, and the acquisition was set up as a second partnership between Rae and his sons.[1] Fate and the tax man had smiled on Rae. It had paid to be an honest businessman, pay your bills on time for the small discounts, and be in the right place at the right time.

In April, Rae announced that the engine company would be moved to Fairfax if he could renegotiate his lease with the Union Pacific subsidiary, which had taken the property back when Fairfax Airport and the Woods Brothers had gone bankrupt in 1934. He also changed the company's name to the "Ken-Royce Engine Company."

By late April, Rae had recovered the purchase price in off-the-shelf sales, the bulk of which came in three orders. One was a $15,000 order from Bellanca; another was a parts order from South Africa; and the third was a $7,000 shipment of engines to the A. B. Gotaverken Shipbuilding Company of Sweden. It had been negotiated by famed flier Gosta Andre who, because of a 1927 flight from Sweden to Cape Town, was called the "Lindbergh of Sweden." The engines were used on the Swedish-built Sportsters, GV-38s.

Rae renegotiated and extended his Fairfax lease, built a 12,000-square-foot L-shaped mezzanine in the existing factory building,[2] and added a 12,000-square-foot metal structure adjoining the north side. Much of the light aircraft work was moved to the mezzanine to make room for the 20 railway freight cars full of engines, machinery, dies, jigs, tools, drawings, and other equipment that rolled west from Cincinnati in July 1938. A handful of key employees who would have been laid off by LeBlond also moved to Kansas City.[3] Bob Rummel, whom Rae trusted implicitly, reluctantly put on another hat, that of the chief engineer of the Ken-Royce Engine Company.

Like its predecessor, the new engine company purchased cylinder "barrels," pistons, cases, crankshafts, and other parts "in the rough." Employees then machined the items with various grinders and wheels to specified tolerances, and assembled the parts with stock components to make a complete engine.

The engine division did not run smoothly at first. The grinding wheels used on the inside of the cylin-

Maurice Shay in the Rearwin engine shop, *circa* 1938.

ders constantly loaded up with the filings, which was perplexing to both Rummel and their manufacturer. They worked fine everywhere else. In fact, they were the same ones LeBlond had used for years in Cincinnati without difficulty. There were experiments with other wheels, but the problems continued and resulted in serious production delays. Sabotage was suspected but could not be proved. Rae finally learned that several of the LeBlond employees who had come from Cincinnati, including the chief engineer and shop foreman, had tried to buy the company from the LeBlonds, and still wanted it. In fact, it was their deal that had fallen through and allowed Rae to buy the company. Rae fired the lot.

In *Howard Hughes and TWA*, Rummel reports that Archie Turpin, an experienced foreman and jig builder, was hired from the Witte Machine Company as the new engine shop superintendent. Turpin brought two employees with him. In a surprisingly short time the production problems disappeared, and the engine division became a smooth-running, efficient operation. Rummel did not view the sudden turn-around following the departure of the former LeBlond employees as coincidence. Nor did others, including Rae and Ken.

One of Rae's long-standing policies was to con-

An interior view of the busy Ken-Royce engine shop, *circa* 1939.
Jim and Grace Combs

The control panel and window into the cell where Ken-Royce engines were tested. Robert W. Rummel

stantly improve his product. It frequently exasperated his sons, engineers, and dealers. Just when a product was ready for market, it was not unusual for Rae to hold it up for an improvement. Royce and Ken argued that he should save the change, whatever it was, for next year's model — so that there would be something new to anticipate, and current customers would not be kept waiting. Rae was particularly stubborn on the issue. He was fond of saying, "We owe them the best we have; *now*, not later."

The practice was carried over to the LeBlond engines. One of Rummel's first tasks was to modernize and increase the horsepower of the three engine models acquired from LeBlond. This required Rummel, who had no prior engine experience or training, to redesign and test many components, including the crankshaft, case, cylinders, and heads.

Assembly foreman Wesley Pipes, left.

The LeBlond 7DF, a 110 hp radial, was developed into the Ken-Royce 7F of 120 hp by increasing the compression ratio, changing the intake manifold, and improving the carburetion. Another modification involved increasing the hardness and wear resistance of the cylinder walls from about 225 Brinnel to nearly 400 by a special heat-treating procedure. The Ken-Royce 7F was awarded Engine Specification No. 52 in early 1939. Certification required an engine to run on a test stand for 150 consecutive hours — a little over six days — without breaking down. No one cared how much oil it used or how badly the parts were worn; it just had to run without stopping for the specified time.

The LeBlond Model 5G of 90 hp and the 7F were also redesigned with pressure lubrication in 1940. Rummel first reviewed all of the literature he could find on rocker box lubrication, and then spent several hours with the foreman of Trans World Airlines' engine overhaul shop, Guy S. "Pappy" VanSkike, a nationally recognized expert. Pappy generously displayed and explained all of the assemblies and detailed components in the transport engine systems to Rummel and Rae, who accompanied him. This guidance helped Rummel to direct the detail design of a similar system for the Ken-Royce engines.

The seven-cylinder Ken-Royce 7G engine with a "club" at rest in the test cell.
Robert W. Rummel

One of the young engineers involved with the engine redesign project was Gene Salvay, another Curtiss-Wright graduate and a native of Kansas City. Salvay wrote to all of the U.S. aircraft manufacturers in 1939 and received the best offer from Rearwin — $27.50 for a five-and-one-half day week. During his first day at work, Rae asked Salvay if he would buy a car designed by an engineer who didn't know how to drive. The youngster laughed and, of course, said he wouldn't. The trap was sprung. Rae then asked him what made him think someone would buy an airplane he designed if he didn't know how to fly it. Salvay swallowed the

**BACKED BY REPUTATION**
*the new*
**KEN-ROYCE 120**

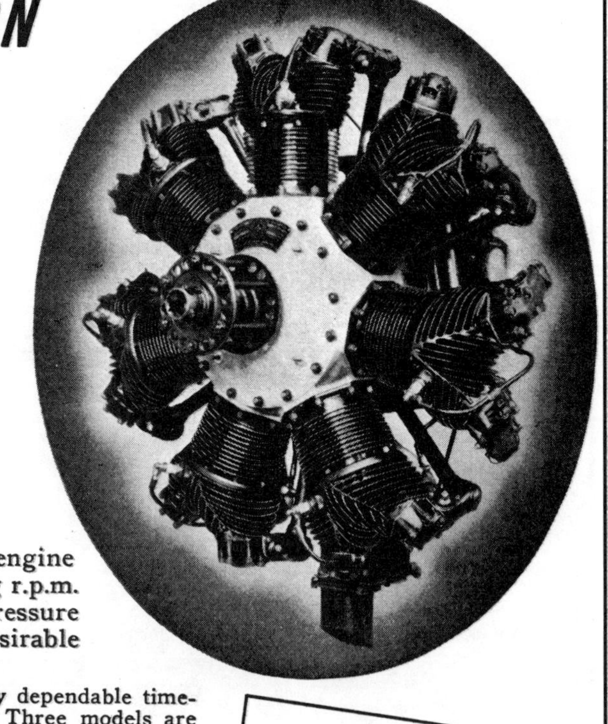

**KEN-ROYCE engines (formerly LeBlond) are in active service in over 20 countries throughout the World. They are now being used by six prominent aircraft manufacturers in the United States, Sweden and Denmark, as well as by the U. S. Army Air Corps.**

**Manufacturers and owners prefer Ken-Royce engines because of their exceptionally long life, low maintenance cost, interchangeable parts, and smooth, clean operation.**

**The new model 7F of 120 horsepower replaces the former model 7DF of 110 horsepower. It has three-bearing crankshaft, cadmium silver master rod bearings, new unusually hard alloy cylinder barrels, and many other costly improvements. Dry weight of this engine is only 285 pounds. Its gasoline consumption at cruising r.p.m. is 7 gallons per hour. Model 7F is available with full pressure baffling, starter, generator, radio shielding and other desirable accessories.**

**Airplane manufacturers find a ready market for ships powered by dependable time-tested Ken-Royce engines, developed over a period of 14 years. Three models are available—70 h.p., 90 h.p., 120 h.p. Present production program makes Ken-Royce engines available at exceptionally low prices. Full details, power curves and prices will be furnished on request.**

**MODEL 7F**
**120 h.p. at 2225 r.p.m.**
**A T C 52**

**REARWIN AIRCRAFT & ENGINES, INC.**
**FAIRFAX AIRPORT, KANSAS CITY, KANSAS, U. S. A.**

Antique Airplane Association, Blakesburg, IA

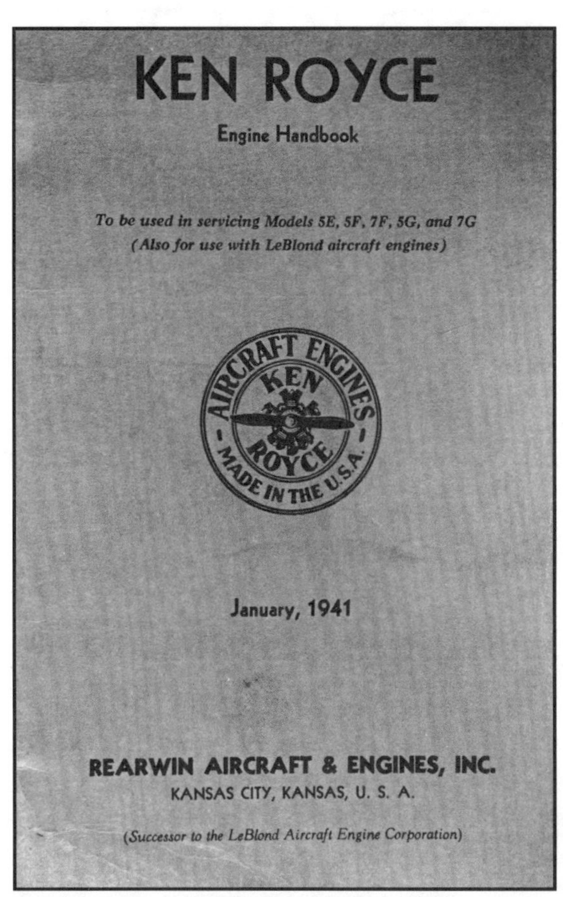


# KEN-ROYCE ENGINES

*are used in*

# MORE THAN 20 COUNTRIES

Throughout the world these smooth running, long lasting, trouble free engines have established a reputation for DEPENDABILITY. Ken-Royce engines (formerly Le Blond) are the result of over fourteen years of expensive development work; and today the various Ken-Royce models are pre-eminent in their respective horsepower classes.

An example of Ken-Royce superiority—Frank Miller, Nashville, Tenn., flew his airplane, powered with a Ken-Royce motor, 970 hours before either top or major overhaul. After this splendid service, the motor was using only 5 gallons of fuel and 1 pint of oil per hour.

Manufacturers now using Ken-Royce engines include Bellanca Aircraft Corporation, Dart Aircraft Corporation, Rearwin Airplanes, A. B. Gotaverken (Sweden). These engines are also used by the U. S. Army Air Corps.

Three Ken-Royce models are available—5E-70 h.p.; 5F-90 h.p.; 7F-110 h.p. (Model 7F is now being re-rated for 120 h.p.)

An August 1939 *Aero Digest* ad.

Antique Airplane Association, Blakesburg, IA

## REARWIN ENGINE GRANTED ATC; PARTS 90% INTERCHANGEABLE

**REARWIN Aircraft and Engines, Inc.**, has been granted a type certificate on a new engine, Model 7F, rated for 120 h.p. at 2225 rpm (A.T.C. 52). This is a development of the LeBlond Model 7DF at 110 h.p. Increased power has been attained principally by increasing the compression ratio and the rpm. Many other changes have been built into the engine, including three bearing crankshaft, cadmium silver master rod bearings to replace the babbitt bearing formerly employed at this point, rocker arm rollers instead of tappets, harder cylinder barrels, etc. The new model will supplement the Model 5E (70 h.p. at 1950 rpm) and the Model 5F (90 h.p. at 2250 rpm).

Simple design features and interchangeability of parts were emphasized during the development of all three models and as a result nearly 90 per cent of the parts are interchangeable on the Rearwin engines. The Model 7F, like, the 5E and 5F, was designed to permit many sub-assemblies which result in ease of production and lower manufacturing costs.

The crankshaft on the Model 7F (interchangeable on all models) is manufactured from drop forged 3240 steel. The shaft is machine finished all over and dynamically and statically balanced by two bronze counterweights. The crankshaft is supported by three ball bearings, the front bearing of which is assembled and locked endwise in the crankcase cover in such a manner as to permit installing the engine in either tractor or pusher type airplanes.

The pistons on the Model 7F, as on the Models 5E and 5F, are permanent mould aluminum alloy castings, heat treated to give the desired physical properties. Pistons have full skirts and three rings above the piston pin, the lower ring functioning as an oil scraper.

Articulated type connecting rods of an extremely simple design are employed. The rods are made from nickel chromium steel drop forgings of H cross section. The link rods, interchangeable on all models would be reversible were it not for the oil hole in the outside which permits splash lubrication of the piston pins.

Crankcases on the Model 7F are machined from heat treated aluminum alloy castings.

Cam follower bushings are manufactured from hollow cast iron bushings ground to close limits. These are pressed into the crankcase and are located in the same transverse plane.

The cylinders on the Model 7F, like those on Model 5F are composite in construction, the barrels being manufactured from 4140 heat treated steel forgings, the heads being heat treated aluminum alloy castings.

Tulip type valves are used. Rocker boxes, interchangeable on all engines are mounted on a pad concentric with the axis of each valve.

Gearcases are interchangeable on production models. Pads are provided at the top of the gearcase casting for mounting the magnetos and, below, a flange is provided for attaching the oil pump. A cylindrical opening in the case serves as the outer housing for the oil pump when the latter is in place.

The oil pump is built up from a lower body, an upper body, and a plate, all parts being aluminum castings. The pressure gears are located in the upper body and the scavenger gears in the lower body. As oil leaves the pressure pump body, it must pass through a cylindrical screen of fine mesh which is held between the upper body and the plate. Once through the screen, the oil can enter the drilled openings in the gearcase which lead to the bearings or to the pressure relief valve.

The Rearwin Model 7F engine is equipped with Bendix Stromberg carburetor. The engine may be equipped with either Model M-3-1 or No. 13 spark plugs made by Champion Spark Plug Company, or with BG Model 4B-1 spark plugs made by the BG Corporation.

All models of Rearwin engines are equipped with dual ignition and are equipped with two magnetos manufactured by the Scintilla Magneto Company. These magnetos have radio shielded ground terminals as standard equipment.

■

WESTERN FLYING - JULY 1939

Antique Airplane Association, Blakesburg, IA

# PRESSURE LUBRICATION

## of Rocker Arms and Valve Mechanism Now Standard on

# KEN-ROYCE ENGINES

## the Engine Used in the Popular BELLANCA CRUISAIR

★ When you buy a BELLANCA CRUISAIR, you get the famous KEN-ROYCE engine which now has, as standard equipment, automatic rocker arm and valve mechanism pressure lubrication system on both 90 hp and 120 hp models. As a result, KEN-ROYCE engines run absolutely clean and maintenance costs are lower than ever. In fact, this system can save you from $40 to $60 every hundred hours on grease jobs alone. In addition increased lubrication efficiency of oil over grease will save a tremendous amount of wear and tear on your engine and increase time between overhauls. *The KEN-ROYCE is the only radial type engine, in production, in its horse-power class that has automatic rocker arm pressure lubrication!*

Other major improvements which make KEN-ROYCE engines better than ever include:

1. Austinetic steel exhaust valves with improved valve guides.
2. Unusually hard cylinder barrels (400 Brinnel) assure many more hours between major overhauls.
3. Tappet adjustments now made in rocker arms. Tappets can now be adjusted with very little effort.
4. Finger type oil screens added to facilitate inspections on Model 7G. Can be removed in 5 minutes.
5. Oil consumption reduced to as low as ½ pint per hour, full throttle.

Production facilities enable us to offer these superior engines at exceptionally low prices. For complete details, power curves and prices write or wire TODAY. PRESENT OWNERS! These improvements can be made in engines now in the field. Write for details and prices.

**REARWIN AIRCRAFT & ENGINES, INC.** KANSAS CITY, KANSAS, U.S.A.

bait. Like many Rearwin engineers, he gave a share of his salary back for flying lessons. That was before he learned that Rae himself was not a pilot. Similarly, engineers and other employees seeking raises frequently ended up with a free half-hour of flight time a week instead of a pay increase. Some "banked" the hours and sold them at a discount to other employees more eager to fly.

A 1939 ad in *Aero Digest* boasted that the Ken-Royce engines were the result of over 14 years of development, that Frank Miller of Nashville, Tennessee, had flown his Ken-Royce-powered plane 970 hours without a top or major overhaul, and that the three models of engines available were being used in more than 20 different foreign countries. In mid-1939, the U.S. Army Air Corps even ordered several 90 hp engines for use in dirigible and balloon observation cars.

LeBlond had seen, in 1937, the tax advantage of selling the engine business, but he also saw that the days of a round engine on the front of light planes were numbered. The upstart, inline opposed engines, were already making inroads. But that didn't render the LeBlond purchase a bad deal for Rae. To the contrary, it was one of the better decisions he had made since resigning from Henry Sudendorf's lumberyard.

REARWIN AIRCRAFT & ENGINES, INC.
FAIRFAX AIRPORT
KANSAS CITY
KANSAS

CABLE
REARWIN

## *Chapter 19*

# Rearwin Aircraft and Engines, Inc.

*IN 1938, the aircraft partnership again earned a pre-tax profit of just over $15,300 on gross sales of $120,000. The Ken-Royce Engine Company did nearly as well, with pre-tax earnings of $14,720 on sales of only $47,900 — a spectacular return on the original $25,000 investment. In addition, over $20,000 worth of new engine orders were in hand. There were more than 900 LeBlond/Ken-Royce engines in operation, and sooner or later each would need service and parts. The 1938 profits of $30,000 were divided equally among the happy partners.*

*It was time to expand; time to develop new airplanes; time to improve and increase the power of the Ken-Royce engines; and time to promote and sell. But fresh capital was needed. That meant, as it had in 1929, incorporation and the sale of stock.*

*The Rearwin co-partners retained Arthur R. Ross, a Kansas City, Missouri, certified public accountant and attorney, to audit the books of the partnerships and assist with the formation of a new Kansas corporation, including the preparation and filing of the required financial data with the Securities and Exchange Commission.*

*On April 27, 1939, the aircraft and engine partnerships entered into an agreement with a pair of New York City security underwriters, Tobey and Company, and Hatch, Piper & Company, Inc., to form a new corporation and raise $240,000* through the sale of stock. The new firm, Rearwin Aircraft and Engines, Inc. would be capitalized with 250,000 shares of $1 par value common stock, and would assume the assets, liabilities, and operations of both partnerships. In return, the Rearwins would receive 115,338 shares of stock; 38,462 each for Rae, Royce, and Ken, and one share each for Royce's wife Jacqueline and Ken's wife Suzanne. All would serve on the Board of Directors. Rae, as president, would receive a salary of $7,500 annually, while Ken, as secretary-treasurer, would be paid $5,000. Royce was still in Salina running the lumberyard and fuel businesses.

The agreement called for the joint underwriters to offer 100,000 shares at $2.50 net to the corporation, with Rae, Royce, and Ken holding an option on the last 45,000 shares, but at the same offering price. The underwriters were to receive a 75-cent commission on each share sold, so the stock would be offered at $3.25. Rae also agreed to list the firm on the New York Stock Exchange upon the sale of the first 50,000 shares to the public.

The new corporation was born on May 17, 1939. The August 24, 1939, prospectus reported that the aggregate "out-of-pocket" cost to the Rearwins for their stock was $139,402 (only about $1.21 a share), but the figure was grossly misleading. The out-of-pocket cost did not accurately disclose the full picture. In fact, the two partnerships had actually transferred assets worth $365,120 to the new corporation. That meant the cost of the Rearwins' stock was actually about $3.16 a share.

The difference was attributable to the purchase of the LeBlond Aircraft Engine Corporation. The Ken-Royce engine partnership had been sitting on a gold mine of untapped profit. The engine, parts, and equipment acquired from LeBlond had been carried on the Rearwin partnership books at Rae's cost ($25,000). According to the audit performed by Ross, that was at least $215,716 *less* than what they had cost LeBlond to acquire and manufacture! Moreover, the engines and parts would be priced at retail before they were sold. The grossly undervalued partnership assets represented worth or unrealized profit, so they were properly marked up by the accounting firm to fair market value prior to the formation of the new corporation.

If fully subscribed, the offering would net the new corporation about $240,000 after expenses. According to the prospectus, the new funds were earmarked for sales promotion, working capital to manufacture engines and build aircraft, the purchase of additional manufacturing equipment, the design and development of new two- and four-place aircraft, and the design and development of new engines.

The sale of stock was scheduled to be complete in 120 days, but the results were disappointing. The public was still skittish of the securities market, particularly new aviation issues, and money was tight. The misleading out-of-pocket figure may have also been a factor. Only about 22,000 shares were sold. The $55,000 of new capital would have to be used sparingly.

**CACHET TO BE USED ON AIR MAIL OUT OF SALINA MAY 19th**

**AIR MAIL SPECIAL**

**National Air Mail Week - - May 15 - 21**

***Observance of 20th Anniversary of Air Mail Service***

**KENNETH R. REARWIN, *Pilot***

***Plane will arrive at Salina Airport 12:27 p. m. Depart at 12:47 p. m.***

Plan to use air mail service on the 19th. It will help to boost Salina for air service and will also advertise the city by the special cachet to be used on all air mail sent out during air mail week, and especially May 19th. Envelopes with special cachet are obtainable at the Assistant Postmaster's window.

**All air mail for the May 19th flight must be in the Post Office by 12:00 noon on the above date.**

AVIATION COMMITTEE, CHAMBER OF COMMERCE
ED MORGENSTERN, *Chairman*
OTHO SCHMIDT, *Vice-Chairman*

CONSOLIDATED – SALINA

Many chambers of commerce still had aviation committees when Ken flew the mail from Fairfax to Salina to observe National Air Mail Week in 1938.

## *Chapter 20*

# A Partnership Dissolved

*HENRY SUDENDORF died in his home in Salina on the afternoon of Friday, February 11, 1939. It was the eve of the 60th anniversary of his marriage to Carrie. She was too ill to attend the funeral, so a private radio wire was set up to carry the service and eulogies to her bedside. Henry had been 81. Carrie died 15 days later at age 86. The excuse Leila had relied on since 1930 for refusing to move to Kansas City was no longer valid, if it ever had been.*

*Throughout the decade, Henry had frequently advised his only daughter that her place was with her husband, but she rationalized his counsel as parental sacrifice. In truth, Leila had lived in Salina all her life and was simply unwilling to leave.*

*Rae's trips to Salina had been frequent, at least in the early years following the move to Kansas City. He lived for a time at the Kansas City Athletic Club, and later spent several years at the Phillips Hotel — surely a lonely and introspective place after working hours, even for a former traveling salesman. Slowly, Rae and Leila grew apart. She occasionally spoke of moving when her parents were gone, but no one believed she actually would, least of all Leila herself. Rae pressed for a resolution in the summer of 1939 after her parents' deaths. Leila, then 58, was comfortable in Salina and was still not interested in uprooting her life, even to be near the first grandchild that Ken had provided. Also, Leila was vaguely aware of the* early financial struggles of the aircraft venture. She unjustifiably believed that Rae had his eyes on her assets, which now included half of her parents' estate.[1] Both sons viewed Leila's unfounded suspicion as simply another excuse for refusing to move. It also provided acceptable justification among her Salina friends for obtaining a divorce.

With Rae's approval, Leila filed for divorce on August 9, 1939. She alleged, in the language of lawyers and the law, that at all times she had conducted herself as a faithful, dutiful, and loving wife, but that her husband had abandoned her for more than one year and been guilty of extreme cruelty, thus defeating and destroying the ends of matrimony.

Less than 30 days later the parties entered into a stipulated property agreement which provided that Rae would pay Leila $5,000, $1,000 in cash and 20 shares of stock in the Planters State Bank. She would also receive sole ownership of the family home, which she and Rae had jointly built, and all personal property and automobiles in her possession. Due to her substantial inheritance and assets, alimony was waived.

Rae kept the businesses and the other property in his name or possession, which included various stocks, as well as title to some 15 lots in Salina and Wichita. The divorce was final on October 16, 1939.

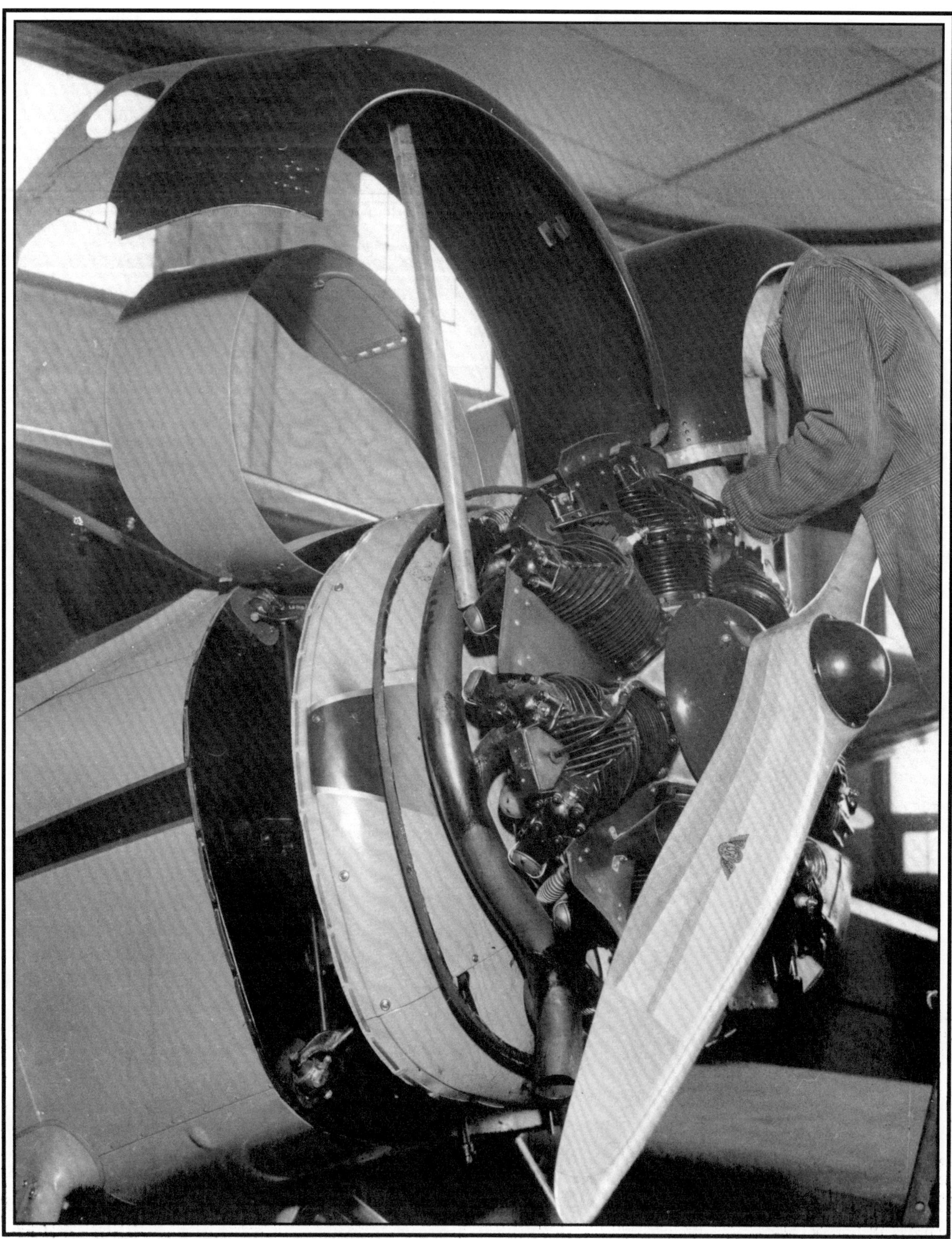
Early Cloudsters had double (outer and inner) cowlings.

Robert W. Rummel

## *Chapter 21*

# The Cloudster

*The light aircraft market began tilting away from tandem seating in the mid-1930s. Royce and Ken had been urging their father to build a side-by-side plane even before returning from a January 1937 aircraft exhibition in New York City's Madison Square Garden. By their count, prospects looking at two-abreast seating outnumbered those interested in the traditional tandem arrangement by three or four to one. Rae, however, was still trying to certify the Speedster, and Royce's persistent prodding became another bone of contention.*

*Although the Speedster was certified in late 1937, sales were sluggish, and the Sportster, while still selling well, was essentially a 1935 design. Rae finally gave in to the dictates of the marketplace in late 1938, and authorized Rummel to develop a side-by-side utility plane using as much technology and tooling as feasible from existing Rearwin designs. Rae initially envisioned simply widening the Speedster. Rummel was anxious for just such a project and suggested the new two-seater should be designed and certified with both the 90 and 120 hp Ken-Royce engines — that is, two models for the price of one. Rae agreed.*

*While Rummel believed that the Speedster held the best prospects for design transfer, almost every aspect of the new plane proved to be different. For example, the wing loading, span lift distribution, lift strut geometry, landing gear, fuselage*

The prototype was the only Cloudster Model 8090 built.
Robert W. Rummel

Below: The Speedster, Sportster, and Cloudster were all being sold during 1939. Robert W. Rummel

structure, engine installation, and cabin were significantly different. One change led to another and, in keeping with the objective of building the best possible plane at the most economical cost, a virtually new aircraft emerged.

The prototype Model 8090, featuring the five-cylinder Ken-Royce 5F engine up front, rolled out the door in about six months. It was first flown by Bill Miller in early April 1939, and, like the redesigned Speedster, quickly passed the stringent spin tests. It was originally dubbed the Rearwin Coupe, but was publicly unveiled a month later as the Cloudster, a name once used but dropped by Donald Douglas. The Cloudster was appointed with plush fabrics from Cadillac overruns, a simulated woodgrain instrument panel, and other conveniences — including an oversized luggage compartment that would hold 50 pounds. The Model 8090 was first displayed at the 1939 National Air Races in Cleveland, and was certified on October 17, 1939 with ATC No. 711, but only one was ever built.[1] The companion Model 8125 was powered by the Ken-Royce 7F radial engine of 120 hp.

Rummel and his engineering staff modified the Model 8125 to carry a third occupant in early 1940. The engine was moved forward about four inches, the fin was enlarged, and the seating was rearranged slightly to accommodate a seat behind the pilot. Its occupant sat sideways, a common arrangement in the 1930s, and the right front seat folded for entry. While he was at it, Rummel designed a full-length NACA cowling hinged along the top for easy access. This eliminated the need for an inner cowling, reducing weight and improving performance. The Model 8135 was spun off in late 1941 with the improved Ken-Royce 7G engine that featured pressure lubrication.

The 90 hp Cloudster was introduced at $3,495, the 8125 at $3,795, and the 8135 at $4,495. However, all three were available for one-third down.

About 20 percent of all Rearwin aircraft production ended up in export pipelines. The largest single

The Cloudster churns the skies over rural Kansas. Robert W. Rummel

foreign order came from Iran (formerly Persia) in 1941. The Aero Club of Iran, a government-sponsored paramilitary group, offered free pilot training to qualified citizens. Those who completed the course were inducted into the Imperial Iranian Air Force. The Club ordered 25 Model 8125s with the new pressure-lubricated Ken-Royce 8G engine.

Ken, who was then the sales manager, had negotiated the contract in Washington, D.C., over a two-month period with a Colonel Kosravani, who headed the Iranian mission. With parts and dockside delivery, the deal was worth $150,000, or about $6,000 per plane, including $300 for crating. It also provided that an Iranian Air Force officer, Major A. Afkami, would be stationed at the Fairfax plant to oversee production, personally fly each plane, and monitor the dismantling, crating, and loading on flatcars. The wooden crates were also to be specially designed so that upon arrival in Teheran they could be converted into housing units — most likely, barracks.

While Iranian envoys kept dangling the prospect of another order for 75 to 100 aircraft in front of Rae and Ken, both regarded it as perpetual, post-contract bargaining calculated to squeeze the already signed agreement. Indeed, at one point, an Iranian negotiator arrived to discuss licensing terms, a concept that was inconsistent with the promise of future purchases. Nothing further ever developed.

Gene Salvay, who had done design work on the Model 8125, and Jack Bucher, a Rearwin Flight School instructor, served as test pilots and flew with Major Afkami on many such flights. According to Salvay, Afkami delighted in flying the new planes up and down the Missouri River at an altitude of about 50 feet.

Harry B. Taylor, a flight instructor and a licensed

Static testing of the Cloudster's seat strength was accomplished with the use of lead weights. Robert W. Rummel

Bill Miller places luggage behind seat of the Cloudster prototype. (This photo was used in advertising.)

The Cloudster with enlarged fin under assembly. Robert W. Rummel

The student learned in the rear of the double-paneled tandem instrument trainer.

Robert W. Rummel

Rearwin salesman and demo pilot Richard "Rich" Palmer and Rae at an airshow, *circa* 1940.

Rearwin salesman and flight instructor Richard Palmer inspects under the full cowling of the Cloudster, *circa* 1939.
Robert W. Rummel

This 1940 Cloudster was donated by the Rearwin family to the San Diego Aerospace Museum. Authentic restoration was completed in 1996.
Bill Wright

Sandbags were piled on the horizontal stabilizer of the Cloudster to test strength, while buckets of sand held the empennage in place.
Robert W. Rummel

An unidentified Rearwin employee works on the Cloudster empennage.
Robert W. Rummel

Major Afkami and one of the 25 Cloudsters sold to Iran in 1940.

airframe and engine mechanic, was contracted by the Iranian government from 1941 to February 1945 to instruct students and maintain the fleet of Cloudsters.

On his return to the United States in 1945, he reported the Iranians had eventually mounted a single 30-caliber machine gun on the left wing strut, outside the prop diameter; that all 25 craft were still flying; and, despite extreme desert conditions, not one had ever sustained an engine failure. According to Taylor, "The Cloudster has become the modern counterpart of the Persian Flying Carpet."

In January 1941, Zack Mosley, the 1933 creator of the popular "Smilin' Jack" comic strip, traded in his Cub Coupe on a three-place Cloudster 8135 (SN872). The plane was custom-painted dark brown to Mosley's specifications, and the Cub's registration number, NC26000, was transferred.

Mosley wasn't as pleased with his Ken-Royce 7G engine as the Aero Club of Iran was with theirs. Unlike the Cub's flat engine, the Ken-Royce dripped oil on the hangar floor, as radial

"Smilin' Jack" cartoonist Zack Mosley with his custom-painted Cloudster purchased new in 1941. Jill Mosley Sandow

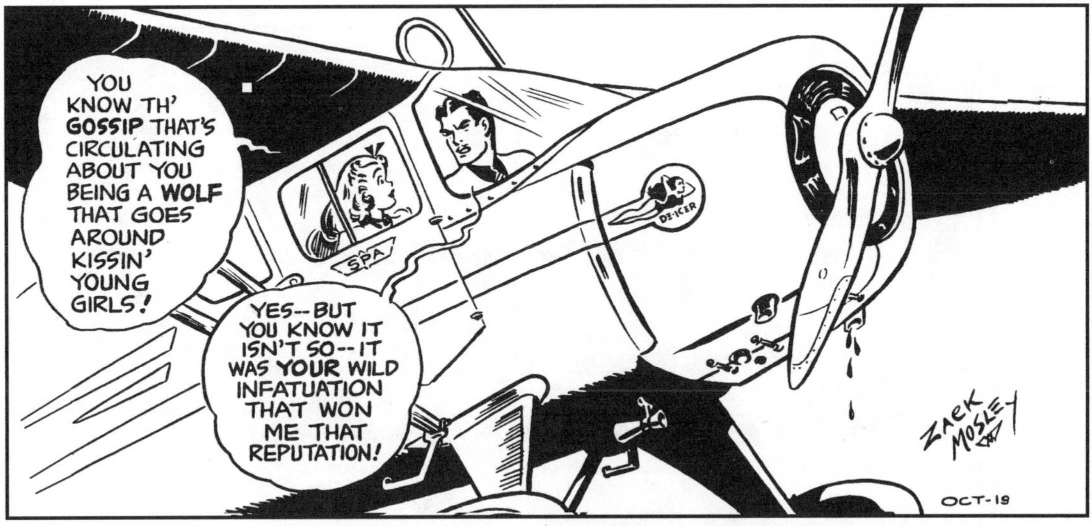


This Zack Mosley cartoon was intended to prompt the Rearwin dealer to stop the oil leak.
Jill Mosley Sandow

Below: Zack Mosley poses with the "de-icer" model used for the logo on the vertical fin of his Rearwin Cloudster.
Antique Airplane Association, Blakesburg, IA

engines sometimes did. The dealer and Rearwin factory personnel sought to solve the problem, and explained "the facts of round engine life" to Zack several times, but he didn't buy it. The plane was regularly featured in his famous cartoon strip, piloted, of course, by "Smilin' Jack." Mosley couldn't resist including an occasional depiction of the Cloudster dripping oil in flight or on a hangar floor.

When President Roosevelt established the Civil Air Patrol on December 1, 1941, six days before Pearl Harbor, Mosley and "Old Linen Sides," as he called the plane, were ready to patrol for Nazi subs off the Florida coast. In fact, he moved his studio

The Cloudster Model 8135 was available as either a two- or three-place plane.
Robert W. Rummel

The three-place Cloudster Model 8135 was converted to a tandem, two-seat instrument trainer — the Model 8135T. About 25 were built.
Robert W. Rummel

Shades enclosed the rear cockpit of the instrument trainer; the instructor retained normal visibility.
Robert W. Rummel

to the Lantana Airport, which was also the base of the local CAP wing.

On April 24, 1942, Mosley and another craft were patrolling beyond sight of the Florida coastline between West Palm Beach and Melbourne. His wingman, flying an Ercoupe, headed east to detour around a thunderstorm. Mosley figured that they wouldn't be able to circumvent the storm and reach land by dark. A nighttime engine failure over the Atlantic wouldn't be good, so he banked west. He later called it the best decision he ever made.

Just as land appeared on the horizon, the engine dropped to about 1,500 rpm. The oil pressure also fell while the engine-head temperature rose. Mosley set up his best glide angle and crossed the beach in semi-darkness at about 300 feet with the partially constructed runway at the uncompleted Vero Beach Airport in sight. The plane was shaking, the cowling was jumping, smoke was trailing, and the engine was now clunking at just 1,000 rpm. The driver of a steam roller smoothing the strip saw the smoke-trailing craft headed in his direction, and jumped off as the plane rolled to a stop just a few feet short of disaster.

As Mosley observed, his was the first CAP coastal patrol plane downed with engine trouble, but there would be others. A piston had swallowed a valve, and the engine was beyond repair. Undaunted, he ordered another Ken-Royce from the factory and was back on patrol in less than two weeks. Six months later he bought a used Stinson Reliant with a 245 hp engine so that he could haul around a 300-pound depth charge. Zack was hardly the "coward" he claimed he was in his writings.

In early 1941, Pan American Airways was looking for a suitable and inexpensive two-seat platform to use as an instrument trainer for pilot training. The trainers then in use not only cost about $20,000 each, but they were also expensive to operate and maintain.

Juan Trippe, who headed Pan Am and was as eternally interested in saving a dollar as Rae, decided to develop an inexpensive trainer with an existing manufacturer. He had personally owned a Sportster fitted with Edo floats since 1937, and knew that Rearwin manufactured a rugged, overbuilt product. He thought that the wide-cabined Cloudster 8135, converted back into a tandem two-seater with doors front and rear for emergency use, would meet his needs. Was Rearwin interested in the job?

Rummel and the rest of the engineering department dove into the project at a hectic pace, and modified the basic Cloudster 8135 powered by the Ken-Royce 7G pressure-lubricated engine to Pan Am specs. Several structural changes were made in the cabin area of the airframe to permit the desired tandem seating arrange-

Seats in the Model 8135T were designed for occupants wearing either seat or backpacked parachutes, with height adjusted by cushions. Robert W. Rummel

Quick removal of the rear instrument panel converted the Model 8135T back to a tandem-seat primary trainer. Robert W. Rummel

This Cloudster restored in England by Phillip Mann as a Pan Am instrument trainer is now back in the United States.

ment. Both seats were designed with cushions that, when removed, would accommodate either seat or backpack parachutes. Two doors fitted on the right side could be opened or jettisoned from either cockpit in the case of emergency, a design expense lesser operators might not have been willing to incur.

The rear compartment was also designed so that it could be fully enclosed by drawing a blackout curtain, while the front seat instructor retained normal visibility. The instruments necessary for "blind flying" were incorporated separately in a rear panel that could be quickly removed to convert the plane back to a primary trainer. The engi-

# MAKE THIS Point by Point COMPARISON!

■ Check the REARWIN CLOUDSTER . . . point by point . . . with any other airplane in its class. When you do, you'll agree with us that REARWIN offers more value per dollar.

Compare the CLOUDSTER'S flashing beauty . . . the dependable, smooth running, 120 hp Ken-Royce motor mounted in rubber . . . the 2 mile per minute cruise with 600 mile range . . . the quiet, insulated, attractively upholstered 42" wide cabin . . . the soft, restful cushions, the smartly appointed instrument panel . . . the swift take-off, the phenomenal climb . . . and the many other features you'll want.

Then, after you've made your point by point comparison . . . choose the airplane that measures up . . . the REARWIN 3-PLACE CLOUDSTER.

The Cloudster is also available as a 2-place coupe with either 90 hp or 120 hp, time-tested Ken-Royce motor. Payment plans are available on either model. Ask for a demonstration *today*.

**COMING!**

Latest addition to the Rearwin line . . . a new 2-place, side-by-side, low-priced airplane will be in production soon. Watch for our announcement.

**REARWIN AIRCRAFT & ENGINES, INC. KANSAS CITY, KANSAS, U. S. A.**

From *Aero Digest*, June 1940.

Antique Airplane Association, Blakesburg, IA

neering, stress analysis, static testing, and CAA approvals took about four months. The first three planes, destined for Pan Am stations in Alaska, San Francisco, and Columbia, were delivered in August 1941.

The versatile craft was designated the Cloudster 8135T and, full of instruments, sold for about $10,000. While the empty weight was increased by 200 pounds to 1,340, gross weight remained at 1,900 pounds. According to Rummel, the Cloudster's central linkage had the feel of a larger passenger plane, which was a decided psychological advantage for neophyte instrument pilots. Other aviation concerns must have agreed. In addition to Pan Am, which bought five, Instrument Trainers were also sold to Parks Air College (five), American Flyers (three), Spartan School of Aeronautics (five), Ailor Sales Corporation, American Aircraft Company, the Civil Aeronautics Authority, and Transcontinental and Western Air (TWA). About 25 were built.[2]

**IT'S GOT EVERYTHING!**

The CLOUDSTER, Rearwin's new side-by-side model has everything you want . . . everything you've been looking for. In appearance, performance, comfort and utility it's tops!

Just look at these features: beautiful finish . . . belly flap . . . hydraulic landing gear with 80 inch tread . . . ball-bearing controls throughout . . . quiet, roomy cabin attractively upholstered . . . handsome instrument panel . . . exceptional visibility . . . 34 gallon fuel capacity in wing tanks . . . cruise of 110 mph with 90 hp motor or 130 mph with 120 hp motor.

A CLOUDSTER demonstrator is coming to your airport. Write or wire the factory for full information.

The SPORTSTER and SPEEDSTER are also ideal for instruction and private use.

You can buy a Rearwin for only $735.00 down.

**REARWIN AIRPLANES**

*Eleventh Continuous Successful Year*

FAIRFAX AIRPORT . . . KANSAS CITY, KANSAS, U. S. A.

"REARWIN popularity is proof of REARWIN superiority"

Left: From *Aero Digest*, June 1939.
Antique Airplane Association, Blakesburg, IA

Below: Antique Airplane Association, Blakesburg, IA

**SEE IT! FLY IT! YOU'LL BUY IT!**

THE NEW 1940 CLOUDSTER IS JUST WHAT YOU'RE LOOKING FOR

WANT REAL POWER PLUS SMOOTHNESS?
Here's a choice of either 90 or 120 lively horses, rubber mounted to eliminate vibration.

WANT A BEAUTIFUL AIRPLANE, INSIDE AND OUT?
Here's symmetry from prop to rudder with interior appointments second to none.

WANT SPEED AND RANGE?
Here's an airplane you can cruise at over 2 miles a minute with a range of over 600 miles.

WANT ECONOMY?
Here's 18-20 miles to the gallon with low oil consumption.

WANT COMFORT AND QUIETNESS?
Here's a cabin 42 inches wide with soft, restful coil spring cushions and lots of leg room. Here's insulation which makes conversation as easy as in your car.

You'll find the Cloudster's got what it takes. A demonstration will convince you. Write for complete information NOW!

See the 3-Place Cloudster at the Miami Air Races

**REARWIN AIRCRAFT & ENGINES, Inc., Kansas City, Kansas, U. S. A.**

**LEARN TO FLY!**

**In the latest 2S Rating heavy type 75 h. p. and 90 h. p. $3,000 Airplanes manufactured by Rearwin Aircraft and Engines, Inc.**

**$3.75** Per Lesson GOVERNMENT LICENSED INSTRUCTORS

Rearwin is now building for the Iranian Government (formerly Persia) 25 Airplanes for military training

**Rearwin Flying School**

Fairfax Airport, K. C., Kansas, FA. 1750

This ad appeared in the *Kansas Citian* dated September 29, 1939.

One Cloudster (NC37719) was impressed during World War II and designated as a UC-102A. It was acquired at Kansas City, Kansas, on May 14, 1943, and was assigned to the 364th Base Headquarters, at Billy Mitchell Field near Milwaukee. The draftee was declared surplus in August 1944 and sent to the 4100th Army Air Forces Base Unit at Patterson Field in Ohio. Several months later it was transferred to the Reconstruction Finance Corporation at Cimarron Field, Oklahoma, but its fate is unknown.

In 1942, the 1,300 employees of the National Housing Company in Dallas purchased a new Rearwin Cloudster equipped with a two-way radio, and donated it to the CAP for antisubmarine patrol duty. It was christened the "National Housers Comet," and was delivered to the CAP on Labor Day.

A total of 124 Cloudsters were built. The Model 8090 was given serial number 101. The balance were issued consecutive serial numbers 801 through 923. The new, full NACA cowling was first installed on SN823, a Model 8135. Flaps and slots were initially tested on SN839, while the elevator tab setting was changed to 14½ degrees up and 28 degrees down on SN841 and the stabilizer leading edge was lowered three-quarters of an inch. The last

***Use Any* YARDSTICK *You Choose***

***the* CLOUDSTER *"measures UP"***

**COMING!** Latest addition to the Rearwin line . . . a new 2 place, side-by-side, low-priced, Class 2S airplane will soon be in production. Watch for announcement.

**Is Your "Yardstick"**

**PERFORMANCE?**

**If so, you'l. [illegible] a CLOUDSTER! Takes off in less than 700 feet in still air with full load . . . climbs like a rocket . . . lands at very slow speed. Ball bearing controls throughout and balanced ailerons assure easy flying as you breeze along at 2 miles a minute . . . and you can cruise 600 miles without a stop. With its service ceiling of over 16,000 feet fully loaded, your CLOUDSTER easily clears any mountain in the United States. The CLOUDSTER'S top-notch performance is tailor-made for efficient . . . safe . . . economical operation under all flying conditions. Make a point-by-point comparison, you'll see "By the YARDSTICK of Performance, the CLOUDSTER measures up!"**

**Powered with choice of 90 hp or 120 hp time tested Ken-Royce motors . . . available in either 2 or 3 place models.**

**REARWIN AIRCRAFT & ENGINES, INC.** KANSAS CITY, KANSAS, U. S. A.

From *Aero Digest*, July 1940. Antique Airplane Association, Blakesburg, IA

# Aero Club of Iran CHOOSES REARWINS!

**From the many competitive training airplanes submitted, the Iranian Government picked Rearwin, 120 H.P. Cloudsters—twenty-five of them. Why? Because the Cloudster has what it takes! On all points—appearance, dependability, construction, performance, economy of operation —the Rearwin Cloudster was first.**

**These airplanes will be used half way around the world on fields a mile or more above sea level and over high, mountainous country. They *have* to be good—and the same features which appealed to the Aero Club will appeal to you. Whether you want an airplane for training purposes or private use, you'll find the Cloudster gives you more for your money every time.**

**Get full information on the 2- and 3-place Cloudsters—their perfectly appointed and sound-proofed interiors, phenomenal climb, 2-mile-a-minute cruise, 600-mile range. Write for color folder today!**

***It's a hit! Orders are pouring in for Rearwin Rangers. 75 h.p. model, fully equipped, only $2295. Ask for a demonstration.***

**REARWIN AIRCRAFT & ENGINES, INC. KANSAS CITY, KANSAS, U. S. A.**

From *Aero Digest*, September 1940. Antique Airplane Association, Blakesburg, IA

Cloudster, a Model 8135 (SN923), rolled out on July 6, 1942, and was delivered two weeks later by Ken to a customer in Pascagoula, Mississippi.

According to Rearwin buff Gary Van Farowe, 36 Cloudsters, including the 25 "Persian Carpets" (SN841-865) and two spare airframes sold to Iran, were exported. Two were sold in Mexico (SN814 and SN837), and one each went to Australia (SN820), Argentina (SN836), Brazil (SN838), Columbia (SN878), the Congo (SN837), Uruguay (SN898), and the Philippines (SN886). Another Cloudster, an instrument trainer, was exported to England after World War II by Phillip Mann, a collector of more than a dozen pre-World War II aircraft. Ken flew in the plane (G-BGAV) while vacationing, and was told by Mann that the Pan Am trainer was the personal favorite of the Duke of York. Mann's collection has since been sold, and the plane is back on this side of the Atlantic.

An authentically restored Cloudster Model 8135 (NC-25553) donated by Ken Rearwin is currently on display at the San Diego Aerospace Museum. Another (NC25451) is on display at the Experimental Aircraft Museum in Oshkosh, Wisconsin, while a third (NC25449) is housed at the New England Air Museum at Windsor Locks, Connecticut, near Hartford's Bradley International Airport. The Airpower Museum at Blakesburg, Iowa, also owns one.

The gear legs and springs on the Skyranger were clean, efficient, and simple.

Robert W. Rummel

## Chapter 22

# The Skyranger, Last of the Breed

*DESPITE UNDERSTANDABLE reluctance, Rae had little choice but to give in to the flat horizontally opposed engines, which were the wave of the future. Even when he bought the LeBlond Company in 1937 he had known the day would come. By 1940, the market for Ken-Royce engines, except for use in Rearwin-built aircraft, was drying up.*

*Shortly after the Cloudster was certified, Rummel and his engineering staff, which now included Keith Dentle and Bion MacWhirter, started on the new model's basic design and engineering work. The concept was a smaller, less expensive, two-place side-by-side monoplane with a Continental 65 hp engine up front that would appeal to both the sportsman and the business pilot. As usual, Rae wanted it to be a notch or two above the Aeronca, Taylorcraft, Luscombe, and Piper models of 1939 — a deluxe personal aircraft that was both comfortable and well-appointed. Rummel and his staff on the second floor of the office structure did not disappoint him.*

*According to Gene Salvay, the engineering section was large enough for about ten drafting tables, a couple of desks, and a flush-mounted wall safe containing drawers for prints and drawings. An "arc" lamp blueprint machine with a fixing "bath" at the side was located in one corner behind a partition. Drawings were*

Above: The Rearwin engineering staff was located on the second floor of the office structure at the left of the hangar.
Wyandotte County Museum, Bonner Springs, KS

Left: Fairfax Airport, May 1938.
Wyandotte County Museum, Bonner Springs, KS

limited to the size of the glass cover on the machine. The mezzanine was sometimes dusty because wooden wings were made on the same floor. Normally, all drawings had to be approved by Rummel before the engineer reviewed them with the production foreman.

The Rearwin Model 165 was first flown by Bill Miller on April 9, 1940, and was introduced to the public in July as the Ranger. However, with complaints from the aircraft engine company of the same name and the appearance of the Continental 75 hp engine, the new plane was certified as the Skyranger Model 175 on August 16, 1940, with ATC No. 729. Simplicity of design and construction permitted salesmen to promise delivery within ten weeks of placing an order, and the fully equipped, well-appointed Model 175 was priced at just $2,295. The 65 hp version was originally offered at $2,195. A stripped-down version was also offered at $1,795 until early 1941, but few were sold.

Rummel's goal of designing the safest aircraft possible led to the incorporation of wing slots on the Skyranger, giving flight and landing advantage — even though he was concerned from a marketing standpoint that the flying public might believe that their presence had been necessary to counter undesirable flight characteristics. One of the initial problems was to design the slot opening so as to produce minimum air flow during cruising speeds. This was accomplished by locating the surface opening at the stagnation points for a wide range of cruising angles of attack.

The slot itself was a simple aluminum sheet

**PARIS FLYING SERVICE**
**PARIS, TEXAS**

November 6, 1940.

REARWIN AIRCRAFT & ENGINES, INC.
Fairfax Airport,
Kansas City, Kansas.

Gentlemen:

We had a very pleasant trip home in our new 75 hp SKYRANGER. Needless to say, we made the 365 miles non-stop with the standard 24-gallon wing tanks and had fuel enough left to give all the boys at the field a ride and then some. This single fact alone puts the SKYRANGER in a class of its own.

Also, we averaged well over 100 mph in spite of the fact we never ran the motor at its full cruising r.p.m. On tests I have run since, the SKYRANGER has shown 105 to 110 mph to be about right at 2400 r.p.m. Congratulations on the fine airplanes you are producing. It is not hard to find a home for a REARWIN.

Cordially yours,
LLOYD M. DAMRON, *Manager*,
PARIS FLYING SERVICE

Above: An unidentified Rearwin employee envisions piloting the final product.

Left: Rearwin salesman Bill Allman demonstrates the Skyranger's cowling was designed for easy engine access. Robert W. Rummel

Ample space between the Continental engine and the Skyranger's firewall permitted ready access to the magnetos and facilitated the installation of a starter and other engine accessories.

Robert W. Rummel

# *Announcing the New* REARWIN RANGER

**IMMEDIATE DELIVERY** on Rearwin Cloudsters. Get your order in at once for this popular 2 or 3 place airplane. Choice of 90 hp or 120 hp dependable Ken-Royce motor. From $3795.00.

## APPROVED and in PRODUCTION

A real cross-country, 2 place, side-by-side airplane, low in price but sky high in value . . . with these expensive, big airplane features:

- Leading edge wing slots for safer flying.
- Unexcelled visibility both in the air and while taxiing.
- 100 mph cruise. 400 mile range.
- 125 lbs. allowance for luggage and equipment.
- 18 gallon wing tank with provisions for another wing tank increasing capacity to 36 gallons and range to 800 miles.
- Roomy cabin, beautifully upholstered and sound proofed.
- Grade A fabric with rubbed finish.
- Class 2S rating.

For a rugged, dependable, cross-country airplane that can "take it," buy the new REARWIN RANGER. Deluxe model, 65 hp motor, fully equipped, $2195. 75 hp motor, $2295. Immediate deliveries. Write for new folder with complete details TODAY!

**REARWIN AIRCRAFT & ENGINES, INC.** KANSAS CITY, KANSAS, U. S. A.

This ad appeared in the August 1940 *Aero Digest*. The "Ranger" was subsequently renamed to avoid confusion with the Ranger engine.

Antique Airplane Association, Blakesburg, IA

A 75 hp Skyranger at Mecca, near the Salton Sea, California, in 1941. The pilot is Ruth Downie. Don Downie

Ken Rearwin (left) with an unidentified Skyranger prospect in Springfield, Missouri, during the summer of 1941.

The tail wheel and rudder assembly on the 1941 Skyranger.
Robert W. Rummel

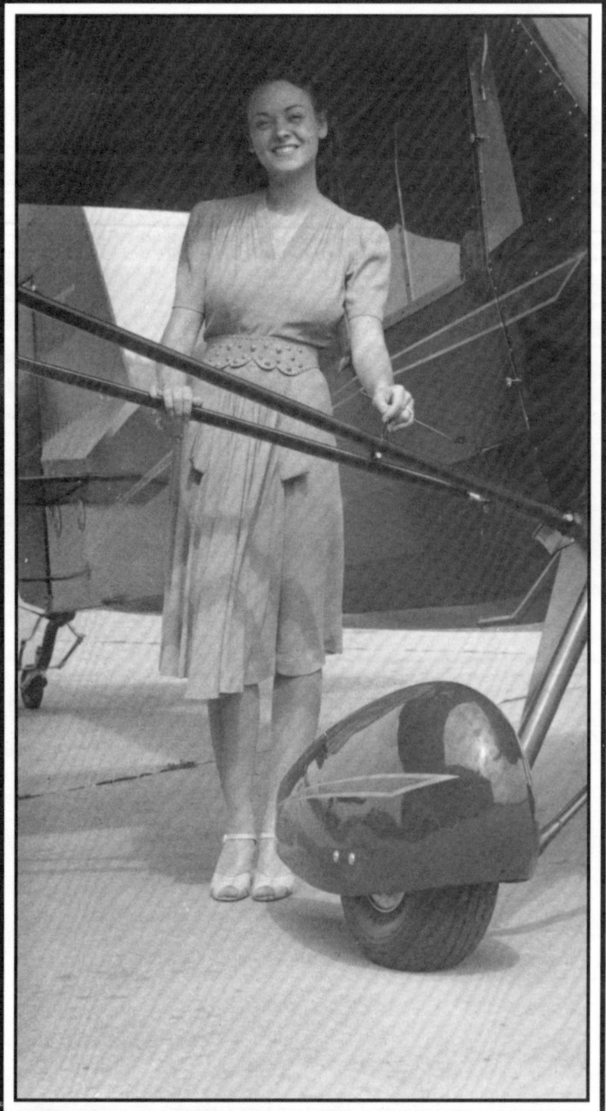

Right and opposite page: Royce's wife Jacqueline frequently posed as a model for Skyranger ads.

wrapped to the correct shape and retained at each end by steel fittings and one bolt. Computing the aerodynamic loads was difficult because little data was available. Thus, to allay any certification concerns, Rummel assumed high load factors and ran the stress tests accordingly without encountering any problems.

The rapid availability of higher-rated engines quickly resulted in a revamped Skyranger. Two 80 hp

The Skyranger was a clean and trim two-place craft. Note the slots on the wings. Only 82 were built by Rearwin before World War II; 276 after the war by Commonwealth.

Orders are pouring in for this new, 2-place, side-by-side, deluxe airplane. Without question, the SKYRANGER is destined to be the sensation of 1941.

Built with the same care and exactness as the famous Rearwin CLOUDSTER, the SKYRANGER embodies all the latest safety features including spin-preventing wing slots. Here is the airplane which ANYONE can fly with perfect confidence and absolute safety.

Outstanding SKYRANGER features include: Class 2S rating. . . . 100 m.p.h. cruise. . . . 500 mile range with 750 mile range available. . . . exhaust silencer. . . . quiet, comfortable, and attractive cabin 40 inches in width.

The trend is to more power. *Be ahead of the Procession with the 75 h.p. SKYRANGER.* Fully equipped, only $2295.00 65 h.p. motor, fully equipped, $2195. Write for new folder today!

If you want a 3-place plane, be sure to see the CLOUDSTER. Takes off in 700 feet with full load. Cruises 2 miles a minute with 600 mile range. Has new, automatic pressure oiling system on Ken-Royce engine. Eliminates greasing by hand. Ask for a demonstration TODAY!

**REARWIN AIRCRAFT & ENGINES, INC.** KANSAS CITY, KANSAS, U. S. A.

International Air Show

EXHIBITOR'S SEASON TICKET

January 28 to February 6, 1938

MR. R. A. Rearwin

is regularly employed as an exhibitor at

Rearwin Airplanes EXHIBIT

INTERNATIONAL AMPHITHEATRE

HALSTED AT 43rd STREET

CHICAGO

95

Vice Pres. Gen'l Mgr No. 802 Exec. V. Pres.

This ticket is not good for re-admission without return check

1 2 3 4 5 6 7 8 9 10

George Hyde, the final assembly foreman in 1942, works on the panel of one of the last pre-war Skyrangers. Hyde was one of few Rearwin employees to move East with Commonwealth. George Hyde Family

versions were subsequently offered in the fall of 1941. The first was the Model 180 powered by the Continental 80 hp engine.[1] The other was the Model 180F, priced at $2,575 FOF. It had the Franklin 4AC-176-F3 power plant up front. Both were approved by an amendment to the original type certificate on October 25, 1941.

The installation of the 80 hp Franklin engines required changes in the cowling and permitted the use of an automotive-type starter and generator. Many owners also wanted radios and other options, all of which added weight. Accordingly, the gross weight was increased by 100 pounds. Some fuselage tubing was also beefed up with safety margins of 10 to 15 percent. The engineering staff then went back and did a complete load and stress analysis, and the drop tests on the landing gear were redone.

The final pre-war Skyranger was the model 190F. It was engined with the 90 hp Franklin 4AC-199-E3 and approved by a second amendment to the type certificate on September 1, 1942. However, only one example was built before World War II, and the diversion of aluminum halted all Rearwin aircraft production. Only 82 Skyrangers (SN1501-1582) had been built by Rearwin.

But that was not the end of the Skyranger. A small batch was built in Kansas City by Commonwealth Aircraft Inc. after the war in late 1945. Much of the jigs and tooling had been used for scrap during the war, so the first 12 (SN1601-1612) shipped to dealers on December 21, 1945, were virtually handmade. Although the 75 hp Model 175 was available for a short time at $2,750, Commonwealth standardized production in February 1946 with the Continental

The tachometer in the Skyranger's faux woodgrain panel turned counterclockwise. Note the antenna reel. Robert W. Rummel

C-185-12 engine rated at 85 hp at 2,550 rpm. With an electric starter, generator, and battery, the new Model 185 was base-priced at $3,195.

Commonwealth built 276 Skyrangers (SN1601-1876) before production ended in October 1946. Less than a dozen were exported. One went to Brazil (PP-THR), two to Uruguay (CX-ACV and CX-AEA), and four to Canada. Including the 82 pre-war Rearwin units, a total of 358 Skyrangers were built — the largest production run of the six basic Rearwin designs.

## *Chapter 23*

# Facing the Forties

*EVEN BEFORE THE bombing of Pearl Harbor, the escalating hostilities in Europe had cast doubt on the future of civil aviation. Many believed as early as 1939 that the country was headed for war unless events took a sudden but unlikely turn for the better.*

*In March 1939, Ken took a 90 hp Sportster to Wright Field, where for two weeks the Air Corps tested its potential as a primary trainer. While the plane met all seven Air Corps basic specifications, the Ryan ST was clearly better suited for the job. In June, however, the Air Corps ordered several Ken-Royce engines for use in dirigibles, and later the same year the Rearwin Flying School received Civilian Airplane Pilot Training (CAPT) contracts to provide primary instruction to students from Kansas City Junior College and Park College, in Parkville, Missouri.[1] On the down side, France's surrender to Nazi Germany in June 1940 would end discussions with French officials about building trainers for their air force.*

*The Cloudster was selling well, and the Skyranger was on the drawing boards, but rapid expansion, development costs, and war-driven increases in labor and material resulted in a minor flow of red ink in 1940. Rae waived his salary and briefly considered raising new capital by selling another 120,000 shares of stock through*

Royce S. Rearwin, 1940.

Above: Royce Rearwin and his wife, Jacqueline, with their first daughter, Linda, 1940.

Right: The Rearwin office staff in March 1940. From left, Doris Hitchcock, Fredrika Gardner, Irene Howard (standing), Viola Becker, and Mary Crimmins.

Viola Becker Bourland

Rearwin employees posed for this 1940 photograph while "The Boss" was at lunch and surprised Rae with it later.

Beckly & Company of New York, but instead turned to defense contracting.

In May 1941, the Ken-Royce machine shop was converted to subcontract work for several national defense contractors. Orders with "priority rights" for bottlenecked wartime materials poured in so fast that shop superintendent Archie Turpin had trouble hiring enough skilled workers to fill them, and Rae recruited skilled machinists from Missouri, Nebraska, and Iowa. By mid-1941 the company was backlogged with orders for punches and dies used in the production of cartridge cases for Remington Arms munition plants in Lake City, Missouri, and Denver, and the U.S. Cartridge Company in St. Louis. It also had orders from Fairfax-based North American for specialized machinery, including foot punches, bullet pullers, wheel balancers and mounts, and compression riveters for B-25 production. Orders for landing gear cylinders from Curtiss-Wright in St. Louis and for hydraulic heads and cylinder caps from Pump Engineering in Cleveland were also in hand. By August 1941, more than $325,000 in defense contracts were in the fold, compared with $61,000 in May 1940. Moreover, Skyranger sales were averaging one a week and orders for instrument trainers were flowing in from CAPT contractors.

In February 1942, the War Department awarded Rearwin a $1.5 million contract to build 100 nine-passenger Waco-designed CG-3A training gliders

Rearwin employees Lester Naylor, Wayne Finch, and "Scottie" Wright relax on Sunday, their only full day off during 1941-1942.
Wayne Finch Family

that were still being tested at Wright Field in Dayton. The design was to be "frozen" in April with production to start by May 1st. Fulfilling the contract would require doubling the existing factory space and hiring several hundred new employees.

Rae promptly announced plans to add 12,000 square feet of floor space to the Fairfax plant. The No. 2 metal hangar was to be moved from the west end of Fairfax to the north side of the Rearwin factory. It would house the aircraft and maintenance operations, while the main building would be enlarged 5,000 square feet by extending the second floor mezzanine over the entire first floor hangar area.

Rearwin employees started building jigs almost immediately. However, on May 2, Ken secured another multi-million-dollar contract at Wright Field for an unspecified number of 15-place, CG-4A troop-carrying assault gliders. Such contracts typically provided for a profit of six percent over the direct cost estimate. Government auditors later determined what percentage of general overhead was attributable to the contract, and added that amount to it.

Rae leased three adjoining buildings on the west side of the 1900 block of McGee Street. The buildings, which contained 65,000 square feet, were owned by one T. H. Mastin but were leased to auto dealer John A. Radcliff. He had no use for them after new car production was suspended, and was undoubtedly delighted to get off the rental hook.

The CG-4 was built with wooden wings and a steel tubular fuselage covered mostly with fabric. It had a wingspan of 83 feet, 8 inches, a box section fuselage, and a hinged nose section that swung upward to permit direct loading into the cabin. The hinged "cockpit" contained dual controls for the pilots, and the cabin could alternately hold 13 fully equipped troops, a standard jeep, a one-quarter-ton truck with crew, or a 75 mm howitzer and crew. It had a gross weight of about 9,000 pounds and was towed behind a C-46 or C-47 at about 150 mph. An improved model, the CG-4A, was

**REARWIN and NATIONAL DEFENSE**

We're glad we can help in the defense of America by building instrument trainers needed alike by airlines and flying schools. Rearwin Instrument Trainers were designed especially for blind flying training and are doing their part in preparing American pilots to navigate on instruments.

Two Rearwin Instrument Trainer designs are available . . . Model 8135T with 120 hp Ken-Royce engine and model 9000KRT with 90 hp Ken-Royce engine. Both engines have full automatic pressure lubrication which guarantees long life and low maintenance. Rearwin trainers operate for less than $2 per hour and carry preference rating.

REARWIN is proud to have a part in NATIONAL DEFENSE.

* * *

PHOTO: Rearwin Instrument Trainer purchased by U. S. Civil Aeronautics Administration. Other Rearwin Instrument Trainers are now being used by Pan American Airways, Parks Air College, Missouri Institute of Aeronautics, Mississippi Institute of Aeronautics, American Flyers, Spartan School of Aeronautics and Ailor School of Aeronautics.

* * *

DO YOU KNOW that the 3-place CLOUDSTER can also be used for instrument training? Write or wire for complete details.

From *Aero Digest*, January 1942. Antique Airplane Association, Blakesburg, IA quickly developed. The wing span was reduced by 20 feet, gross weight went up by 500 pounds, and the craft could be towed at 180 mph.

The CG-4 series ferried some 25,000 troops, 3,500 jeeps, and 3,200 tons of ammunition, gasoline, and other supplies to various theaters during World War II, but at a heavy cost. Nearly 20 percent of 5,000 glider pilots were killed, injured, taken prisoner, or listed as missing in action. With some justification, such craft were soon dubbed "Flying Coffins."

Rae welcomed the glider, tow release, and other defense contracts, particularly because aircraft production, except for civil defense purposes, was all but suspended. Indeed, Fairfax Airport had been purchased in February 1941 for $600,000 by the city for North American B-25 production, and then was closed in August to all civil aircraft other than Rearwin planes approved for CAPT or CAP units.[7]

With the glider contracts in the fold, Rae inventoried his situation. Instinct told him the time to sell might never be better.

*Part Three*

# Finesse and Finality

Partners Royce, Rae, and Ken, *circa* 1938.

# Chapter 24

# A Time to Fold 'Em

*RAE ANDREW REARWIN decided to get out of the aircraft and engine business early in 1942. Precisely why is unclear. Most likely, there was no single reason. He had turned 64 in March, an age when most men customarily reflect on mortality and seek retirement under palm trees (or whatever shade they can afford). The borderline workaholic was still paces ahead of most younger men, but the gap was narrowing.*

*Rae had entered the aircraft business in 1928 to make money, pure and simple. The Great Depression had waylaid that goal, but he had stubbornly clung to it, struggling, waiting, and sacrificing for the aviation boom that was always just around the corner. That plan, too, had exploded on December 7, 1941.*

*The Second World War had resulted in healthy defense contracts, but it would end someday. Rae believed that others (Taylorcraft, Aeronca, Cessna, Luscombe, Beech, Piper, Mooney, and Funk, to name just a few) would be ready after the war with improved models; that Stearmans, SNJs, and Ryan trainers would be available at rock-bottom prices; and that the pent-up boom market for private aircraft would be short-lived. Many firms would wither. He had seen it happen before in the auto industry.*

*Rae also understood that the sun had set on the small round engine. The hori-*

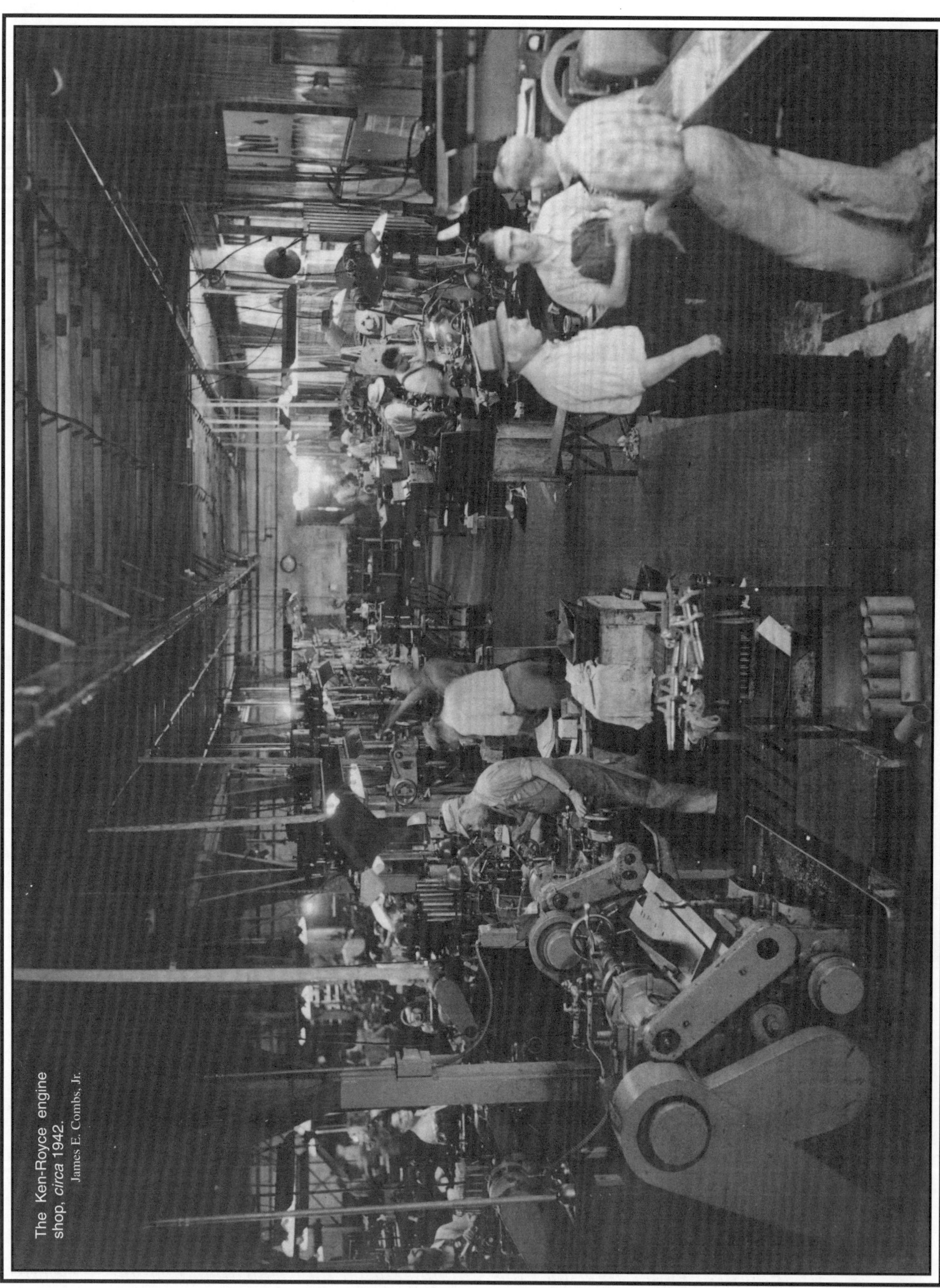

The Ken-Royce engine shop, *circa* 1942.
James E. Combs, Jr.

The Rearwin machine shop in early 1942. Note the Ken-Royce engine cylinders stored above the "HOSE" sign.

zontally opposed Franklins, Continentals, and Lycomings were coming into their own. Even his own Skyranger used one. They were more efficient, more reliable, and less expensive. Unless Rae was willing to develop a new engine of his own, and he was already far behind the curve, the Ken-Royce engine business would end with the war. The time to sell was now, while it arguably had some value.

Finally, over the years Rae had deluded himself into believing that he had entered aviation to provide a legacy for his sons. He said so with increasing frequency. Royce and Ken were both intelligent, dedicated, and hardworking. They complemented each other in many respects. Royce, like his father, had an innate ability for things mechanical, while Ken was more inclined toward the front office, accounting, sales, and administration. Royce was intense, at times volatile, while Ken rolled with the waves. The two were not a bad combination; in fact, they had a nice balance. But neither son was the complete Rae. Neither was fueled by the intensity that flamed in their father and that was necessary to carry on in the fiercely competitive business. This is no criticism of Royce and Ken. Rae's will had been forged on the harsh Kansas prairie of the 1880s. He thrived on challenge. The sons, however, had been born to relative comfort and position. They needed little, least of all change or challenge. They were simply cut from a different bolt at a different time, a truism that Rae surely recognized even if he had entered the aviation business with the vague notion that they would someday take over. In fact, neither son was especially interested in doing so, either alone or in concert with the other.

*Looking for Mr. Goodbuyer*

Rae did not list the firm with a broker or investment banker. There was, to his reasoning, no need to pay a commission to sell a hot property with several million dollars of wartime contracts in the fold, substantial cash in the bank, and no long-term debt. Indeed, "For Sale" signs were often mistaken for overeagerness. Rae simply let it be known in the proper circles that the business might be available, and suitors were soon calling. They included George W. Pitter and George Daugherty of the Willys-Knight Company in Toledo; A. M. Merkel, president of the American Fidelity and Casualty Company of Richmond, Virginia; the Singer Sewing Machine Company; Steinway Piano Company; Defendaire Corporation of New York City; and Eugene Core, an investment broker from Core, Klingsmith & Grimani of Detroit, allegedly acting for an undisclosed principle.

Despite several discussions, no one had talked turkey before Core arrived in Kansas City in June 1942. He claimed to represent a buyer for the 115,000 shares of stock Rae, Royce, and Ken were willing to sell at $2.75 each, but there were two conditions. Core said he needed a 30-day option to put the deal together. Rae knew that meant Core didn't have a buyer in hand, but hoped to find one during the option period. Core also added that Rae would have to pay a commission of ten cents a share, or $11,500. Rae countered. He was amenable to a short option and would even pay the commission, but he had two conditions of his own. First, he and Ken would be employed by the purchaser for three years; second, if the option was not exercised on time, Core waived all claims for any commission or finder's fee. Suspecting others were waiting in the wings, Core agreed.

The parties entered into a three-page option agreement dated June 5, 1942, which would expire at midnight June 19th — a two-week period. At Rae's request it did not refer to the commission terms, which were to be kept confidential in the event that Core did not perform. There was no need to let other prospects know Rae had agreed to pay one which, of course, reduced the net price. It was a seller's market; let the buyer pay. The commission terms were covered in a side-letter, also dated June 5. However, the option was never exercised.

Unknown to Rae, Core subsequently contacted Frank Harder of Allen & Company, a New York brokerage firm, with an offer to split the fee if he helped to find a purchaser during the two-week period. Harder had a client in mind, but he was not about to willingly share the commission with Core. Harder waited a respectable time after Core's option expired, "found" his potential buyer, and went to Kansas City in August searching for a deal and the commission he knew that Rae had been willing to pay.

Harder's client was Frank Cohen, a munitions manufacturer with offices on New York City's Fifth Avenue, who controlled Philadelphia-based Empire Ordnance. Acquiring Rearwin Aircraft and Engines, Inc. would not only ring up more short-term war profits, but would also make Cohen well positioned at war's end when the munitions business would all but vanish. Cohen gave Harder a green light to negotiate the best deal possible, and he'd take over from there.

Rae offered to sell the block of 115,000 stock shares at three dollars a share net, meaning Allen & Company's commission would either be paid by Cohen, or the price had to be increased to cover it. Rae and Ken would also resign. Harder, no doubt, was taken aback. That was $345,000 up front without a commission. Cohen would expect better than the terms of the Core option which, after the commission but excluding the post-sale employment costs, was only about $304,750.

But Harder was also aware of the negotiations Rae had with Defendaire in June or July after the Core option fell through. Whether he had heard about them through the New York City grapevine or because Rae had used the proposed deal as leverage with Harder is not known. The negotiations centered on a flat price of $300,000 for the stock, with both Rae and Ken being retained as employees for three years; Rae at $15,000 a year, and Ken at $1,000 a month. The total package was worth $381,000, but Defendaire dallied. It was Harder's opening. He told Rae his client was not interested in purchasing unless he and Ken stayed on for at least three years. His client, he explained, had seen too many transitioning firms fail because of a lack of management continuity. Accordingly, Harder countered with a flat price of $300,000 for the stock, and employment contracts for three years at $1,500 a month for Rae and $1,000 for Ken.

Rae had made the same offer to Defendaire, but they were not in sight. Moreover, the total package offered by Harder, including employment, was worth $381,000 instead of the $345,000 Rae had sought without the employment contracts. He and Harder went to work on the details.

### *The Contract of Sale*

The agreement for the sale of Rearwin Aircraft and Engines, Inc. to Frank Cohen was actually a contract for the transfer of stock that was executed by the parties on August 28, 1942, in Kansas City, Missouri, in the offices of Borders, Wimmell, and McCreight, Rae's attorneys. Partner R. B. (Bob) McCreight handled the transaction and acted as an escrow agent for the initial $30,000 deposit and postdated resignations from the existing Rearwin Board of Directors. Later payments were to be cleared through the Security National Bank. There were 139,141 shares of stock outstanding at the time. Rae, Royce, and Ken each owned 38,462 shares, or a total of 115,986. The corporation also owned 1,500 shares of treasury stock that had been purchased for employee options, including 165 subject to call by Bob Rummel. The remaining 22,248 outstanding shares were publicly owned.

The four-page contract covered the sale of 115,000 shares for $300,000, about $2.61 a share. The deposit was to be held by McCreight for 30 days, at which time another $70,000 was due. A third payment of $100,000 was also due on or before November 28th. When made, 45,000 shares of stock held in escrow by McCreight would be delivered to Cohen or his nominee. The final $100,000 was to be paid not later than March 28, 1943. At that time the remaining 70,000 shares and the Rearwin Board resignations would be delivered to Cohen. The sale would then be complete.

The sellers committed not to issue any stock during the interim and to permit Cohen to audit and approve the firm's financial condition as of July 31, 1942, within 30 days. Cohen could back out if he didn't like what he saw. Finally, Rae, Royce and Ken agreed not to use the name "Rearwin" in the aircraft manufacturing business for a period of five years.

On the same day, and in Cohen's presence, the corporation also entered into written employment contracts with both Rae and Ken. They were to be employed for a period of three years, Rae at $1,500 a month and Ken at $1,000, with the nature of their duties to be determined from time to time by the corporation or its new officers.

### *Squeezing the Deal*

The balance sheet for July 31 indicated the book value of the outstanding stock was $3.48 a share, or $2.94 if the $475,000 assigned to "goodwill" and other intangible assets was discounted. Moreover, the company had a multi-million-dollar contract for military gliders, the $400,000 contract with Remington Arms Corporation to make dies and punches, and the contract for glider tow releases. It was a fat deal for Cohen and a modest one for Rae, who wanted out while the time was right.

Cohen's auditors did their thing, and the parties met next on September 18 at the Muehlebach Hotel in Kansas City, Missouri, where Cohen and one of his munitions partners, Raymond Voyes, were staying. Cohen informed Rae, in the presence of Royce, Ken, and McCreight, that the auditors' report was acceptable and satisfied that condition of the agreement. He even added that a $25,000 variance would not have mattered.

For some reason, perhaps not wanting to irritate or openly insult Cohen with a lack of trust, neither McCreight nor Rae asked for Cohen's written approval of the firm's financial condition. Perhaps it was simply an oversight or they were diverted by Cohen's proposal to transfer all of the Rearwin stock on the payment of the next $70,000 installment. Cohen wanted immediate control. Rae said that was not a problem; all Cohen had to do was write a check for the full $270,000 balance. Cohen said he was willing to release the initial $30,000 deposit, but he did not have the total balance. He would pay the $70,000 due September 28, but he proposed that the Rearwins accept an interest-bearing note for the remaining $200,000. Rae didn't buy it. He insisted they stick to the terms of the August 28 contract.

Neither Rae nor Cohen were novices at negotiation. Rae knew Cohen realized the purchase was sound, that Cohen was not about to forfeit his $30,000 deposit, and that, if he really didn't have the money when due, which was hard to swallow, he would come up with it. Rae was now wary. Cohen had sought full control of the company for a mere $100,000. Rae was disappointed, if not insulted, that Cohen had believed there was even a chance he would agree to such a proposal.

It had not escaped the attention of Cohen's auditors that there was more than $105,000 in corporate cash rusting in the bank on August 31 and that paid-in-surplus available for dividends exceeded $107,000, the equivalent of about 77 cents a share. With the stock and control of the Board, Cohen could declare a dividend of about 75 cents a share, use the $86,000 or so that he would receive to partially pay for the stock, and borrow working capital.

Cohen had struck out, but he was still targeting Rae for another deal which, realistically, may have been all he was shooting for in the first place. It was a classic ploy: Let the rube bask for a while counting on the deal; then threaten to pull the plug, while leaving the door open a crack for a sweetener. It works some of the time, particularly if the mark is vulnerable — say, a 65-year-old with a three-year employment contract dangling.

## *Chapter 25*

# Closing the Sale

*COHEN WIRED Rae at the Phillips Hotel in Kansas City on September 26, 1942, alleging for the first time that his auditors had advised him that the glider contracts referred to in the August 28 agreement were not in good standing, and that poor cost-control accounting procedures had made it impossible to conduct a proper audit. The telegram went on:*

> *. . . these obstacles preclude me from purchasing your stock under (our) agreement. I regret this as I had looked forward to making your company the base of our expanding program.*

*The final sentence, of course, was calculated to keep the door ajar. Rae understood.*

*A telegram and certified letter sent separately by Cohen to McCreight the same day quoted the telegram to Rae and concluded with a demand for the return of the $30,000 deposit held in escrow. It also authorized McCreight to return the already-signed resignations of the Rearwin Board of Directors to Rae.*

*Rae attempted to contact Cohen to find out what the real problem was, but was unable to reach him — another part of the ploy. Rae knew it wasn't the books or the company's financial condition that stopped the deal. Indeed, current assets ex-*

ceeded current liabilities by almost two and one-half to one, and there was no long-term debt. Rae would not believe that Cohen couldn't raise the $70,000 due September 28. Cohen's partner Raymond Voyes took the call. The issue, it seemed, was still control. Cohen now wanted equal representation on the board when he made the September 28 payment. Apparently, Cohen believed the corporation might declare a cash dividend from the paid-in-surplus before he got his hands on the last 70,000 shares of stock that were to be delivered with the final payment due in March 1943.

Rae considered the request for equal board representation reasonable if Cohen would add $100,000 to the September 28 payment. He told Voyes he would forward Cohen a revised agreement later in the day, which Voyes confirmed by wire that evening:

> Frank Cohen has this day wired you in order to avoid waiver of rights under agreement of August 28 between you and him. However, my understanding is that you are drawing up a modification of the agreement to meet the changed conditions which arose and you will have this agreement in our office Monday morning so that we can reopen and complete purchase.
>
> Raymond Voyes

The financial terms of Rae's new proposal were essentially unchanged. The only significant modification involved joint control. Rae proposed that upon the payment of $170,000 by October 1, the board resignations of Ken's wife and Bob Rummel would be effective, and Rae would cause Cohen, Voyes, and C. H. Dolan, a Cohen nominee, to be elected. An evenly-split six-member board would result in a standoff and protect both camps pending completion of the sale. Concurrently, however, the resignations of the three new Cohen directors would be deposited with McCreight and become effective in the event Cohen defaulted on any future payment. As in the initial agreement, Cohen was to receive 45,000 shares upon payment of $200,000 and the final block of 70,000 shares when the last payment was made. Rae also agreed that Voyes could be elected president and Dolan appointed as general manager. In effect, the company would operate temporarily under the scrutiny of the chairman of the board, who would still control more than 50 percent of the outstanding stock and half of the board of directors. The plan could work.

By now, Rae was extremely wary of Cohen; accordingly, he added several other clauses confirming matters that had either been understood or previously agreed upon, but were not in writing. First, he or Ken had to sign or countersign *all* checks, and single expenditures in excess of $10,000 had to be approved by at least four of the six members of the new board. Second, he added a paragraph requiring Cohen to acknowledge that he was satisfied with the books and financial condition of the corporation, and that the various representations previously made by the sellers in the August 28 contract were true and correct. With justified foresight, he also added redundant paragraphs again requiring Cohen to acknowledge his awareness of the employment contracts between the corporation and Rae and Ken, and that the corporation owed Rae $30,000 and Ken $7,500 in notes for deferred salary and loans previously made to the corporation that were due and payable December 1.

Rae also tightened the payment terms, making the final $100,000 payable in four monthly installments of $25,000 each, starting December 30 and ending March 28. Finally, he added a three-year employment contract for Royce at $500 a month, and attached copies of all three employment contracts. Cohen's pitch had backfired.

The modified agreement was airmailed to Cohen on September 30, with a pointed letter from McCreight. It referred to the Muehlebach meeting two weeks earlier and read in part:

> . . . you stated very emphatically in response to inquiry by Mr. R. A. Rearwin that your auditor's report on Rearwin Aircraft and Engines, Inc. was entirely satisfactory and fulfilled all of the conditions of the agreement. . . .
>
> I think that as a fair minded man you will concede that the War Department contracts mentioned in the agreement were in good standing on August 28, 1942 and, for that matter, are still in good standing at this time. No notice of cancellation has been made up to this time to the Company.
>
> In order that there may be no mistake as to the facts in existence, we feel that they should be set forth here in response to the unwarranted statements contained in your letter.

Cohen received the revised proposal and letter on Monday, October 1. He most certainly was disappointed. The compromise was fair and reasonable to the point that Cohen knew he could not push Rae's buttons any further without possibly breaking the deal, which he didn't want to do. He also realized the muzzle was now pointed in his direction. The matters outlined in McCreight's letter were true and, if Cohen didn't complete the deal, there was little chance of getting his deposit back, with or without a legal battle. In fact, he was already technically in default of the August 28 agreement and, if Rearwin was so inclined, he could pull the plug at any time, keep the deposit, and find a new buyer. Nevertheless, Cohen felt there had to be a way to slice a larger piece of the pie for himself.

Harder telephoned Rae and McCreight and assured both that Cohen wanted to close the deal. In fact, he said Cohen wanted to pay off the entire balance immediately and assume full control at once. Would that be a problem? If Rae and McCreight slapped each other on the back, their celebration was short-lived. There was a minor hitch. Cohen didn't have the $270,000 cash! Harder dangled the bait. He explained he could raise the money for Cohen from a bank in Arkansas, but Cohen wouldn't pay Harder's fee of $10,000 for doing so.

It was decision time for Rae. He didn't necessarily buy Harder's story. He still could not believe that Cohen didn't have, or couldn't raise, the money himself. Rae was probably tempted to throw in the towel, keep the deposit, and start over. Indeed, one prospective purchaser he had recently talked with had expressed disappointment about the pending deal and said he was ready if it fell through. Cohen would certainly sue for the return of his deposit, but Rae wasn't so much worried about that as he was a suit for an injunction and specific performance. That could tie up a new sale for two or three years, maybe more. Rae was also certain that Cohen was counting on him analyzing the situation exactly that way. Although Rae and McCreight were confident that they would ultimately win any lawsuit and keep the deposit, protracted legal wrangling could scare off other purchasers until it was resolved.

Cohen won the first round. Rae agreed to reduce the aggregate purchase price of the stock by $10,000, even though he and McCreight suspected that the sum actually represented Allen & Company's finder's fee for putting the deal together, rather than for arranging financing. Cohen had merely wiggled out of paying the commission. But Rae had two stipulations of his own. Royce was to be employed for three years at $500 a month, as proposed in the September 30 counter-offer, and Ken's salary was to be maintained at $500 a month for the duration of the employment agreement even if he was involuntary inducted into the military. Harder called back later in the day and said they had a deal. Could they meet in Kansas City on October 7 to wrap it up? Round two went to Rae. Royce, who was not covered by the original agreement, would now receive $18,000 in salary over the three-year term of his employment — a net increase of $8,000.

Cohen and his entourage arrived in Kansas City as scheduled. Predictably, he had new demands. He wanted the Rearwins to sell the remaining 986 shares of stock they owned and another 75 shares they controlled through family members at the same per share price as the other 115,000 shares. He also wanted a written agreement that the Rearwins would not purchase any stock in Rearwin Aircraft and Engines, Inc. during the period of their employment with the firm and a warranty that they did not own any other shares. Rae agreed and side letters were prepared. Clearly, Cohen had gained respect for Rae's business acumen, and he didn't need any minority stockholder suits from the shrewd farmer's son. The unusual requests, however, elevated Rae's antenna another notch.

As customary, the Rearwins warranted that other than in the ordinary course of business there had been no substantial change in the financial condition of the company since August 28 and, except for a 200-unit decrease in the number of CG-3A gliders which was offset by an increase of 150 CG-4A gliders, the glider contracts were unchanged and in good standing. The parties also amended the August 28 contract to reflect the modified $290,000 purchase price, which now approximated $2.52 a share. A certified check for the balance of the purchase price, increased to include the additional 1,061 shares, was deposited in escrow at the City National Bank of Kansas City. Except for the election of a new board of directors, the sale was completed on October 7, 1942.

A special meeting of the board was convened at 12:01 a.m. on October 8, 1942, in McCreight's office, with the current directors waiving notice of the meeting. Rae, Royce, Ken, and Ken's wife Suzanne, who would deliver a third child six days later, were present. Bob Rummel, who had previously replaced Royce's wife on the board, was not.

The four directors resigned and five new ones

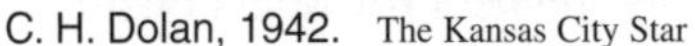

C. H. Dolan, 1942. The Kansas City Star

Kenneth's wife Suzanne, *circa* 1940.

were elected: Cohen, C. H. Dolan II, Benjamin Dowd, Raymond Voyes, and H. S. Nakdimen. Cohen would serve as chairman, Dolan as president and general manager, Voyes as vice president, and Nakdimen as secretary. Rummel resigned later the same morning.

Dolan had been a member of the famed Lafayette Escadrille during World War I, and had remained in aviation, serving as an adviser and inspector for the Chinese Air Corps in the early 1920s. He had also conducted route surveys for several airlines, worked for Eastern Airlines and International Aircraft Export Corporation, and then joined Cohen and Voyes who, apparently as partners, controlled Empire Ordnance.

Voyes was also a World War I pilot, but for the French. At one time he had managed North Beech Field near New York City, the predecessor to La Guardia Airport, where Ken had met him during the pontoon tests for George Cluett II in 1936. Voyes and Dowd were also vice presidents of Empire Ordnance, while Nakdimen was a former vice president of his father's bank in Fort Smith, Arkansas. Rumor had it the bank had loaned Cohen money to ensure the son would be employed in one or more of Cohen's defense businesses and thus escape the draft, unfortunately a common practice during World War II.

Rae posted a signed letter on a bulletin board at the Fairfax plant in the morning announcing the sale and urging the employees to continue their loyalty to the new owners. The sale was also reported in the *Kansas City Kansan* on October 12. While the article centered mainly on Dolan's background, it announced that Rae, Royce, and Ken would continue as employees, and that the Rearwin name would be retained. So much for the formalities — Cohen and Dolan had other plans.

*Chapter 26*

# Loose Ends

*EUGENE CORE soon learned that Allen & Company, through Harder, had brokered the sale of the Rearwin stock. He threatened to sue everyone in sight. According to Core, it was his contact with Harder that had resulted in the sale, and the contact had taken place during the two-week option period. It didn't matter that the option had not been exercised. He alleged that Harder, Rae, and Cohen had simply conspired to wait out the option so that Allen & Company could keep the full commission and Rae would end up with a better package — $390,000 versus $337,500. He was wrong. Rae was completely unaware that Core had contacted Harder about finding a buyer and splitting the commission until Core cried foul. Core demanded half the $11,500 commission, less reasonable expenses.*

*Allen & Company had to settle. Such suits not only soiled a company's reputation, but the firm could not permit Cohen, a valued client, to become entangled. Harder knew that Rae appreciated the considerable time and expense involved in fighting the case and said that his firm would settle with Core if Rae would come up with half. Rae fumed, but countered with an offer of $1,000 conditional upon Core and his partners first providing Rae with a full release. Allen & Company, wary of pushing its luck with Rae, agreed.*

Harder wrote Bob McCreight, Rae's attorney, on November 30, 1942, enclosing the signed releases from Core, Kleinsmith, and Grimani, which Harder had secured by first paying Core in full. With unusual politeness, Harder requested that McCreight or Rae send a check payable to Allen & Company for $1,000. Rae could not be blamed if, with the releases in hand, he told Harder to take a hike. There was no practical way Harder could sue or force payment. If the thought crossed Rae's mind, it was quickly dismissed. His word was worth more than $1,000. He paid.

Dolan now began his assault. In mid-October, he directed Royce, who lived in Salina and was wrapping up personal business and details related to the liquidation of the lumber and coal company assets,[1] to report to work virtually without notice. Dolan then seized on the fact that Royce was detained in Salina for several days. He told Royce that he was in violation of his employment contract and, unless he agreed to cancel it and work on an "at will" basis, he would be fired. Royce refused and took his family to Florida. Next, the name "Commonwealth Aircraft Company" replaced "Rearwin Aircraft and Engines, Inc." on January 7, 1943.

Meanwhile, Rae protected his flank. He suspected that Cohen and Dolan might not be exactly prompt in paying off the $37,500 in corporate notes he and Ken held, even though the treasury was cash-heavy. Rae discounted the notes at Farmers National Bank in Salina. As between Commonwealth and the Rearwins, the bank was an innocent third-party purchaser protected by law. Moreover, on a Salina handshake, Rae guaranteed bank president Raymond Geiss that he wouldn't lose a dime; Rae would make the notes good if the bank couldn't collect from Commonwealth. More likely than not, Rae also opened a substantial account.

By now, Cohen recognized and respected Rae's experience and business judgment. Whether Dolan knew it or not, Rae's duties included monitoring the overall operation and reporting directly to Cohen if things were amiss. This put Rae in an awkward position, as Cohen knew it would. But Rae concluded that his allegiance was to Cohen, as he had put up the money and owned the stock. Rae squirmed uneasily as he saw chief engineer Rummel shunted aside almost immediately in favor of a Dolan cronie. Rummel's considerable talents were virtually wasted.[2] Rae was also increasingly disturbed by wastefulness and foolhardy extravagance that were compounded by false economies. In one case, Dolan ordered jigs and dies that were temporarily idle to be cut up, rather than purchasing scrap metal that was readily available to defense contractors at reasonable prices. These jigs and dies could have been used later, or sold. Moreover, while Rae had run a squeaky-tight-to-a-fault ship, Dolan had almost tripled the size and cost of the maintenance crew within several weeks. He also added what Rae felt were unnecessary administrative positions. Such practices were totally contrary to Rae's constitution, and he churned.

Rae also observed that Dolan seldom arrived at work before noon. Although he regularly stayed until nine or ten in the evening, he was unavailable to his staff, customers, and government representatives for substantial periods of the day. The relationship between Dolan and the Rearwins, as well as with other former Rearwin employees, became strained, to say the least. Obviously, Dolan tolerated Rae and Ken simply because they had come with the deal.

Ken became so disillusioned that in early 1943 he told a friend, TWA Treasurer John Lockhart, that he was thinking of quitting, moving to California, and taking a position offered by Convair in San Diego. Lockhart told Ken to forget Convair: he was perfect for the assistant treasurer's job at TWA. An interview with Lockhart's boss, executive vice president E. Lee Talman, was arranged. Talman offered Ken the job, which paid $500 a month. That was only half what he was making at Commonwealth, but it looked good. Ken was fed up with Dolan and wanted out. Rae advised Ken to go for it, but counseled him to write Cohen first to get released from his employment contract. Cohen refused to let Ken go. His letter stated that Commonwealth was going to design and build planes after the war, and Ken would be needed since he knew the civil aircraft business. Rae advised Ken to think the matter over, but said that he should probably honor his contract. Ken then wrote Cohen withdrawing his request to resign.

Several weeks later, and perhaps not coincidentally, Rae decided that it was time to inform Cohen about Dolan's wasteful practices and inept management style. Obviously, Rae knew the information would get back to Dolan one way or another, particularly if he orchestrated it. Rae drafted a letter to Cohen while his own secretary was off. It was prepared by a new typist in the steno pool. She was carefully instructed by Rae to make only two copies, no more, and to give both to him. He would personally mail one to Cohen and keep the other. The poor young typist believed she would be fired by Dolan for typing the letter, and she was probably right. She made a third copy and gave it to Dolan that evening without Rae's knowledge — or so she thought. Rae was not only a wily businessman, he was also a pretty fair judge of character, and he suspected she would make another copy.

Predictably, Dolan was livid and arrived at work early the next morning. When Ken showed up, the Rearwin-friendly gate guard, whom Ken had hired, apologized profusely but refused, under the threat of losing his job, to let Ken through. He was also under orders to get Ken's badge. Ken asked why.

The guard replied, "Did your Dad send a letter to Mr. Cohen last night?"

Ken was surprised. "Yes, he did, but how did you know?"

Any answer, of course, was irrelevant. Ken gave up his badge and walked over to the Simmons Mattress Company, which was located in the former American Eagle plant. He asked an acquaintance if he could use the telephone, and called Lockhart at TWA. Ken told Lockhart he had just been fired and asked if the assistant treasurer's job was still open. Lockhart said it was; he'd been waiting for an answer, and said that Ken should report immediately — meaning "now." Ken asked to start the following Monday. Reluctantly, Lockhart agreed; after all, it was Thursday.

Rae was also fired when he arrived. He was tempted to ask Dolan about the overdue payments of the discounted notes, but he held his tongue. He would call the bank soon enough.

Whether or not Dolan telephoned Cohen before firing Rae and Ken is not known, but it didn't matter. Cohen had no choice but to back Dolan. The Commonwealth board of directors quickly passed a resolution stating:

> Resolved that the officers of this corporation be and they hereby are instructed to hold up any further payments to R. A. Rearwin on his employment contract dated August 28, 1942.

An identical resolution was passed concerning Ken, who was fired because Dolan believed Ken knew about or had participated in writing the letter. He was right; Rae had shown his handwritten draft of the letter to Ken. While the son could not talk his father out of sending it, he did convince Rae to tone it down a tad. Rae feigned surprised later in the day of their firing when Ken told him he had the job with TWA locked up — and only a few weeks after Cohen had refused to let him out of his contract.

After more than 14 years, R. A. Rearwin was out of the aircraft manufacturing business and unemployed. He would never return to it. He had been shot down by a former Lafayette Escadrille pilot, but who could be sure that Rae hadn't intentionally crossed in front of his sights? Ken was now free to start at TWA, and the palms of Southern California continued to beckon the 65-year-old. But he was not yet ready to fade into the sunset. First, he had to make a call to the Farmers National Bank in Salina, and then talk to a lawyer about a trio of sure-fire breach of contract lawsuits. He might enjoy watching Dolan's cork pop, but he would have to be content with savoring the mental image. Score two rounds for Rae.

The breach of contract actions were filed in April while Rae commuted to Salina to wind up the liquidation of the lumberyard and fuel businesses and manage his other interests there. In the meantime, Ken arranged for TWA to pirate Rummel, who was only too glad to leave. At first, Commonwealth refused to pay the notes owned by the Farmers State Bank, but relented in short order. The breach of contract actions were also settled before the end of the year with mutual releases of all claims. Cohen had filed counter-suits alleging fraud and other matters. However, when the dust cleared, the settlement money — about $28,000 — flowed from Commonwealth to Rae, Royce, and Ken. Excluding the salaries received during their brief employment, the Rearwins received about $320,000 for the firm from Cohen — and they no longer had to work for Dolan.

From 1929 to October 1942, the various Rearwin aircraft firms had designed, built, and sold approximately 507 planes, nearly 20 percent of which were exported to some 20 different countries scattered on six continents.[3] Rae's companies also built more than 300 Ken-Royce engines, put aircraft on snow skis and pontoons, designed the Instrument Trainer, put hundreds of new pilots in the air, and trained scores of mechanics and other workers for aircraft plants and shops. Many of the young engineers, pilots, and mechanics who cut their teeth at Rearwin moved on to distinguished, life-long careers in aviation.

Bob Rummel, the chief engineer at Rearwin for some five years, wrote in *Howard Hughes and TWA*:

> While things were not always a bed of roses at

Rearwin, I respected the Rearwins and thoroughly enjoyed the work. The concentrated experience gained there probably could not have been duplicated anywhere else. It was with a sense of gratitude to the Rearwins for the opportunities they provided and a keen sense of disappointment concerning the new management that I left Commonwealth.

Gene Salvay, who worked in the Engineering Department for Rummel, reminisced in 1995:

The year and a half I spent at Rearwin was very exciting. Remember, everyone in that engineering department was in their 20s, and we turned out some fantastic aircraft designs. Sure, we had problems. By today's standards, the facilities and conditions were crummy. But I really enjoyed my time at Rearwin. It just seems like we all loved to go to work.

Bob Faris moved from apprentice to purchasing manager and worked at the Fairfax plant for nearly four years:

I have a very fond memory of my experience with Rearwin Aircraft and Engines, Inc. and R. A. Rearwin. I was given a most unusual opportunity, considering my very young age (16) at that time, and the Rearwin phase of my life has served my aviation career well over the succeeding fifty years in the industry and several thousand hours as a pilot.

Jim Combs of Farley, Missouri, a former production worker, summed up in 1983:

Of all the jobs I ever held, working at Rearwin Aircraft was the grandest of all . . . perhaps it was because those times were the grandest of all. We at Rearwin were like one big family, we visited back and forth . . . the parties we used to have . . . nothing elaborate or fancy . . . I remember one picnic at Lakewood Park in Bonner Springs, with sack races . . . and (Rae) right there in the middle of it all. The sun never did shine any brighter than those days at Fairfax Airport.

*Chapter 27*

# Commonwealth Aircraft, Inc.

*RAE HAD CLAWED through the Depression for 14 years before selling to Cohen in October 1942. Just four years later, however, the company he founded was out of business at the very height of the post-war aviation boom. Cohen and Dolan may have profited from the war, but peacetime competition was another matter.*

*In December 1942, shortly after the sale, Dolan and Gilbert Novotney, the new Rearwin secretary-treasurer, negotiated to lease the American Royal Arena, a livestock exhibition hall owned by the Kansas City Stock Yards Company. The show floor where prize cattle and gaited horses once pranced on tanbark exceeded 250,000 square feet. Every inch was needed for the glider contracts Rae and Ken had negotiated, and the McGee Street property was abandoned.*

*The first glider was towed from Fairfax on February 17, 1943, and flown for 30 minutes by Major B. B. Price, a Dayton test pilot. In June, the Army Air Corps awarded Commonwealth another multi-million-dollar contract. Dolan boasted it would make the company the second-largest producer of the 15-place CG-4A troop carrier. An article in a local paper also reported that Commonwealth was looking forward to the post-war era, its engineers were already busy on post-war aircraft projects, and that Commonwealth would erect its own plant building at Fairfax* after the war. By late 1943, nearly 2,000 employees, including some 700 women, were busy on two shifts working on the gliders and other defense contracts.

The original glider contracts were completed by July 1944, and massive layoffs followed. Less than a month later, however, the firm received a contract to establish field depots to repair gliders damaged during training exercises. That was followed in the fall by another multi-million-dollar contract for more gliders, and Commonwealth quickly sought to recall its workforce. However, the contract was canceled prior to its fulfillment as the war in Europe ground to an end.

Commonwealth built a total of 1,470 CG-4A gliders, ranking third behind the Ford Motor Company's Iron Mountain plant (4,190) and Northwestern (1,510). There is no doubt that Cohen made money on the contracts Rae and Ken had set in place, but whether he held on to it long after V-J Day is debatable. Commonwealth Aircraft, Inc., was out of business just 15 months later.

There are several reasons for Commonwealth's demise. Many key aircraft employees had either abandoned ship or been tossed overboard. Not one engineer who had worked on the Skyranger was left to carry on and, despite press reports, little had been

A Waco glider built at Fairfax.
George Hyde

Reed Pigman, President of American Flyers.

Frank Cohen with Ken and Rae beside one of the first gliders; note the position and angle of the Venturi tube.

Below: The Commonwealth Trimmer never reached production.
NASM, Smithsonian Institution, Washington, D.C., 1A-20969

Commonwealth built about 14 Skyrangers at Fairfax in late 1945/early 1946 before moving the plant to Long Island, New York.

Commonwealth Skyrangers on the snow-covered tarmac at Fairfax, December 1945.

done to update the 1942 Skyranger for the post-war market. In addition, much of the tooling and jigs had been damaged, discarded, or used as scrap, and the marketing and sales network the Rearwins had put in place was a shambles. No one had bothered to resurrect it, and neither the domestic nor export markets had ever heard of Commonwealth. Cohen had been right in 1943 when he refused to let Ken out of his employment contract. He was needed, but that was history.

A small, mixed batch of 75 and 85 hp Skyrangers were built at the Fairfax plant in the winter of 1945 while Cohen and Dolan, for some obscure reason, prepared to relocate to the former Columbia Aircraft factory at Valley Stream, Long Island, New York, obviously at considerable expense. The ill-conceived move took place in early 1946, and seriously interrupted production and sales at the very start of the short-lived post-war boom.

At about the same time, Commonwealth sold the rights, drawings, remaining tooling, and parts to the various Cloudster models and the 120 hp Ken-Royce 7G engine to Reed Pigman's American Flyers, then based in Ardmore, Oklahoma. The flight school had purchased five Instrument Trainers prior to the war, was still heavily involved in instrument instruction, and wanted to maintain a ready source for Cloudster and round engine parts. What happened to the rights to the Ken-Royce biplane, the Junior, the Speedster, and the Sportster, as well as the other Ken-Royce engines, is not clear.

Designer Gilbert Trimmer also interested Cohen and Dolan in developing a small twin-engine amphibian called the Trimmer C-170, which drained time, attention, and money from other projects. It was powered by a pair of Continental C-85-12 engines, but only one experimental model (NX 41853) was built. The organization was headed for disaster. Few of the skilled Kansas City employees were interested in moving to Long Island, and that was just fine with Dolan. Production at the new plant, which suffered from mismanagement and a lack of aviation experience, was limited to the Model 185 Skyranger with the Continental C-85-12 up front.

Commonwealth built 276 Skyrangers (SN1601-1876) at Fairfax and Long Island before the final blow came in the form of a disastrous labor strike in October 1946. Meanwhile, Cessna, Piper, Luscombe, Aeronca, and others eagerly filled the demand for personal, two-place aircraft. Commonwealth had lost its toehold in the marketplace, there never was a market for the Trimmer, and no labor union was going to dictate to Commonwealth's management how much the employees were paid or how the company was run. Commonwealth closed its doors in November 1946. Others, too, would fall by the wayside as the highly competitive post-war aircraft boom rapidly cooled in mid-1947. However, Rae Rearwin, age 69, was basking in California sunshine and regularly attending birthday parties for five grandchildren.

*Chapter 28*

# Among the Palms

*AS STIPULATED IN THE 1938 partnership agreement between Rae and his sons, the net proceeds from the sale of the corporate stock, as well as that from the settlement of the breach of contract suits (less attorney's fees of $1,800), were divided equally among the three. True to his word, Rae established separate trusts of about $100,000 for Royce and Ken in early 1943. The principal was prudently invested in rock-solid common stocks managed by Rae, while the dividends were paid directly to the beneficiaries.[1] During the following decade, each trust earned in excess of $60,000, while the corpus, despite market fluctuations, increased in value by more than 50 percent. Combined with the earnings from the trusts established by their grandfather, neither son needed to work if he chose not to, nor did their father.*

*Rae not only had his own share of the sale to Cohen, but the proceeds from the nearly contemporaneous liquidation of the lumberyard, coal and petroleum business, and other assets. Through careful investing, Rae also still owned real estate and a handsome portfolio of high-grade securities.*

*The real estate consisted of the two commercial structures built during the 1920s across from the lumberyard and several residential properties acquired in Salina* and Wichita during the same period. The rents, as well as cash flow from depreciation, had been a fairly dependable source of income during the Depression. In 1942 their aggregate net rental income exceeded $7,000.

Rae's careful investing in common stocks had also helped to keep him afloat during the upstream struggle through the 1930s. His repurchase of Western Star stock in the late 1920s had paid off with uninterrupted dividends of nearly $700 a year throughout the Depression decade, and they were continuing. He had also invested in General Motors, Goodyear Tire, Texaco, and Consolidated Oil, which collectively paid dividends in excess of $4,000 in 1942. Indeed, the proceeds from the notes discounted at the Farmers National Bank were, comparatively speaking, pocket change. In the terms of the 1990s dollar, the farm boy from Lincoln was worth more than a million dollars in 1943, and his separate estate would actually be so valued more than a quarter-century later.

In 1943, Rae married Grace S. Smith, a Kansas City school teacher born in Chetopa, Kansas, on March 4, 1905. Meanwhile, both sons volunteered for military service, Royce in the Army and Ken in the Navy, but neither served overseas.

Rae and Grace, who retired from teaching, succumbed to the lure of Southern California in 1944. Two years later, they built a comfortable two-story home in the

Royce S. Rearwin, *circa* 1945.

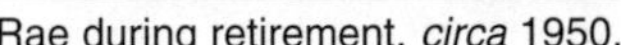
Rae during retirement, *circa* 1950.

Rae kept in shape even during retirement.

U.S. Navy officer Ken Rearwin, *circa* 1945.

Right: Rae with granddaughters Dianne (left) and Linda, *circa* 1947.

Below: Grandfather Rae in Beverly Hills with Kenneth's children, Penny, Steve, and David, *circa* 1948.

The Cadillac and palm trees suggest that this photo of Rae and Grace was taken in California in 1949 or 1950.

community of Beverly Hills, about 1,200 air miles west-southwest of Rae's boyhood home in Lincoln, Kansas. Royce moved to California with his family after the war. Ken, who had been stationed in San Diego as a Navy lieutenant, stayed in Southern California after his discharge in early 1946.

As if by magic, the workaholic switch was turned off. Rae enjoyed retirement. It turned out to be a quarter-century of leisure, travel, doting on grandchildren, managing trusts, dabbling in real estate, collecting rents and dividends, and shifting investments with the ebb and flow of business fortunes and the economy.

Ironically, Rae earned nearly as much in retirement as he had during his working years, primarily in the stock market, and in particular, on the frequent swings of tobacco stocks. He bought heavily when the floor fell out after the tobacco-cancer link was first exposed and widely publicized. He was convinced that smokers would not give up their vice and was well rewarded for his insight. Rae also became involved in community affairs, was an active

Rae and Grace Rearwin in front of their Beverly Hills home, *circa* 1966.

Shriner, and was a supporter and patron of the Antique Airplane Association and the Airpower Museum, Inc., both of Blakesburg, Iowa.

With his health failing in 1967, Rae expressed a desire to be laid to rest in his Masonic apron, which was embroidered with the dates of the various degrees earned after 1906, including the Scottish Rite in 1919. Grace could not find the original, so she wrote the Salina Lodge for a duplicate. The Lodge secretary noted in his reply that Rae had become a life member in 1957, and thus had the unusual distinction of being a member for more than 60 years.

On July 20, 1969, Rae watched from his bed with the rest of the world as Neil Armstrong stepped onto the surface of the moon. His shriveled, former six-foot-two-inch frame was ravaged by pain and the infirmities of more than 91 years. Surely he marveled at the time, distance, and the once unfathomable miracles now taken for granted that bridged the Kansas frontier of the 1880s to the one where Armstrong stood.

Fate had been good to Raymond Andrew Rearwin. He had been deposited naked on the doorstep of man's greatest era, the threshold between the field and horse civilization of a thousand years and the concurrent ages of steel, oil, electricity, exploding atoms, and all they wrought, including the fulfillment of man's most ancient dream, Flight. One could not have ordered better.

Rae had learned, while waiting to quench an overpowering thirst as a boy on the Kansas prairie, that each in his own time and way must climb, circumvent, or retreat from whatever appears on his horizon. Perhaps his mountains had not been as steep or as tall as those confronting others; maybe the rivers he crossed were not as swift or as wide. What mattered was that the dying man knew within himself that the dirt farmer's son had not shrunk from life's opportunities nor done less than his best to surmount the challenges that came with them. He had, indeed, taken full advantage of the time allotted between the happenstances of birth and death.

The end came at home on November 19, 1969, but Rae missed it. He was sleeping. A few days later he was buried in a new Shriner's apron at Forest Lawn Memorial Park, in Glendale, California.

Ken Rearwin, left, and Royce attended the Twenty-Fifth Anniversary Antique Airplane Association Fly-In at Blakesburg, Iowa, over Labor Day Weekend, 1996. Ken is 83; Royce 86. Mary Beth Bach

# Afterword

*IN RETROSPECT, our father was one of the smartest, hardest-working, and most business-oriented individual either of us have known in our 80-plus years. He rode through his working life at full throttle. Even when he reached his sixties, most younger men could not match his seemingly boundless stamina.*

*Although Dad was quite successful in Salina, he was never one to rest on his accomplishments. He was always on the lookout for ways to expand and improve his operations, and he was quite proud to have plugged the losses of the Western Star Mill in the early 1920s. So, following Lindbergh's flight and our many trips to Wichita, it is not surprising that he turned to aircraft manufacturing as a new challenge and a fresh outlet for his interests and energies.*

*But Dad was much more to us than a businessman. He was our father — and we remember him as such. To be sure, he was strict, both in accordance with the times and with the responsibility of any parent. But he was also fair and, despite working 10 or 12 hours a day, six days a week (and sometimes on Sundays), he somehow made time for us. We certainly never felt neglected.*

*In addition to learning the traditional "life lessons," we spent many pleasant times with Dad while he taught us marksmanship, hunting, fishing, golf, and other* pastimes. He was also generous. He backed our mother's insistence that we take music (piano, trumpet, and violin) lessons at an early age. Indeed, while it did not help our abilities, he purchased a gold-plated trumpet and, while in Vienna in 1926, invested in an especially fine Guarnerius violin that today would cost many thousands of dollars.

Mother also benefitted from Dad's generosity. She always had outside help for household and domestic chores, and her own automobile — long before Dad provided us with our own brand-new 1927 Pontiac Roadster which, of course, enhanced our status among Salina's most popular teenage girls. Conversely, as we grew, he expected us to "pull our weight" around the filling station and the lumberyard — not as a matter of economy, but as a learning experience.

Dad believed that there was money to be made in aviation, and that he would earn his share. That goal was thwarted by the Great Depression. Nevertheless, Dad faced the resulting obstacles head on and actually found pleasure in solving and surviving the problems of those dire times. His good friend, Chet Housel, once said to us, "Your dad works like a dog and never knows when he's licked." Chet was right. One thing is sure — early on, we both learned the "work ethic" from Dad, and 50- to 60-hour work weeks came naturally. So did attending college.

Dad was a remarkable and complex man. He gave his best and demanded the same from those around him. He would come down hard on incompetents and laggards, but he could also be understanding and generous with someone in a jam. He was impatient, sometimes explosive, but always proud and a man of his word.

We wondered many times how our father survived those dark economic days and the lonely years in Kansas City. He told us he simply put his troubles on the nightstand every evening and got a good eight hours' rest. Refreshed, he tackled his problems again the next morning.

Our father clearly enjoyed sharing the limelight cast by aviation, rubbing shoulders with famous fliers and other manufacturers, and just plain being a part of the Fraternity of Flight. Although it is unlikely that he ever considered the matter, Dad and the quality aircraft and engines he put in the air during aviation's formative but not so "golden" age have truly earned a lasting place in that history.

Royce S. Rearwin
Kenneth R. Rearwin
September 1996

# Notes

## Part One — The First Half Century

**Chapter 1, pp. 3-5.**

1. Salina's first airport consisted of 160 acres of rolling farmland located south of East Crawford Street. According to the *Salina Journal*, the site was purchased in October 1928 "as a direct result of the challenge flung some months ago by Will Rogers, famous comedian, on the occasion of his appearance here." It was closed in 1966, and all operations were transferred to the former Schilling Air Force Base.
2. Lindbergh was not the first to fly the Atlantic. That feat had been accomplished as early as 1919. He was, however, the first to fly it solo and non-stop from New York to Paris.
3. *Wings*, which opened in 1927, with Clara Bow, Buddy Rogers, and Richard Arlen, was followed in 1928 by about 20 other feature films about aviation.
4. The sale was made to finance the construction of a new factory at Fairfax Airport and to purchase the Wallace Touroplane Company of Chicago, which manufactured a unique three-place cabin monoplane with folding wings.

**Chapter 2, pp. 7-11.**

1. The college was later moved to Albany, Missouri, then to Franklin, Indiana, and finally to Defiance, Ohio.

**Chapter 3, pp. 12-17.**

1. The abandoned Upper Mill was a popular picnic, boating, and recreational area until the site was razed in April 1932.

**Chapter 5, pp. 24-29.**

1. Ironically, even the other lumberyards purchased Trailmobiles, but not from Rae. Unwittingly, they bought from his sub-agents.

**Chapter 6, pp. 30-38.**

1. The Dow-Jones Index more than quadrupled from about 71 points in early 1921 to just over 300 by late 1928.

## Part Two — The Airplane Years: 1928-1942

### Chapter 7, pp. 41-48.

1. Royce, having assessed the weather, mistakenly concluded the flight would not take place and went to a fraternity party in Wichita.
2. Even though the engine was not operated at full power, Halsey calculated the speed at 131 mph. The plane was also tested to an altitude of 12,500 feet with designer Landgraf and welder Smokey Nelson riding in the front cockpit, but the flight was discontinued because of the cold air temperature.

### Chapter 8, pp. 49-59.

1. Braniff was born in Salina in 1884 and moved to Kansas City, Missouri, with his family in 1891. He was president of Braniff International Airways in 1954, when he died in a Shreveport, Louisiana, aircraft accident at age 70.
2. The intrepid Martin sat on a canvas sling stretched tightly between two bamboo poles, just ahead of the radiator and engine. Flaps (ailerons) mounted on each side of the bamboo framework about midway between the lower and upper wings were used to tilt the rickety craft in turns, while vertical control was obtained by another pair of flaps (elevators), one at the front and the other at the rear. Martin crashed the fragile airplane on his first attempt, repaired it overnight, and then made several successful flights. Leila Rearwin was a school classmate of Martin, but it is not known whether she witnessed the flights.
3. Dr. Brock, an optometrist, was also the first pilot to fly to the capitals of all 48 states.

### Chapter 10, pp. 66-70.

1. Rearwin sales manager Dodson Goss, with Royce as a passenger, flew a Ken-Royce biplane in the Depression-shortened 1930 Tour. Royce also flew a new Sportster on the three-day Tour to nine western Kansas cities in 1935.

### Chapter 11, pp. 71-80.

1. Only 40 women pilots met the minimum entry requirements of at least 100 solo hours of flying, including at least 25 on cross-country flights of more than 40 miles from the point of departure.
2. Young Royce and Ken were present when Nichols arrived at Fairfax in the Fledgling with her mechanic. The event was memorable for both. Royce, then 19, thought Nichols was a "slick looking chick." Ken, 16, had his back to the idling plane and was literally tackled to the ground by Nichols's mechanic as he started to step backwards into the swinging propeller.
3. The Dow-Jones Index had been steadily declining for several months, but on "Black Tuesday" it fell another 30.57 points, losing about 12 percent of its value on that one fateful day.

### Chapter 12, pp. 81-97.

1. Ong wrote in his autobiography, *Ride The High Wind*, "I hadn't done much for Rae Rearwin, although I tried my best. He had been very fair with me, despite the aggravation I know I caused him."
2. Royce and Rearwin salesman Dodson Goss had previously flown the plane to the reservation and demonstrated it for Standing Bear, who wanted to buy. However, the Sioux elders, who controlled his purse strings, would not approve the purchase.
3. Long, a former World War I pilot-observer, founded the Dallas School of Aviation in 1926 and held commercial pilot's license No. 476. He also operated Dallas Aero Service and several airline routes, which were sold to Braniff Airways in 1939. Long died at age 81 in August 1976.
4. She delivered one to the Kinner Motor Company in Glendale, California, in 1930.

### Chapter 13, pp. 99-111.

1. A "Group 2 Approval" was a less expensive form of government certification that could be issued for a limited production run, for test purposes, or to cover major modifications to an aircraft model that was previously certified with an Approved Type Certification (ATC).
2. The Aeromarine had enclosed push rods with rocker box covers and initially sold for just $350. However, the firm had underestimated its development costs and the market. Despite rapid price increases to $600, the firm soon withered.

### Chapter 14, pp. 112-116.

1. To obtain volume discounts, Rae's firms and Cessna Aircraft regularly purchased tubing, rubber molding, and other materials jointly under the name of one firm and then reshipped part with a bill to the other. Rae also bought materials and supplies from bankrupt firms and, when possible, resold what was not needed.

### Chapter 15, pp. 117-124.

1. Webber did the basic design work on the Speedster on his own time during 1932-1933. As with the Junior, he sold Rae a "package," including his own services through certification, for $2,500.
2. Rae twice added $500 to the deal to keep young Webber on the project through certification. However, with no end in sight, and perhaps disillusioned, Rae did not hold Webber to his "to certification" commitment.
3. The Speedster was certified on November 28, 1937, with ATC No. 653.
4. It was Kling's 29th birthday.
5. While Royce made a presentation to the Miami Chamber of Commerce Industrial Committee, both the *Herald* and *Tribune* featured articles about the possible move that centered on the advantages of better weather and the proximity to the markets of Latin America.
6. The flight was related to the first International Miami-Havana Air Race held on December 13. Passengers were not permitted in the over-water race, so Ham and Rae flew along anyway as non-participants.
7. The Speedster prototype (NC12588) is rumored to still exist, but is not currently registered. It apparently awaits restoration.

### Chapter 16, pp. 125-142.

1. The Key brothers, Al and Fred, from Meridian, Mississippi,

also purchased a new Sportster in September and became one of the first dealers. The pair had previously set the world endurance record by staying aloft in a Curtiss Robin for almost 28 days.

2. Harold Price, Glasgow, Montana, bought a snow ski version in December 1937 for the avowed purpose of hunting coyotes in Montana's back country. Price claimed that the roar of the engine jumped the coyotes from their lairs and, with the bounty at $10 a pelt, he would recover the cost of the plane by April.
3. It did. Several pontoon-equipped planes were sold in Canada and Alaska, as well as in the lower 48.
4. Only nine Warner-powered Sportsters were built.
5. Trippe was born in 1899 and educated at Yale University.
6. The fourth New Zealand Sportster was reportedly destroyed in an accident.

**Chapter 17, pp. 143-147.**

1. The hangar, which had 25-foot ceilings and an attached two-story office building on one side, had been built in 1929 at a cost of over $115,000. It offered twice the floor space of the A.R. Jones Building.
2. Ken had high grades in high school and was one of ten students nationwide to receive an Austin Scholarship in 1931. It covered tuition and expenses at Northwestern University for four years. A year's post-graduate study abroad was canceled due to lack of funding by Northwestern during the Depression.
3. A *Fortune* magazine article from the time reported Rearwin was one of only four aircraft firms to turn a profit in 1937.
4. On still another occasion, Miller took off in a new Sportster dressed in white, but returned in black. Someone had left the oil filler cap off. Miller had to open his door for visibility when his windscreen was blackened, inviting the oil in. He had not checked the cap himself, so no fingers were pointed.

**Chapter 18, pp. 149-157.**

1. At the time, there were only 13 other companies in the United States manufacturing certified aircraft engines.
2. A few workers used a rope to slide from the mezzanine to the hangar floor. The practice ended when one poor soul discovered too late that a large steel hook had been attached to the end of the rope.
3. The engine division, which initially employed 25 workers, increased total Rearwin employment to over 70.

**Chapter 20, pp. 160-161.**

1. The other half had been put into separate but equal trusts for Royce and Ken.

**Chapter 21, pp. 163-177.**

1. The prototype was designed with a single, direct linkage belly flap thought necessary to slow the plane. However, flight tests proved it was not needed, and it was eliminated.
2. Rummel also modified the Sportster into a less expensive instrument trainer, the Model 9000 KRT. Without instruments, it sold for $3,795 in 1941, while the Model 8135T, also less "blind flying" dials, sold for $6,495.

**Chapter 22, pp. 179-187.**

1. One was sold to the Ford Motor Company Employees Flying Club at Dearborn, Michigan, in March 1941.

**Chapter 23, pp. 188-192.**

1. Tommy Blanche, a 19-year-old freshman at Kansas City Junior College, was the first such student. With the publicity and fanfare Rae customarily arranged for such occasions, Blanche took a 30-minute lesson in a Sportster from flight instructor "Mac" McDonald on November 29, 1939.
2. The airport was returned to civilian use after World War II, but it was permanently closed on April 1, 1985, to make way for a new General Motors plant.

## Part Three — Finesse and Finality

**Chapter 26, pp. 205-208.**

1. Nearby natural gas fields now heated most homes, and the war had stifled the lumber and service station operations. Rae had also decided to sell or liquidate them.
2. Rummel was seldom involved in the Commonwealth glider production process. Instead, he spent much of his time designing new civilian and military aircraft concepts, none of which interested Dolan. Apparently, it was Dolan's method of keeping Rummel busy and out of the way.
3. The number of Rearwin-designed aircraft built increases to almost 800 if the Swedish-built Sportsters (12 to 14) and the Commonwealth Skyrangers (276) are included.

**Chapter 28, pp. 214-217.**

1. Rae subsequently released management and control of the trusts to each son.

*Part Four*

# Appendices

# *Appendices*

*Appendix A*

# Whatever Happened to . . .?

**A*SHCRAFT, Don***, *was a top-notch airframe and fuselage welder. He earned a private pilot's license at the Rearwin Flying School and later became a line captain for Braniff Airlines.*

***BARTSCH, August***, *a German immigrant, fabricated aluminum fuel tanks while employed at Rearwin. He subsequently hooked up with TWA in Kansas City and worked as a mechanic and maintenance engineer until retirement.*

***BECKER, Viola (Bourland)***, *started working for Rearwin Airplanes in January 1936 and resigned from Commonwealth in September 1944 to move to Los Angeles. She worked as Rae's secretary-stenographer, as the office manager, and processed the licensing, financing, and exporting of all Rearwin aircraft. She also handled most of the orders for parts and engine overhauls. Mrs. Bourland now lives in Independence, Missouri.*

***BOWMAN, Hart***, *worked for the Dallas School of Aviation after leaving Rearwin in about 1932. He later opened his own flight school, and subsequently was the airport manager at Love Field in Dallas. However, he claimed to be proudest of having introduced Walter Beech and Olive Ann Mellar to each other. Bowman passed away in Dallas in 1972.*

Hart Bowman.

Flying School instructor John "Jack" Bucher "armstrongs" a prop.
Jack Bucker

"Chico."

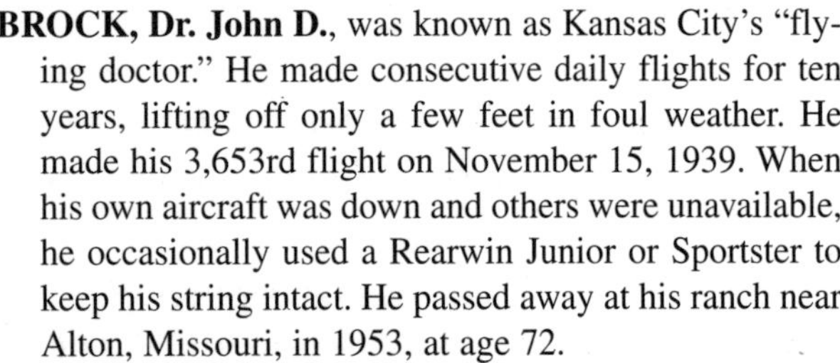

**BROCK, Dr. John D.**, was known as Kansas City's "flying doctor." He made consecutive daily flights for ten years, lifting off only a few feet in foul weather. He made his 3,653rd flight on November 15, 1939. When his own aircraft was down and others were unavailable, he occasionally used a Rearwin Junior or Sportster to keep his string intact. He passed away at his ranch near Alton, Missouri, in 1953, at age 72.

**BUCHER, John (Jack)**, a Rearwin flight instructor and test pilot in the late 1930s, managed the airport at Prescott, Arizona, for several years. At age 80 he still pilots aircraft in the Colorado City, Colorado, area.

**CARTER, Kenneth**, became a top designer of landing gear for Lockheed Aircraft Corp. He is deceased.

**CHICO**, a native of the Philippines, seldom disclosed his last name. He was employed as a Rearwin assembler in the mid-1930s. However, as Charlie Nixon recalls, "Chico did anything anyone asked of him — and cheerfully." He returned to the foreboding uncertainty of the Philippines in 1940.

**CLARK, John J. (Jack)**, returned to Travel Air for a short time after his layoff from Rearwin, but at $35 a week, and married Ramona. He then worked for Boeing as a project engineer for 39 years without another layoff. He is retired in Wichita.

**COMBS, James E., Jr.**, left Rearwin in late 1942 to enlist as a private in the Army Air Corps. He emerged four years later only to find Commonwealth loading the last of the equipment for Valley Stream. Jim worked in a number of machine shops before opening his own, Spartan Engineering Co., in Atchison, Kansas, which he still heads.

**COOKE, Oscar**, the owner of the last known Rearwin Junior, passed away in Billings, Montana, in 1995, at age 94.

**DENTLE, Keith**, was hired as a Rearwin draftsman in December 1939. He left in 1940 to work for the Glenn L. Martin Co. in Baltimore, where he was involved in design work on the Martin Mars, the PBM flying boats, and the B-26 bomber. In 1945 he went to work for the Bureau of Aeronautics and then the Naval Air Systems Command, retiring in 1980 as the Director of the Design Analysis Division. He resides in Falls Church, Virginia.

**DOLAN, C. H. (Charles/Carl)**, was president and general manager of Commonwealth, Inc., after it purchased Rearwin. At his death at age 85 in 1981, he was the last surviving member of the 38 famed World War I Lafayette Escadrille pilots. He was officially credited with downing two aircraft, but claimed eight. After Commonwealth's demise he became a consultant to the Senate Aviation Subcommittee. He was recalled to active duty as an Air Force colonel during the Korean War in 1951, and served as a liaison representative to the Sperry Gyroscope Company. He died in Hawaii.

Carl Dolan.

Barnstormer Ben Gregory was based at Fairfax. Lou Holland Collection, Kansas City Museum, Kansas City, MO

Noel Hockaday, with the "Comet." NASM, Smithsonian Institution, Washington, D.C., 95-15041

**FARIS, Robert C. (Bob)**, left Rearwin in 1941 for Culver Aircraft, then in 1944 enlisted in the Navy. After the war Bob purchased the Culver manufacturing rights, inventory, and tooling and, while servicing some 700 Culver owners, opened a Mooney aircraft dealership. He sold the Culver rights in 1956 and operated Precision Metalcraft, Inc. in Wichita, which manufactured and sold parts to the Air Force and various aircraft manufacturers. The firm was sold in 1986 and Bob returned to college during retirement, completing both bachelor's and master's degrees at Wichita State University while organizing Farin Financial and Farin Management Group, mortgage investment firms. He still flies a Bonanza purchased new in 1960 and has logged more than 7,000 hours. He lives in Wichita with his wife Marge.

**FIRMIN, Joel A.**, born in Alto, Texas, on May 1, 1920, was laid off by Commonwealth in 1946, and went to work the next day at Rex Welding and Engineering. He was employed as a machinist most of his working career, and now lives in Dekalb, Missouri.

**FORMAN, Marvin**, a Rearwin engineer, later worked for North American and Rockwell International on the Sabreliner, B-1, and Apollo projects. He passed away in Palos Verdes, California, in June 1995, at age 76.

**GREGORY, Ben**, barnstormed the Midwest in a Ford Trimotor carrying up to 14 passengers, and later thrilled airshow spectators with a nighttime extravaganza in his neon-tubed, smoke-belching Ford Trimotor named *The Ship From Mars*. Gregory flew over a half-million passengers during his career and survived seven crashes (three in Trimotors). He died at age 84 on February 17, 1974.

**HAASE, Alfred**, a German immigrant, worked in the Ken-Royce engine shop from November 1938 until July 1941. Rae helped him obtain U.S. citizenship. He subsequently worked for Rupert Die Casting and Tool Company and retired as the tool room superintendent. He passed away in 1994, at age 86, while vacationing in Albuquerque.

**HALSEY, George**, left Rearwin in late 1928 and in 1931 was the Fairfax Operation Manager for Midland Air Express, an air taxi service that served several communities between Kansas City and Cheyenne.

**HOCKADAY, Noel R. (Hock)**, was born in Kinmundy, Illinois, on May 24, 1905, and entered the aircraft industry as a welder for the E. M. ("Mattie") Laird Airplane and Wallace Aircraft companies in Chicago. He moved to Kansas City with Stan Wallace in early 1929 when Ed Porterfield's American Eagle Aircraft Corp.

absorbed Wallace. He left Porterfield in 1936 after the Flyabout 35-W was certified, and worked for Lockheed Aircraft in Burbank until 1941. While there, he moonlighted as the president of Hockaday Aircraft Corp. and, with engineer W. H. Yarick, designed and built the Hockaday Comet in 1945-1946. The two-place, side-by-side metal and fabric high-winged monoplane was powered with a 130 hp engine and designed to sell for $3,000. Although Hockaday promoted the Comet extensively, there is no evidence it was ever certified or successfully marketed.

**JOHNSON, Frank B.**, was a Rearwin structural engineer from 1938 to 1939. He worked briefly at Porterfield on the CP-50 and Collegiate, and then joined Convair as a group engineer on the B-24, B-32, and B-36 projects. After the war he became the chief design engineer for Convair's Stinson division, which turned out the Voyager and STOL L-13. Johnson joined Lockheed Burbank in 1946, was an assistant project engineer on the C-130, and in 1960 transferred to the Lockheed Missile and Space Center where he held several engineering management positions on the Polaris and Poseidon projects. He retired from Lockheed in 1976, and passed away at home in Norcross, Georgia, in 1991, at age 79.

**JONES, Albert R. (Bert)**, weathered the Great Depression. Unlike many, his debt structure was manageable and the country still needed oil and natural gas, which were pumped to Chicago, Denver, and Texas through pipelines. Jones reportedly sold a substantial portion of his holdings to the Phillips Petroleum Company, and he served on the Phillips and Colorado-Interstate Gas Company boards for a number of years. At age 77 in 1952, he was also the president of five oil companies, including the A. R. Jones Oil and Operating Company.

**JONES, Ray**, was a Rearwin test pilot and flight instructor in 1936, but a "barnstormer" at heart. He was killed during an aerobatic accident at Wichita Municipal Airport on July 20, 1936, three weeks after leaving Rearwin. He was 28.

**KEYS, Troy**, resigned from Commonwealth in late 1942. He worked as a foreman and plant manager for the Benson Manufacturing Company for 20 years, and then as an estimator for the Union Machine Tool Company until 1972. He enjoyed ten years of hunting, fishing, and retirement before his death on January 9, 1983, at age 78.

**LA GRONE, John Kerr (Tex)**, sold his fixed-based operation at Fairfax in 1942 and went to work at North American testing Fairfax-built B-25s, his first employment since 1919. He died at home in Kansas City on April 12, 1953, 9 days short of his 62nd birthday.

**LANDGRAF, Fred**, designed and certified the Curtiss-Wright Sportsman in 1931, was the chief engineer at Lewis American Airways in Denver in the late 1930s, and was a project engineer at Douglas Aircraft in El Segundo from 1938 to 1943, where he designed landing gear. Fred then opened his own firm and developed the Landgraf H-2 single-seat helicopter. He also worked for Ryan Aircraft in San Diego on a number of experimental projects until retirement in 1970. He died of a heart attack in San Diego on July 12, 1973, at age 69.

**LA RENE (Foote), Jean**, died in her late fifties at Hidden Valley ranch near Lockhart, Texas, on May 28, 1960, a few days after suffering a stroke. She was a charter member of the "99s" — the International Organization of Women Pilots.

**LE CLAIRE, John B. (Jack)**, resigned from Rearwin in 1935 to take a drafting job at TWA and wait for a flying position. He subsequently served as a line pilot and captain flying DC-2s, DC-3s, Martins, Lockheed Constellations, and the Boeing 707 prior to retiring in 1968. Jack and his wife still live in the Kansas City area.

John Kerr "Tex" LaGrone. Wyandotte County Museum, Bonner Springs, KS

Jean LeRene, *circa* 1930. Wyandotte County Museum, Bonner Springs, KS

**McDONALD, Charles R. (Mac)**, learned to fly as a U.S. Navy Ensign. He left Rearwin to reenlist, and later served as a director and vice president of the Missouri Aviation Institute.

**MILLER, William E. (Bill)**, was employed as a pilot for the Federal Aviation Authority in Kansas City, Missouri, from 1940 to 1960. He retired to a 160-acre spread near Piper, Kansas, where he farmed and raised cattle, winning several awards for innovative water and soil conservation techniques. He spent more than 12,000 hours in the air. Bill was also active in the formative days of the "Rearwin Club" and was a long-standing member of both the OX-5 Aviation Pioneers Hall of Fame and Quiet Birdmen — the "Anciente and Secret Order" organization founded for aviators in January 1921 by General H. H. Arnold. Bill Miller died of heart problems on December 6, 1972, at age 59.

**MOSLEY, Zack**, the creator of the syndicated "Smilin' Jack" cartoon strip that appeared in the *Chicago Tribune* and *New York News* for 40 years, died in Stuart, Florida, on December 21, 1993. He was a colonel in the Civil Air Patrol, Base 3, at Lantana, Florida, and a member of the Quiet Birdmen.

**NAYLOR, Lester**, Rearwin production worker, passed away in Halstead, Kansas, in June 1993, at age 82.

**NICHOLS, Ruth Rowland**, a Wellesley College graduate known as "The Society Flier," was a charter member of the "99s." She worked for Fairchild Aircraft and Aviation Country Clubs and was a founder of *The Sportsman Pilot* magazine. By 1931 she held three major international women's aviation records and, flying for New York and New England Airways in 1932, was reputedly the first female airline pilot. In 1958, she became the first woman to fly an Air Force jet in excess of 1,000 miles an hour. She died at age 59 in New York City in October 1960, leaving notes indicating suicide.

**NIXON, Charles W.**, a native of Topeka, had one goal when he graduated from high school in 1937 — to get into aviation. He did, through the Rearwin apprenticeship program. His 45-year career included work for Cessna, the Federal Aviation Administration, and Beech. He worked as a principle inspector during the development of the Citation, and is now retired in Springfield, Missouri.

Bill Miller. William E. Miller Family

This oil portrait of Ruth Nichols was first published in 1931.

Charles W. Nixon, *circa* 1944. C. W. Nixon

Bill Ong.

**ONG, William A. (Bill)**, continued as a racing pilot during the mid-1930s and participated in six Thompson Trophy races. However, with a wife and two sons to support he gave up racing and, after a brief stint in insurance, became the sales manager at Beech. He organized the Ong Aircraft Company in 1937, which built a four-place, high-winged monoplane dubbed the Continental that flew in 1938 but never reached production. Ong also operated a Piper Cub agency and flying school, trained CAPT students during World War II, and was instrumental in establishing several community airports in Kansas and Missouri. He won second place in the 240-mile SOHIO race during the 1946 National Air Races in Cleveland, averaging 345.8 mph in a P-51 Mustang. He also managed Richards Field, was the founder of the Aero Club of Kansas City and the local OX-5 Chapter, and served as president of both the National Aviation Trades Association and the National Aeronautics Association. His 54-year career in aviation ended with his death in 1979.

**PORTERFIELD, E. E., Jr. (Ed)**, was born in Kansas City, Kansas, on November 7, 1890, the son of a Circuit Court judge. Ed was a Ford dealer after World War I and traded a used Model T to barnstormer Blaine Tuxhorn in 1925 in exchange for flying

E. E. "Ed" Porterfield, Jr. Rob Bach

lessons in a "Jenny." Later the same year he opened Porterfield Flying School at Richards Field and started building biplanes (the American Eagle A-1 was first). He moved his flying school and plant to Fairfax in 1928. Porterfield spent World War II building Waco combat gliders at plants in Kansas City and Fort Smith, Arkansas. He retired shortly after the war ended, and died of heart problems three years later on August 29, 1948.

**PRESTIA, Arthur B.**, sometimes simply known as "AB," was a former employee of Arrow Aircraft. He worked in the Rearwin welding, assembly, and inspection departments during the late 1930s. He resigned at the start of the glider projects, hooked on with TWA, and became a flight engineer on Constellations, traveling primarily between New York and Rome. He is retired in Shawnee Mission, Kansas.

**REARWIN, Elizabeth**, Rae's mother, died in Lincoln, Kansas, on July 11, 1936, at age 91, 4 years after her husband John. She had lived in Kansas 56 years.

**REARWIN, Grace S.**, lived in the Beverly Hills home for 25 years after Rae's death. She passed away on October 14, 1994, at age 89.

**REARWIN, John**, Rae's father, died in Lincoln, Kansas, on March 21, 1932, at age 83, without ever having returned to New York. Rae served as the executor of the estate, which he divided among his three sisters.

**REARWIN, Kenneth R.**, obtained a leave from TWA in 1944 to enlist in the Navy, and was discharged in San Diego in 1946 as a full lieutenant. He and his wife Suzanne had three children, Stephen (1939), David (1941), and Penelope (1942). Ken sold residential real estate for a short time after the war instead of returning to TWA. He joined Merrill Lynch in San Diego in 1947 and in 1949 opened the firm's La Jolla office. He became a partner in the firm's San Francisco office in 1958, but returned to San Diego in 1966 and managed that office until retiring in 1973. Ken has also been active in community and charitable affairs, serving on the San Diego Board of Education for seven years and a member of the California Coordinating Council for Higher Education for six years. He was also president of the Parker Foundation for 18 years, a trustee of the San Diego Aerospace Museum, and a vice president of San Diego's Timken Museum. He lives in La Jolla and at age 83 still regularly plays tennis.

Kenneth R. Rearwin (scale model of a Speedster on desk).

**REARWIN, Leila**, died suddenly at home on October 28, 1948, presumably of heart failure related to her childhood bout of rheumatic fever, content she had never moved from Salina. She did not remarry.

**REARWIN, Royce**, served briefly in the U.S. Army and

moved to California after the war. He and his wife Jacqueline had two daughters, Linda and Dianne. Royce is an active gun collector and a supporter of various gun clubs, including the National Rifle Association. He currently lives near Santa Barbara, California.

**ROCHE, John F.**, worked briefly in the engineering department on both the Speedster and Sportster projects in 1935-1936. Jack LeClaire recruited Roche to the TWA engineering department where he worked for 40 years, retiring as Director of Aircraft Engineering Systems. He is retired and lives in Kansas City, Missouri.

**RUMMEL, Robert W. (Bob)**, went on to a distinguished 35-year career with TWA, 19 of those as a personal aviation consultant to Howard Hughes. During that time Bob served as TWA's chief engineer, held successive positions as vice presidents of engineering and jet planning, planning and research, and technical development, and contributed to the development of the air transport fleet from the Martin 202A through the Lockheed 1011 and Boeing 747. He retired from TWA in 1978 and established a successful aerospace consulting firm. Bob has also served as a NACA and NASA consultant (1953-1975), on the White House Program Evaluation Committee (1965-1967), and as Chairman of Aeronautics and Space Engineering Board (1981-1982). In 1986 he was appointed by President Reagan to the commission responsible for investigating the *Challenger* space shuttle accident. Among many professional honors, he was elected to the National Academy of Engineering in 1973, and he was awarded the Distinguished Public Service Medal from NASA in 1979. Bob and his wife Marjorie, married in 1939, currently reside in Mesa, Arizona. They had five children.

**SALVAY, Melvin E. (Gene)**, moonlighted for Ed Porterfield in 1941 while working at Rearwin, and moved to North American and B-25 production when World War II broke out. As the war slowed, he and George Stark designed the experimental single-place Skyhopper, first flown in 1945. Gene moved to Southern California with Rockwell in 1946 and, with Bill Morrisey from Douglas Aircraft, designed and built the "Nifty" in his spare time. It first flew in 1949 and, after development by others, evolved into the Varga Kachina. At North American-Rockwell, Gene worked on the B-45, C-82, Sabreliner T-39A, and B-1 bomber projects. He joined Lockheed in 1977 and spent seven years as a project director at the "Skunk Works," retiring in 1984. Salvay is also a serious aircraft modeler. He designed and marketed several authentic scale models, including replicas of the Rearwin Speedster, Sportster, Cloudster, and Skyranger. He lives in Southern California.

**SLOBODNICK, Tony**, born April 12, 1912, worked at Rearwin from September 1937 through November 1940, both as a cable splicer under Troy Keys and in the finished assembly department for Wesley Pipes. In his "spare time" he cranked props for Flight School instructors and students. Tony returned to farming after World War II, retired in 1979, and now resides in Grand Junction, Colorado.

**STARK, George**, a Rearwin draftsman-engineer, was laid off in August 1941, worked briefly for Beech, and started at North American on the B-25 project six days before the Pearl Harbor attack. He moved back across Fairfax to Commonwealth in 1944, and then to TWA in early 1946. While at Commonwealth, Stark and Gene Salvay designed and built the single-place, 50 hp Skyhopper in their spare time, and a decade later marketed it as a plans-built. Stark moved to California in 1955 and worked for North American on the F-107 project. He sold his interest in the Skyhopper to Salvay. However, he later designed the Sportaire, a two-place, side-by-side, plans-built project based on a design that Salvay had started but dropped. It first flew from Torrance Airport in 1959. Stark is retired from North American and lives in Anaheim, California.

**STORY, Jack B.**, worked for the Ford Reliability Tours as an announcer and public relations man in 1931 and 1932, and as a goodwill ambassador and announcer on the Midwest Rodeo circuit for Montgomery Ward & Co. during the Depression. He died in Dallas in 1967.

Royce S. Rearwin.

Robert W. Rummel. R. W. Rummel

Cable splicer Tony Slobodnick.
William E. Miller Family

**SUDENDORF, Blanche P.**, born in Toulon, Illinois, on August 30, 1875, died on October 13, 1934, at age 59. She and Edward had been married 24 years.

**SUDENDORF, Edward H.**, retired and sold his remaining interest in the Western Star Mill in 1932. He died in his home at 528 South Santa Fe Avenue, Salina, on December 31, 1951, two days after his 82 birthday.

**WEBBER, Douglas H.**, left Rearwin in 1935, two years prior to the certification of the Speedster, for a faculty position at Parks Air College, East St. Louis, Illinois. He taught there as a Professor of Engineering and Design until 1953.

**WEEKS, William Henry**, left Rearwin in 1937 and was Chief of the Aircraft Engineering Division for the Civil Aeronautics Authority in Kansas City, Missouri, until 1953. He then served as the Chief of the Federal Aviation Administration's Engineering and Manufacturing Division in Washington, D.C., until retiring in 1966 to become a consultant to several aircraft manufacturers. He obtained a commercial rating in 1939, and multi-engine and instrument ratings in 1944, logging over 2,500 hours in some 50 aircraft models. Weeks resides in Fort Smith, Arkansas.

George Stark. George Stark

Antique Airplane Association, Blakesburg, IA

# *Appendix B*

# The Rearwin Club 1960-1996

*THE "REARWIN CLUB" is currently organized under the mantle of the Antique Airplane Association (AAA) headquartered in Blakesburg, Iowa. It is dedicated to the preservation, restoration, and flying of Rearwin aircraft, including the Commonwealth Skyrangers built in 1945-1946. It also serves as a hub for the exchange of historical information, technical data, and news among the worldwide owners of Rearwin- and Commonwealth-built aircraft.*

*The Club was originally founded in 1960 by the late Robert E. "Pat" Patterson of Wichita, Kansas, then the owner of a Cloudster and a pair of Sportsters, one of which was being restored. Patterson had no pipeline to other Rearwin owners, so he wrote a brief article about the formation of the new type club and its goals which appeared in the December 1960 issue of the* ***Antique Airplane Association News****, then published by the AAA in Ottumwa, Iowa. The March 1961 issue of the* ***News*** *reported eight members, including Kenneth Rearwin and former Rearwin test pilot and flight instructor William E. "Bill" Miller. As of 1996, there were more than 150 members.*

*Miller quickly became one of the Rearwin Club's most devoted and enthusiastic supporters. He authored a nine-page article entitled "The Rearwin Story" for the June 1961* ***News*** *that stimulated interest in both the club and Rearwin aircraft. Over the next two years, Bill also wrote some 20 "Rearwin" columns for the* ***News****. Glenn Buffington, a*

From left, Ken and Royce Rearwin and Roy Good with son, at Blakesburg, Iowa, August 21, 1982.

former Rearwin Flying School student of Miller's, also wrote an article entitled "Rearwin Roster" that appeared in the May 1962 issue of *Sport Aviation* and increased interest in the vintage Rearwin designs.

Kansas City's Noel Gouldsmith, Jr. the owner of a multi-award-winning Cloudster, also authored a series of Rearwin articles for the *News* in the late 1960s, while Miller, Ken Rearwin and others arranged for a reunion of former Rearwin employees that was held in Kansas City on January 16, 1967. Cloudster owner George "Bald Eagle" Williams, of Portage, Wisconsin, and his brother Ken, the owner of a Sportster 9000KR, also carried the Rearwin banner to scores of Midwest fly-ins during the late 1960s and 1970s.

Miller's death in 1969 resulted in a brief period of inactivity, but Seattle's Ray Taylor, the brother of AAA founder Robert L. "Bob" Taylor and the owner of a Sportster (N18722) then under restoration, volunteered to coordinate club activities, including research and correspondence. He did so until his death in March 1973, while Williams continued to write for the *News*. The Sportster is now owned by Ray's nephew, Barry Taylor, and is based at Antique Airfield, Blakesburg.

Williams took charge again in 1974 and, with Gary Van Farowe serving as technical director, headed the Rearwin Club until 1977, publishing the *Rearwin Flyer*. Club member Roy Good purchased the aircraft type certificate (No. 711) for the Cloudster series, as well as the existing parts, tooling, and prints, from Reed Pigman's American Flyers in 1977. A year later he donated the Cloudster rights and parts to the Airpower Museum, Inc. Van Farowe was instrumental in inventorying the Cloudster blueprints and parts for the Museum. He still owns several Cloudsters and continues to assist Rearwin Club members with historical information and technical advice.

Another period of inactivity took place in the late 1970s. However, with the approval and support of brothers Royce and Ken Rearwin, the Rearwin Club formally associated with the Antique Airplane Association headed by Taylor in 1981, and the first issue of the *Rearwin Register* appeared in June. It is published about every nine or ten months and continues to serve as a source of news, assistance, and communication for Rearwin owners from Sweden to Australia. Publication is supported by the Rearwin family, subscriptions, and club memberships.

Roy Good and son Larry also purchased the rights, parts inventory, and much of the tooling and jigs for the Ken-Royce 90 and 120 hp engines from Pigman in the late 1970s. With financial participation from Ken Rearwin, the pair donated the engine rights and over 50,000 pounds of parts, tooling, and jigs to the Airpower Museum in 1982. Since then, the Museum has sold parts and provided technical data to the dwindling number of owners of the now scarce LeBlond and Ken-Royce engines.

The popularity of the increasingly rare Rearwin aircraft continues to grow as a new generation of antiquers "discover" the honest quality, performance, and safety engineered into the Rearwin designs of the 1930s and '40s. Rearwin aircraft are now prized possessions and, properly restored, are consistent award winners on the fly-in circuit.

Decades of support by the Rearwin family, as well as the continuing interest fostered by the Rearwin Club and aircraft owners, assures deserved recognition and survival of the breed. The Rearwin Club and Airpower Museum are headquartered at Antique Airfield, P.O. Box 127, Blakesburg, Iowa 52536.

Above: Rearwin Club alumni at the 1968 reunion — Maurice Shay, Jack LeClaire, Troy Keys, Wesley Pipes, Kelsey Chaney, and Bob Faris. Jack LeClaire

Left: Ken Rearwin, Noel Gouldsmith, Jr., Bill Miller, and Antique Airplane Association founder Robert W. Taylor at the first "Rearwin Reunion" held in Kansas City on January 16, 1968.
Antique Airplane Association, Blakesburg, IA

Roy Good, Moore, Oklahoma, flew this 1940 Cloudster Model 8135 with "wheel fenders" on the Midwest fly-in circuit. This photo was taken at Ottumwa, Iowa, in 1970. Rearwin Club

This 1939 Cloudster was owned and flown for many years by the late George Williams, Portage, Wisconsin. Rearwin Club

Bill Haselton finished restoring this Sportster (N14485) in August 1964. Rearwin Club

George W. Genevro, Carlsbad, California, and Ron Bell owned this 1941 Skyranger 175, N32402, in 1988. A Lycoming 0-235C engine was installed in 1963. Rearwin Club

This 1940 Cloudster 8135 about to touch down at Daniels Field, Harrisburg, Oregon, in 1984, was then owned by Hal and Carol Skinner, Springfield, Oregon. Rearwin Club

Noel Gouldsmith, Jr., Independence, Missouri, custom-painted his Cloudster, a regular on the Midwest fly-in circuit. Rearwin Club

Don't be fooled by the sign. The aircraft is a Commonwealth Skyranger 185, NC93280, SN1845, built at Valley Stream, Long Island, New York, in 1946. It was owned by Richard D. Denkema when this photo was taken at Antique Airfield in 1974. Rearwin Club

Ken (right) visited with New Zealand Sportster owner J. Nixon in 1987.

"Bob" Rummel, former chief engineer at Rearwin, donated this kiosk to the San Diego Aerospace Museum; Ken Rearwin is at the right.

Alan Buchner, Fresno, California, restored and still owns this 1936 Rearwin Sportster. Rearwin Club

A 1938 Menasco-powered Speedster owned by R. O. Bevins, Hinsdale, Illinois, when photographed.
Antique Airplane Association, Blakesburg, ia

This Sportster, owned by Ken and Shirley Williams, was photographed at Antique Airfield, Blakesburg, Iowa.
Antique Airplane Association, Blakesburg, IA

Sportster designer Henry Weeks and Ken Rearwin posed with a Cloudster at Bartlesville, OK, *circa* 1987.

The Sportster prototype is owned by the Airpower Museum, Inc.
Antique Airplane Association, Blakesburg, IA

The last known remaining Rearwin Junior was owned and flown by Marion McClure, Bloomington, Illinois, before sale to Oscar Cooke.
Antique Airplane Association, Blakesburg, IA

This Rearwin 9000 Sportster was owned by Ken Jerolman when the photo was taken.
Thomas S. Cuddy, II

Walt Lepson's Sportster was photographed on final approach.
Ira Ward

Royce Rearwin (right) with Skyranger at the Liberal, Kansas, aviation museum, 1982.

Antique Airplane Association President Bob Taylor owned this Sportster (NC20746) when the photo was taken at Amana, Iowa, in November 1958.
Antique Airplane Association, Blakesburg, IA

Rearwin Skyranger Model 190F, owned by Lyle Laughlin of Pittsburg, Kansas, was photographed at the 1989 Antique Airplane Association Fly-in held in Bartlesville, Oklahoma.
Antique Airplane Association, Blakesburg, IA

Ken Rearwin presents an award to Cloudster owner Bill Ammentorp, Houston, Texas, at the 1989 AAA National Fly-in.
Antique Airplane Association, Blakesburg, IA

*Appendix C*

# Rearwin Factory Brochures, Aircraft Specifications, and Articles

**Contents**

# *The* KEN-ROYCE

DIMENSIONS

| | |
|---|---|
| Overall Length | 25 ft. |
| Maximum Height | 9 ft. 11 in. |
| Overall Span | 35 ft. |
| Total Wing Area | 300 sq. ft. |

CONSTRUCTION

Fuselage—Welded Chrome Molybdenum and Carbon Steel Tubing.

Wings—Spars of Laminated Spruce, not routed; Ribs of Spruce capstrips and Basswood webs; solid web Drag Ribs with compression member of Spruce at top and bottom capstrip; leading edge of formed Spruce covered with Birch plywood; trailing edge of formed sheet Duraluminum; wing tips of curved steel tubing; wing fittings cadium plated; wings fabric covered.

Tail Surfaces—Welded steel channels and tubes.

Landing Gears—Bendix wheels and brakes with Rearwin Special air-oil shock absorbers. Tail skid or wheel optional.

Ailerons—Friese type on upper wing only.

Fin—Welded direct to fuselage.

Stabilizer—Adjustable from pilots cockpit.

Controls—All controls masts are internal. The elevators are operated by push-pull tubes; the rudder by flexible cables; the ailerons by torque tubes and flexible cables. No pulleys are used. Dual controls may be installed if desired.

POWER PLANT

Curtiss Challenger Motor, 6 cyl., air-cooled, radial, 170 H. P., 1800 r. p. m.

FUEL DATA

| | |
|---|---|
| Gasoline Capacity (upper wing) | 20 gal. |
| Gasoline Capacity (fuselage) | 30 gal. |
| Oil Capacity | 5 gal. |

EQUIPMENT

Instruments: Pioneer.
Tail Skid or Wheel optional.
Rearwin Special Air-oil Shock Absorbers.
Navigation Lights built into the tips of upper wings.
Starter—Optional.

LOAD

| | |
|---|---|
| Weight Empty | 1415 lbs. |
| Useful Load | 885 lbs. |
| Pay Load | 374 lbs. |
| Gross Weight Loaded | 2300 lbs. |

PERFORMANCE

| | |
|---|---|
| High Speed (full load) | 130 m. p. h. |
| High Speed (pilot alone) | 135 m. p. h. |
| Cruising Speed (full load) | 107 m. p. h. |
| Landing Speed (full load) | 45 m. p. h. |
| Cruising Range (full load) | 550 miles |
| Climb at Sea Level (full load) | 1000 ft. per min |
| Climb to 10,000 ft. (full load) | 17 min. 15 sec. |
| Take off Time (pilot alone) | 5 1/5 sec. |
| Take off Time (full load) | 8 2/5 sec. |
| Absolute Ceiling (full load) | 24,000 ft. |

*All tests made with same setting of propeller and no wind.*

**REARWIN AIRPLANES**
*INC.*
FAIRFAX AIRPORT
**KANSAS CITY**
U.S.A.

THE Rearwin Ken-Royce, a three-place Biplane, is the result of careful refinement of design rather than radical departure from conventional practice. Its distinctive, clean-cut lines appeal at once to the casual observer. If you are one who flies you will be impressed with the unusual visibility from either cockpit, the comfortably arranged controls, and its remarkable performance. The low parasite resistance of the Ken-Royce makes it a fast and economical means of transportation. In take-off, climb, speed or maneuverability, it will out-perform any ship in its class. A flight will convince you.

A Beautiful Ship—Master of the Airways—Safe—Comfortable—Extremely Fast

# REARWIN KEN-ROYCE

## *The Aristocrat of the Air*

## A 3-Place Biplane of Outstanding Achievements

Intensive value marks Rearwin Ken-Royce apart as the irresistible buy among planes of its class of fineness and brilliant record. Built to a high standard of engineering, its record has proven its airworthiness. Clean cut, distinctive lines, with parasite resistance reduced to a minimum, feature this beautiful airplane.

The Rearwin Ken-Royce flies so perfectly that the pilot feels at home instantly and will exclaim at its remarkable performance. It is built with the greatest care in every detail. All materials are the very best of their kind. It is custom built. The beauty of the Ken-Royce is outstanding . . . its trim, streamlined appearance attracts attention on every airport. The stability and controllability of the Ken-Royce are exceptional. To the lover of sport it holds interest with its speed. To the conservative it appeals with its gentle landings at 35 miles per hour. Economical in operation, outstanding in performance, beautiful in appearance, the Ken-Royce is the biggest "buy" in fine airplanes today.

## Winner of Over 100 Performance Tests

**Ken-Royce stock airplanes have won more than 100 first prizes, including the National Race from Miami, Florida, to Cleveland during the 1929 National Air Races; The Sportman's Pilots Race at Chicago during the 1930 National Air Race Meet; Free for all Pony Express Race and the race over Pike's Peak, an altitude of more than 14,000 feet, at the 1930 Colorado Springs Race Meet, an outstanding proof of Ken-Royce superiority at altitudes of from one to three miles.**

### REARWIN KEN-ROYCE FACTS IN BRIEF

*Dimensions*

| | |
|---|---|
| Overall Length | 25 ft. |
| Maximum Height | 9 ft., 6 ins. |
| Overall Span | 35 ft. |
| Total Wing Area | 300 sq. ft. |

*Construction*

*Fuselage*—Welded chrome molybdenum and carbon steel tubing.
*Wings*—Spars of laminated spruce; leading edge of formed spruce covered with birch plywood; trailing edge of formed sheet Duraluminum; wing tips of curved steel tubing; wings fittings cadium plated; wings fabric covered.
*Tail Surfaces*—Welded channels and tubes.
*Landing Gears*—Bendix wheels and brakes with Rearwin Special rubber and oil shock absorbers. Semi-air wheels and tail wheel may be installed if desired.
*Ailerons*—Friese type on upper wings only.
*Stabilizer*—Adjustable.
*Controls*—All control masts are internal. The elevators are operated by push-pull tubes; the rudder by flexible cables; the ailerons by torque tubes and flexible cables. No pulleys are used.

*Instruments*—Pioneer
Navigation lights built into tips of upper wings.

*Power Plant*
Continental, Curtiss Challenger, Kinner and Wright engines.

*Fuel Data*

| | |
|---|---|
| Gasoline Capacity (upper wing) | 20 gals. |
| Gasoline Capacity (fuselage) | 35 gals. |
| Oil Capacity | 5 gals. |

*Load*

| | |
|---|---|
| Weight, Empty | 1495 lbs. |
| Useful Load | 885 lbs. |
| Pay Load | 355 lbs. |
| Gross Weight, Loaded | 2380 lbs. |

*Performance With 170 H. P. Engine*

| | |
|---|---|
| High Speed | 137 M.P.H. |
| Cruising Speed | 115 M.P.H. |
| Landing Speed | 35 M.P.H. |
| Cruising Range | 500 Miles |
| Climb at Sea Level | 1,000 ft. per Minute |
| Climb to 10,000 feet | 17 Min., 15 Sec. |
| Take-off Time | 5 1/5 Sec. |
| Absolute Ceiling | 22,000 ft. |

# REARWIN AIRPLANES INC.

FAIRFAX AIRPORT KANSAS CITY, KANSAS

# *The* REARWIN "JUNIOR"

## *Brings a New Day to Aviation*

### FLY FOR A CENT A MILE

The Rearwin Jr. is an inexpensive airplane of outstanding quality, built to meet the ever-increasing demand for a plane with desired performance to sell at a very low price. Picture an airplane of about one-third the weight of the old type plane made possible by skilled engineering and new materials of great strength. It is an efficient, chummy, two-place tandem monoplane that can be operated much cheaper than an automobile—an outstanding achievement in the Rearwin Jr.

We have put forth an extreme effort to construct a superior airplane. We built into it the conveniences which we knew would be appreciated. That is why the Rearwin Jr. has a baggage compartment, adjustable stabilizer which may be operated from either seat, removable dual controls, rugged extra-wide landing gear with air wheels and shock absorbers, front and rear individual wind shields, perfect visibility and spacious comfortable seats with plenty of leg room. Strength and safety are added by substantially welding the seats to the fuselage. This superior quality of construction adds life and safety, which are most important elements to be considered in the purchase of an airplane.

Because of its remarkably sturdy construction, superb flying characteristics and exceptionally slow landing speed, it can be brought down with safety in a very small field. Its quick take-off is also exceptional, adding much safety to flying. It possesses almost unbelievable performance, stability, and economy of operation. The

stability of the Rearwin Jr. enables it to be flown mile after mile with hands off control, and the many undesirable flying characteristics that are so common to airplanes have been eliminated.

The Rearwin Jr. is built for cross country flying, with its liberal gas capacity and small fuel consumption, frequent landings for refueling are unnecessary. It is a real airplane, an airplane of sterling worth and value. It is ideal for sport flying and student training. The upkeep is low. One can learn to fly in much less time in the Rearwin Jr. and at a much lower cost per hour. In every detail it is designed to make flying and servicing by the owner as inexpensive as possible.

Another outstanding feature of the Rearwin Jr. is the center section which allows the stress to be carried through it in a way that makes possible the installation of a very wide door. No struts or cross members interfere with pilot or passenger entering the Rearwin Jr. with or without parachute.

This plane is conceived and constructed by the same organization which produced the famous Ken-Royce, the winner of over 100 performance tests. The Rearwin Jr. is just as outstanding in its class as is the Rearwin Ken-Royce in the field of higher priced planes.

You will appreciate, too, the new detachable winter inclosure which is available at only slight additional cost. With it you can enjoy the Junior as an open plane in the summer and as a warm, comfortable cabin plane in the winter. This inclosure may be quickly installed or detached.

To appreciate the extreme value of this plane, it must be seen and flown. You will admire its clean cut lines and advanced streamlining, and you will marvel at its remarkable performance. Then you will want to own one of these smart, inexpensive planes. Think of the pleasure and profit derived from a Rearwin Jr. You can travel anywhere in it with safety and ease. The whole country becomes your back yard. With its low price and low operating cost (about one cent per mile), many people are enjoying benefits of air travel.

## Rearwin "Junior" Facts

Conventional design.
Power plant—Aeromarine 50 h.p. or Szekely 45 or 50 h.p.
Cut-a-way center section for better visibility.
Easily entered, roomy and comfortable.
Baggage compartment.
Dual controls easily removable.
Stabilizer adjustable from either seat.
Front and rear individual wind shields.
Beautiful finish in attractive colors.
Rugged, wide landing gear, 72" tread, shocks, air wheels.
Gasoline capacity—12 gallons.
Weight—583 lbs.
Wing surface area total—182 sq. ft.

DIMENSIONS

Length ........ 21′ 8″
Span ........ 36′
Height ........ 7′ 6″

PERFORMANCE

Take-off ........ 7 seconds
Landing speed ........ 25 miles
Climb ........ 700 feet per minute
Cruising speed ........ 78 miles per hour
Top speed ........ 91 miles per hour
Cruising radius ........ 3½ hours
Gas consumption ........ 3½ gals. per hour
Absolute ceiling ........ 16,400 ft.

DEALERS

The high quality and low price of the Rearwin Jr. has increased its market materially. Backed by Rearwin Airplanes, Inc., established four years ago, financial stability is assured.

# LEARN TO FLY!

## *only $75.00*

The REARWIN FLYING COURSE is the easiest and the most practical. There are many reasons for this claim. The famous REARWIN JR., used in training students, is the simplest and easiest airplane to handle. It is remarkably responsive—easy to control, dependable always.

The Rearwin Flying School is a subsidiary of the Rearwin Airplanes, Inc. With this close affiliation you gain the advantage of observation and practical experience in the fundamentals of airplane construction in an airplane factory. To every individual interested in flying this is indeed a wonderful advantage.

# *Easy to Learn to Fly*

The average person has all the qualifications to fly successfully—after our course of instruction. There is no secret to flying—the principles are as simple as A, B, C, once you master the fundamentals. Flying an airplane is just as simple as driving an automobile without the traffic hazards.

Once you learn the simple controls you have unlimited confidence in your ability as a pilot. All this has been proven, in countless cases, with REARWIN instruction. This instruction is tremendously fascinating. Your interest increases each day until your course is completed, at which time you are qualified to apply for the government license you desire — Private Pilot, Limited Commercial or Transport.

NOTE: If you desire a Transport License it will be to your advantage to own a REARWIN JR., for you will "build up" your time at the lowest possible cost.

The Rearwin Jr., *which can be flown for about 1c per mile,* is the most economical airplane to operate.

# THE FAMOUS REARWIN Jr.

***Used exclusively in training Students--- the most desirable and easiest to fly***

The Rearwin Course of Instruction is simplicity itself. You learn easily and quickly under the guidance of experts. They have the ability to convey instruction in a manner that makes everything easy to understand.

***You get Training in Primary and Advanced Flying as Follows:***

| | |
|---|---|
| Take-Offs | Stalls |
| Straight and Horizontal | Fish-Tails |
| Turn and Banks | Spirals and Spins |
| Glides | Landings |
| Climbing Turns | Forced Landings |
| Side-Slips | Solo |

*Our airplanes are licensed by the United States Department of Commerce and inspected daily by licensed mechanics.*

Our instructors have had long experience and their sole interest is in your development as a pilot. The Rearwin Jr. is the most practical airplane for instruction and training purposes.

There are several fundamental reasons for making this statement. The Rearwin Jr. takes off so quickly and lands so slowly that a beginner immediately finds himself "at home." It is a chummy airplane. The instructor can talk to the student and give him all the main points while flying. This is a big asset in mastering the art of flying quickly and naturally.

The Rearwin Jr. is enclosed for cold weather flying, enabling students to fly the year around. Our school is located at Fairfax Airport, the crossroads of the air, on one of America's best equipped airports. This affords unusual opportunities.

Rearwin instruction fits students for all licenses, and you receive the added advantage of training at our large manufacturing plant where the Rearwin Airplanes are built.

# 37% INCREASE IN AIRPLANE TRANSPORTATION IN 1932!

The newspapers have given wide publicity to the great increase in airplane transportation in 1932 compared to the year before and other years. This increase, in a year of sluggish business in other industries, is the best evidence that air transportation has definitely taken its place as a great phase of American activity.

The future of aviation is assured! This expansion is a prelude to still greater expansion. The demand for experienced men as mechanics and pilots will become greater and greater. Rearwin Instruction is "in tune with the times." The cost is low but the training is most comprehensive and complete. The great days ahead for air transportation—the development of the airplane for personal and commercial uses, all mean exceptional opportunities for trained men.

All instruction is under the same experts responsible for the success of our manufacturing organization—technicians, mechanics, engineers, pilots, etc.

*. . . . For Further Information Write Us . . . .*

## Rearwin Flying School Corporation

**Fairfax Airport** **Kansas City, U. S. A.**

FACTORY OF REARWIN AIRPLANES, INC., AND REARWIN FLYING SCHOOL.

# REARWIN "JUNIOR" OWNERS ARE SATISFIED OWNERS

AFTER you have purchased a plane it is too late to look around and see if perhaps some other make wasn't a better buy. Look now, carefully. And look at the Rearwin "Junior," a normal powered airplane. See for yourself why every owner of this new and finer airplane is so satisfied with his choice.

Here is a product which represents true value—from basic design to the finished job. The Rearwin "Junior" is built around an unusually sturdy fuselage. Its landing gear, also, is the most rugged for an airplane of its size. An approved type 45 h.p. motor gives the "Junior" a source of reserve power which, as a rule, is obtainable only in larger craft.

A few of the features which recommend the Rearwin "Junior" to the prospective plane owner are: cutaway center section which provides perfect visibility, dual controls, full-size tandem cockpit, semi-airwheels, shock absorbers, perfect streamline, rich finish, cent-a-mile operating cost, 72-inch landing gear, luggage compartment, stabilizer adjustable from both seats, and performance far above anything in its class.

Make a note of these details and remember them when you compare the "Junior" with other low-priced airplanes. Wing spars of spruce, center section leading edge of formed spruce covered with birch plywood. Trailing edge of formed sheet duralumin. Wing tips of covered steel tubing. Wing fittings cadmium plated. Welded chrome molybdenum and carbon steel tubing. Wing span 36 feet, length 21 feet 8 inches, height 7 feet 6 inches. Weight empty 525 lbs., loaded 1,025 lbs. Wing loading 5.55 lbs. Power loading 22.5 lbs. And performance! Take-off in 7 seconds. Climb 700 feet per minute. Top speed 100 m.p.h. Cruising radius 400 miles.

We will be pleased to point out to interested dealers how the low price of the Rearwin "Junior" will increase their market materially.

**REARWIN AIRPLANES, Inc.**
FAIRFAX AIRPORT - KANSAS CITY - KANSAS

## THE REARWIN "JUNIOR"

From *Aero Digest*, August 1931.

# REARWIN *Speedster*

**LIST PRICE $3,295.00**

*Model 6000*

THE New Rearwin Speedster is indeed a masterpiece! Three years have been spent in perfecting its design to combine speed and advanced streamlining with comfort, safety, and ease of control. We have at last achieved an airplane of distinguished beauty and classic harmony. Symmetry is in every line of the clean, graceful fuselage. Fine craftsmanship is apparent in every detail.

The aristocratic modeling of the Speedster is not for the eye alone, however. In keeping with its ultramodern appearance is its speed. Like a slim arrow, the Speedster offers a minimum of wind resistance but the ultimate in performance. The in-line, inverted motor is completely concealed by a streamlined cowling which adds materially to the speed and enhances the beauty of the entire design. The powerful engine assures quick take-off and responsiveness at all times to your every touch. The unusually wide 70-inch landing gear is freed from all struts and wires by the application of a new, exclusive principle. As "knee action" guarantees smooth riding to the automobile, so the Speedster's special landing gear assures stability and smoothness in landing. To facilitate speed and to add to attractiveness, the wheels and landing gear have also been cleverly streamlined.

Close scrutiny of details on the Speedster only increases one's admiration. Within each wing is skillfully placed a 17-gallon gasoline tank of reinforced aluminum. The mechanism of the controls is concealed beneath the floorboard. The cowling is stamped out of a single piece of light, firm, durable aluminum. Non-friction ball bearings of quality reduce wear on controls and increase the smoothness and ease of operation. The Speedster's comfortable tandem seats, unmarred visibility, responsive con-

*The new Fire-Proof Factory occupied exclusively by REARWIN AIRPLANES.* 30,000 *square feet of floor space. One of America's most efficient Airplane manufacturing establishments. Your Rearwin Airplane cannot become an "Orphan". This is our eighth year of successful manufacturing.*

trols, rich upholstery and lining, and perfectly appointed instrument panel answer the demands of the most fastidious.

The Speedster is the spirit of strength, speed, and modern artistry. Comfort is unsurpassed, ease of operation revolutionary, economy unbelievable, safety features paramount. The Speedster is an easy to fly, easy to land, safe airplane.

We offer a choice of two reliable motors. With the 95 h. p. Cirrus inverted, the Speedster flies much faster than any other two place commercial airplane of similar horse power. The 125 h. p. inverted Menasco gives still finer performance.

To those who make their selection with careful discrimination and are seeking for the utmost in streamlined design combined with comfort and outstanding performance, we confidently introduce the New REARWIN SPEEDSTER.

## SPECIFICATIONS

**Rearwin Speedster, Model 6000**
**Powered with 95 H.P. Inline Inverted Cirrus Engine and 125 H.P. Inline Inverted Menasco Engine**

| | Menasco | Cirrus |
|---|---|---|
| Wing Span | 32 ft. | 32 ft. |
| Length Overall | 22 ft. 2 in. | 22 ft. 2 in. |
| Height Overall | 6 ft. 8 in. | 6 ft. 8 in. |
| Wing Area | 145 sq. ft. | 145 sq. ft. |
| Power Loading | 13.4 lbs. per h.p. | 17.4 lbs. per h.p. |
| Wing Loading | 11.50 lbs. per sq. ft. | 11.50 lbs. per sq. ft. |
| Empty Weight | 1052 lbs. | 1052 lbs. |
| Useful Load | 616 lbs. | 616 lbs. |
| Pay Load | 220 lbs. | 220 lbs. |
| Gross Weight | 1668 lbs. | 1668 lbs. |
| Fuel Capacity | 34 gallons | 34 gallons |
| Oil Capacity | 2.5 gallons | 2.5 gallons |
| Maximum Speed | 166 miles per hr. | 144 miles per hr. |
| Cruising Speed | 140 miles per hr. | 120 miles per hr. |
| Landing Speed | 46 miles per hr. | 46 miles per hr. |
| Rate of Climb | 750 ft. per minute | 600 ft. per minute |
| Cruising Range | 600 miles | 600 miles |

| | |
|---|---|
| Airspeed Indicator | Dual Controls |
| Compass | Brakes |
| Altimeter | Fire Extinguisher |
| Tachometer | Tail Wheel |
| Oil Pressure Gauge | First Aid Kit |
| Oil Temperature Gauge | Cabin Door Lock—Yale-Type |
| Switch | Upholstered Cabin |
| 2 Fuel Gauges | 50-lb. Luggage Compartment |

Adjustable Front Seat

# REARWIN AIRPLANES

FAIRFAX AIRPORT KANSAS CITY, U. S. A.

***Eight years of Successful Airplane Manufacturing***

Represented by

# *The* REARWIN *Sportster*

LIST PRICE $2,095.00

*Model 7000—A. T. C. 574 and Model 8500—A. T. C. 591*

## Oustanding Appearance, Performance, Economy, Comfort, Safety, Long Life

THE REARWIN SPORTSTER is designed to meet the demands of thousands of fliers—it is not built to meet a price. All the years of Rearwin experience and engineering skill are back of this new plane. It represents the very latest in modernistic lines—a beautiful sport model that has won immediate approval from coast to coast.

You will be impressed with the high quality of the Rearwin Sportster. It has all the refinements which are looked for in a much higher priced airplane, even to such a small detail as the Yale-type lock on the door. Fliers everywhere are delighted with the Sportster's clean, graceful lines and streamlined contour from rounded nose to tapering rudder; with its narrow fuselage and sturdy hydraulic landing gear. The smooth lustrous finish is outstanding. The Rearwin Sportster is styled in the tempo of the most expensive planes.

A specially designed stabilizer adjustment and carefully analyzed balancing of weight assures easier dual and solo flying, "hands off," from either comfortable seat. The Sportster's reserve power and great lift will take you safely in and out of small fields even in high altitudes and over the highest mountain ranges in the United States. It will carry you four hundred seventy-five miles in four and three-quarters hours on 24 gallons of gasoline. But you, yourself, must fly the Rearwin Sportster before you can fully appreciate all of its splendid flying characteristics.

Think of it—Twenty miles to a gallon of gasoline! And oil consumption is remarkably low! Tires will last for hundreds of hours. It is actually much cheaper to fly a Sportster than to drive a car! In the same length of time, you travel *twice as fast,* cover *three times the distance,* and have ten times the fun!

No gymnastics on entering or leaving, for the Sportster has V-type wing struts. Its commodious cabin is one in which you can ride with complete relaxation the entire day and feel fit as a fiddle when you emerge. You'll appreciate the wide, high-backed, comfortably upholstered seats that provide head, shoulder, and leg room for everyone, even the tallest. You'll be delighted with the convenience of two baggage compartments which provide for 50 pounds of luggage including a full sized Gladstone bag. You'll like the large, double-slide windows which enable you to regulate ventilation, and the green Pyralin ceiling which eliminates uncomfortable heat and glare from the sun's rays. The unsightly gasoline tank, usually found in front of the pilot in airplanes of this price class, has been removed. This saving in space increases leg room and permits the placing of the instrument panel well forward, leaving a place for a convenient map shelf. Best of all, in the Sportster's quiet cabin, you can easily converse with your companion in natural tones.

The Sportster, a medium weight airplane of over 1400 pounds, is ideal for everyone to fly. Rapid take-off, remarkably slow landing, 70-inch tread Hydraulic Landing gear, unusual stability in rough air, visibility in every direction, aileron and rudder control even in absolute stalls, five cylinder dual ignition dependability in all kinds of weather—all of these make the Rearwin Sportster a marvelous airplane for school work, sport flying, or business use. Better balance, perfected visibility, and greatly increased safety are decided advantages gained by having the 24-gallon gasoline tanks built right into the wings. Two gas tanks equipped with reliable gauges inside the cabin add dependability just as do the twin magnetos; and front and rear outlets from each tank guarantee an unfailing flow of gasoline, nose up or down.

The Rearwin Sportster is built to give lasting service. The oil and springs of the streamlined hydraulic landing gear absorb the shocks and bumps of rough fields and naturally lengthen the life of the ship. In the wings, Chrome-Moly X braces, to which the lift struts are attached, give great rigidity and unusual strength. The extra heavy guage aluminum gasoline and oil tanks represent the utmost skill in aluminum welding—leaks are unknown. All cowling, the cabin, seats and seat backs, wing leading and trailing edges, are of genuine aluminum or dural. V-type struts brace each other and prevent vibration. Bushings are generously used to prevent wear. The Sportster's covering is of strongly-woven, grade A fabric, painted with many coats of finest "dope" and pigment. This high quality finish will last for years under any weather condition.

The Rearwin Sportster is a low priced airplane, costing little to fly. It is just what the flying public wants. See your nearest Rearwin Representative, or write us at the factory.

## SPECIFICATIONS

**Rearwin Sportster, Models 7000 and 8500**
**A. T. C. No. 574**
**Powered with 70 H.P. and 85 H.P. LeBlond Engines**

| | 70 H.P. | 85 H.P. |
|---|---|---|
| Wing Span | 35 ft. | 35 ft. |
| Length Overall | 22.3 ft. | 22.3 ft. |
| Height Overall | 6.75 ft. | 6.75 ft. |
| Wing Area (Effective) | 166 sq. ft. | 166 sq. ft. |
| Power Loading | 20.14 lbs. per h.p. | 16.6 lbs. per h.p. |
| Wing Loading | 8.50 lbs. per sq. ft. | 8.50 lbs. per sq. ft. |
| Empty Weight | 853 lbs. | 830 lbs. |
| Useful Load | 557 lbs. | 580 lbs. |
| Pay Load | 220 lbs. | 220 lbs. |
| Gross Weight | 1410 lbs. | 1410 lbs. |
| Fuel Capacity | 24 gallons | 24 gallons |
| Oil Capacity | 2 gallons | 2 gallons |
| Maximum Speed | 110 miles per hr. | 116 miles per hr. |
| Cruising Speed | 98 miles per hr. | 103 miles per hr. |
| Landing Speed | 35 miles per hr. | 35 miles per hr. |
| Rate of Climb, Full Load | 625 ft. per min. | 700 ft. per minute |
| Cruising Range | 475 miles | 475 miles |
| Length of Take Off Run | 280 ft. | 250 ft. |
| Take Off | 10 seconds | 8 seconds |
| Wheels | 7.00 x 4 | 7.00 x 4 |

## STANDARD EQUIPMENT

| | |
|---|---|
| Collector Ring | First Aid Kit |
| Altimeter | Cabin Door Lock—Yale-Type |
| Tachometer | 2 Luggage Compartments—50 lbs. |
| Oil Pressure Gauge | Dual Controls |
| Oil Temperature Gauge | Hydraulic Landing Gear |
| Switch | Wired for Navigation Lights |
| 2 Fuel Gauges | Safety Belts |
| Fire Extinguisher | Fuselage Lining |

Cushions and Seat Backs

## SPECIAL EQUIPMENT

**With Sportster Models 7000 and 8500**

Goodyear 18x8x3 Wheels and Brakes or
Bendix Wheels and Brakes with General Streamline Tires

| | |
|---|---|
| Navigation Lights | Carburetor Heater |
| Speed Ring | Tail Wheel |
| Battery | Special Instruments |

*Convenient Time Payment Plan is Available*

PRICE $3,895.00

# REARWIN SPEEDSTER–Model 6000M

THE NEW REARWIN SPEEDSTER is indeed a masterpiece! Its perfected design combines speed and advanced streamlining with comfort, safety, and ease of control. We have at last achieved an airplane of distinguished beauty and classic harmony. Symmetry is in every line of the clean, graceful fuselage. Fine craftsmanship is apparent in every detail.

The aristocratic modeling of the Speedster is not for the eye alone, however. In keeping with its ultra-modern appearance is its speed. Like a slim arrow, the Speedster offers a minimum of wind resistance but the ultimate in performance. The in-line, inverted motor is completely concealed by a streamlined cowling which adds materially to the speed and enhances the beauty of the entire design. The powerful engine assures quick take-off and responsiveness at all times to your every touch. The unusually wide 70-inch landing gear is freed from all struts and wires by the application of a new, exclusive principle. As "knee action" guarantees smooth riding to the automobile, so the Speedster's special landing gear assures stability and smoothness in landing. To facilitate speed and to add to attractiveness, the wheels and landing gear have also been cleverly streamlined.

Close scrutiny of details on the Speedster only increases one's admiration. Within each wing is skillfully placed a 17-gallon gasoline tank of reinforced aluminum. The mechanism of the controls is concealed beneath the floorboard. Non-friction ball bearings of quality reduce wear on controls and increase the smoothness and ease of operation. The cowling is stamped out of a single piece of light, firm, durable aluminum. The Speedster's comfortable tandem seats, unmarred visibility, responsive controls, rich upholstery and lining, and perfectly appointed instrument panel answer the demands of the most fastidious.

The Speedster is the spirit of strength, speed, and modern artistry. Comfort is unsurpassed, ease of operation revolutionary, economy unbelievable, safety features paramount. The Speedster is an easy to fly, easy to land, safe airplane.

With the 125 h.p. Menasco inverted, the Speedster flies much faster than any other two place commercial airplane of similar horsepower.

To those who make their selection with careful discrimination and are seeking for the utmost in streamlined design combined with comfort and outstanding performance, we confidently introduce the New REARWIN SPEEDSTER.

## SPECIFICATIONS

**Rearwin Speedster, Model 6000M**
**Powered with 125 h.p. Inline Inverted Menasco Engine**

| | Menasco |
|---|---|
| Wing Span | 32 ft. |
| Length Overall | 22 ft. 2 in. |
| Height Overall | 6 ft. 8 in. |
| Wing Area | 145 sq. ft. |
| Power Loading | 13.4 lbs. h.p. |
| Wing Loading | 11.50 lbs. sq. ft. |
| Empty Weight | 1052 lbs. |
| Useful Load | 616 lbs. |
| Pay Load | 220 lbs. |
| Gross Weight | 1668 lbs. |
| Fuel Capacity | 34 gallons |
| Oil Capacity | 2.5 gallons |
| Maximum Speed | 166 miles per hr. |
| Cruising Speed | 140 miles per hr. |
| Landing Speed | 48 miles per hr. |
| Rate of Climb | 750 ft. per minute |
| Cruising Range | 600 miles |

| | |
|---|---|
| Airspeed Indicator | Dual Controls |
| Compass | Brakes |
| Altimeter | Fire Extinguisher |
| Tachometer | Tail Wheel |
| Oil Pressure Gauge | First Aid Kit |
| Oil Temperature Gauge | Cabin Door Lock—Yale-Type |
| Switch | Upholstered Cabin |
| 2 Fuel Gauges | 50-lb. Luggage Compartment |

Adjustable Front Seat

# REARWIN AIRPLANES

FAIRFAX AIRPORT *Established 1927* KANSAS CITY, U. S. A.

Represented by

**Model 8090—Ken Royce 90 H.P.**
**$3,495.00**

**Model 8125—Ken Royce 120 H.P.**
**$3,995.00**

# *The Rearwin Cloudster* » » » »

## A NEW HIGH IN AIRPLANE VALUE

SPORTSMAN pilots and business executives have long desired a high performance, 2 or 3-place side-by-side cabin airplane combining great utility with moderate price.

Flying school operators have also wanted an inherently safe, side-by-side "all-around" airplane for instruction, cross country training, and fast inexpensive charter service. The Rearwin Cloudster is the answer. A handsome, streamlined airplane with the latest refinements, ruggedly built to surpass the most rigid specifications, yet the Cloudster handles as smooth as silk.

On the ground or in the air, the Cloudster's streamlined design and mirror-like rubbed finish are bound to catch and hold your attention. And the Cloudster assures you of safe, comfortable air transportation at speeds up to more than two miles a minute at a cost of less than one cent per passenger mile.

Careful construction in our large modern factory by skilled workmen using the finest materials available guarantees long life with low maintenance costs and slight depreciation.

Full equipment is standard on the Cloudster—there is nothing else to buy. We are proud of the Cloudster—a worthy addition to the Rearwin line.

### ☆ *Performance*

Fine performance is important in an airplane. And when you fly a Cloudster, you enjoy performance no other airplane in its price class can match. The Cloudster has a Ken-Royce engine—the greatest assurance of performance that any airplane can have. The Cloudster performs so marvelously that every hour at the controls is a memorable experience. Just take the stick of a new Cloudster and learn for yourself why the pilot's seat is always in demand. You'll appreciate the quick, eager response to the throttle—the fine balance and handling ease. A comparison of horsepower in relation to weight and wing area will show you why the Cloudster's performance is so phenomenal. There's reserve power for small fields, high altitudes, or hot weather.

While it is unusually stable and safe for amateurs to fly, the Cloudster is a real cross country airplane. It will carry you along at cruising speeds up to 125 miles per hour, depending on horsepower and model, and has a range of well over 600 miles, thus eliminating frequent stops for fuel. And when you do come into a field, you'll be surprised how slowly the Cloudster lands.

### ☆ *Comfort*

The Rearwin Cloudster is one of the most comfortable airplanes on the market, regardless of price. The large cabin is easily entered from either side through wide, solid doors, each equipped with smoothly sliding windows. Its spacious interior provides complete relaxation and enjoyment. Your family, friends, and business associates will enjoy the Cloudster's roominess, comfort, and easy riding qualities plus its beautiful, long wearing upholstery and luxurious appointments. They'll also like the wide, level floor and such conveniences as clever assist cords and ash tray. The smart instrument panel with walnut grain finish increases the attractiveness of the interior. And all instruments are carefully arranged so that they are clearly visible to both pilot and passenger. Dual sticks, placed well

*The 42 inch wide cabin is unusually comfortable with head, shoulder and leg room for everyone. Upholstering is of the finest, while cushions and seat backs have soft air-foam padding.*

*The eighty inch tread gear guarantees perfect control on the ground, and the oil and spring shock absorbers with seven inch travel insure feather-soft landings.*

forward and gracefully curved, enable ladies to wear conventional dresses with perfect freedom when they pilot the Cloudster. All cables, pulleys and control arms are out of sight. Effective insulation gives quiteness, prevents extremes in temperature, and makes conversation easy. Vibration at all engine speeds has been eliminated. The large baggage compartment, behind the seat, is easily accessible in flight. Eight cubic feet capacity enables you to carry 50 pounds of luggage with full fuel tanks and much extra equipment.

Soft, billowy seats with air-foam rubber cushioned padding are as comfortable as your favorite arm chair.

The Cloudster may be flown all day without fatigue to pilot or passenger—a new experience in relaxation and comfort in an airplane of its price.

## ☆ Economy

The Cloudster is sky high in value, yet down to earth in price. One of its many economies is its initial cost, when you consider what you get for your money. Compare the Cloudster with any other ship in its field. You'll discover that Rearwin again gives more airplane value for every dollar invested. Low maintenance is another important economy. The Cloudster, built to last, built to stand up under hard use, saves the owner the expenditure of time, energy, and cash.

Any Rearwin owner will tell you that a Rearwin has a reputation for outliving other airplanes and that maintenance expense is practically non-existent. Another saving is in the low depreciation—high resale value found in all Rearwin models. Not only the quality of the product, but also the good name of a long established company stand guard over the buyer's investment. In operation, too, the Cloudster is easy on the purse-strings, averaging twenty miles or more per gallon of fuel at cruising speeds up to more than two miles a minute. Oil consumption is low. Compare the low first cost, high resale value, economical operation, inexpensive maintenance of the Cloudster with other airplanes—You will find you can't afford to own any other ship in its price or horsepower class.

## ☆ In the Air

You must fly the Rearwin Cloudster to fully appreciate its many splendid flying characteristics. You'll find it so stable that it can fly "hands off" indefinitely. Yet with ball bearing controls throughout it is sensitive and responsive to your every touch. Even at slow speeds, controlability is excellent. Due to the well balanced control system, variable loads are easily felt with changes in air speed. This safety feature, appreciated by experienced pilots, is particularly beneficial to amateurs.

Put the Cloudster in a spin and hold it there for six turns, then release the controls and watch it come out by itself in a fraction of a turn—another safety feature of great importance.

Visibility is unusually good, either taxiing or in the air. In flight, the Cloudster's nose is well below the horizon, and when coming in, the entire landing area is visible during the approach. After the throttle is closed for a landing, longitudinal balance is quickly corrected by one or two turns of the elevator tab control.

Landings on the Cloudster's specially designed hydraulic gear are feather soft—and taxiing even in strong cross winds is easy with the 80 inch tread landing gear.

## ☆ Construction

The Cloudster carries on the Rearwin tradition of strength. It will stand up under hard use on any kind of field. We welcome you to our plant in order that you may see how well our airplanes are built. Wings are exceptionally strong. At the strut point, the front spar is 2⅛″ thick, the rear spar 1⅞″. Ribs are built with short bays for added ruggedness. The fuselage is of chrome molybdenum tubing, perfectly welded into a rigid bridge-like structure. The rugged hydraulic landing gear with wide 80 inch tread has been drop tested for much more than the approved load. The gear will withstand vertical drops of unusual distance. Ball bearing controls are used throughout the control system, including aileron, rudder, and elevator hinges. Ailerons are statically balanced, while rudder and elevator are dynamically balanced. A heavy gauge 17 gallon reinforced aluminum fuel tank is built into each wing giving total capacity of 34 gallons. Front and rear gravity feed lines on each tank guarantee a reliable flow of gasoline to the motor. In the cabin is an accurate gauge for each tank. These wing tanks give greater safety and more leg room in the cabin as well as unobstructed forward vision. The gas shut-off is conveniently located on the lower left of the instrument panel. V type lift struts attach to chrome moly steel X braces in the wings. These X braces give the wings great rigidity and unusual strength.

Full NACA cowling with streamlining of landing gear and wing struts adds to the Cloudster's smart appearance. Only the highest grade dopes and lacquers are used and the hand rubbed finish gives a lasting lustre that assures longest life to the fabric. The Cloudster is a custom built airplane conforming to Rearwin's high standard of quality.

## ☆ Utility

Today, people want airplanes that can be used for cross country trips, even in windy weather. Flying a beautiful Cloudster along your chosen sky path, over cities, rivers and mountains will be one of the most satisfying sensations you ever experienced. It's even more so when at the completion of your trip you find your Cloudster has averaged over 20 miles per gallon of fuel, and two miles were covered almost every minute. Yet you arrive fresh and rested, clean, cool and alert, ready for business or pleasure. A Cloudster will enable you to cover a large business territory of several states quickly and safely—or it will bring your favorite week-end spot within close range. And with the Cloudster's fast cruising speed, you're sure of getting home even in adverse wind or weather.

For whatever purpose you use your airplane—business, pleasure, instruction, or charter—you'll find the Cloudster has the UTILITY you desire. It has a rare combination of beauty, speed, range, and versatility.

The Cloudster doesn't *act* like ordinary airplanes. There's something about the way it takes off—the way it handles—the way it streaks across country—the way you see out of it—that's different. Once you fly the Rearwin Cloudster, even for a short time, you will be restless until you get your hands on the stick for keeps. Fly it and see for yourself.

**Available as either two or three place airplane**

★ ★

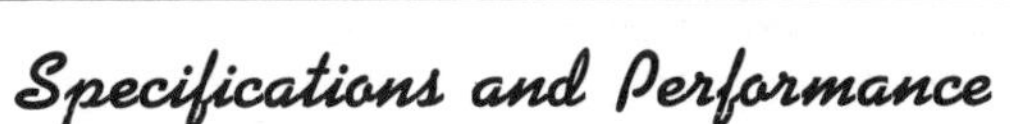

## Specifications and Performance

**REARWIN CLOUDSTER MODELS 8090 and 8125**
**Government Approved—Type Certificate No. 711**

| | English | Metric | English | Metric |
|---|---|---|---|---|
| Model | 8090 | 8090 | 8125 | 8125 |
| Engine | Ken-Royce | Ken-Royce | Ken-Royce | Ken-Royce |
| Horsepower | 90 h.p. | 90 h.p. | 120 h.p. | 120 h.p. |
| Wing Span | 34.146 ft. | 10.4m | 34.146 ft. | 10.4m |
| Length Overall | 21.5 ft. | 6.6m | 21.5 ft. | 6.6m |
| Height Overall | 7.33 ft. | 2.2m | 7.33 ft. | 2.2m |
| Wheel Tread | 80 in. | 2.032m | 80 in. | 2.032m |
| Wheels | Goodyear 18x8x3 | | Goodyear 18x8x3 | |
| Brakes | Goodyear mech. | | Goodyear mech. | |
| Wing Area (inc. aileron) | 161.8 sq. ft. | 15.032 sq. m. | 161.8 sq. ft. | 15.032 sq. m. |
| Power Loading | 18.16 lbs./h.p. | 8.23 kg/hp | 15.0 lbs./h.p. | 6.8 kg/h.p. |
| Wing Loading | 10.10 lbs./sq.ft. | 49.3 kg/sq.m | 11.125 lbs./sq.ft. | 54.3 kg |
| Empty Weight | 1000 lbs. | 453.6 kg | 1040 lbs. | 471-7 kg |
| Useful Load | 635 lbs. | 288.0 kg | 760 lbs. | 344.7 kg |
| Gross Weight | 1635 lbs. | 741.6 kg | 1800 lbs. | 816.5 kg |
| Baggage | 50 lbs. | 22.7 kg | 50 lbs. | 22.7 kg |
| Extra Equip. | *25 lbs. | **11.3 kg | 144 lbs. | 65.3 kg |
| Fuel Capacity | 34 gal. | 128.7 lit. | 34 gal. | 128.7 lit. |
| Fuel Consumption | 5 gal./hr. | 18.9 lit./hr. | 7 gal./hr. | 26.5 lit./hr. |
| Oil Capacity | 2.25 gal. | 8.5 lit. | 3 gal. | 11.4 lit. |
| Maximum Speed | 125 m.p.h. | 201 k.p.h. | 145 m.p.h. | 233.3 k.p.h. |
| Cruising Speed | 110 m.p.h. | 177 k.p.h. | 125 m.p.h. | 201 k.p.h |
| Landing Speed | 48 m.p.h. | 77.2 k.p.h. | 48 m.p.h | 77.2 k.p.h. |
| Cruising Range | 675 miles | 1086 km | 625 miles | 1006 km |
| Rate of Climb | 750 ft./min. | 3.8 m/sec. | 1000 ft./min. | 5.1 m/sec. |
| Service Ceiling | 14,000 ft. | 4267.2 m | 17,000 ft. | 5181.6 m |

*With 24 gallons of fuel, extra equipment of 85 lbs.
**With 90.8 liters of fuel, extra equipment of 38.6 kg.

★ ★

**REARWIN CLOUDSTER—MODELS 8090 and 8125**
**STANDARD EQUIPMENT**

Airspeed Indicator, Altimeter, Tachometer, Oil Pressure Gauge, Oil Temperature Gauge, Compass, Switch, 2 Fuel Gauges, Exhaust Manifold, Carburetor Heater, NACA Cowling, Pressure Baffling, Carburetor Air Cleaner, Altitude Mixture Control, Plexiglas Windshield, Brakes, Parking Brake, Tail Wheel—8-inch, Navigation Lights, Battery, Ball Bearing Controls Throughout, 2 Cabin Doors with Yale Type Locks, Dual Controls, Luggage Compartment (size 8 cu. ft.—37½x22⅛x16, 50 lbs. capacity), Complete Cabin Upholstery, Air Foam" Cushions and Seat Backs, Fire Extinguisher, Tool Kit, Engine Manual, First Aid Kit, Safety Belts and Log Books.

**SPECIAL EQUIPMENT**

Cabin Heater, Generator, Landing Lights, Radio, Electric Starter, Flares, Float Fittings, Special Instruments, Wheel Pants, Metal Propellor.

**SKIS—EDO FLOATS**

**CONVENIENT TIME PAYMENT PLANS AVAILABLE**

# World wide enthusiasm expressed by Rearwin Flyers!

"The Sportster has met with unanimous approval of the club's members, all of whom have tried it out. The public reaction has been surprisingly good. We are confident now of increased activity among our members and the addition of some new members, people to whom our former light plane did not appeal."

RICHARD E. LINDSAY,
Aero Club of Sarasota, Inc.,
Sarasota, Fla.

"Here are some figures on the low cost of operating a Rearwin for student training that will interest you:

| | |
|---|---|
| Gasoline and oil | $ 794.80 |
| Tires, repairs, etc. | 201.35 |
| Storage | 180.00 |
| Depreciation | 494.90 |
| Total | $1,671.05 |

"Number of hours used—782. Total cost per hour, including all expenses—$2.13."

JOE IMESON,
St. Louis, Missouri.

"I have been flying for 22 years and can't say that I have enjoyed flying any aircraft more than the Rearwin. I have found it an excellent machine in every way and find it very easy to give dual instruction. All our senior members enjoy flying in it and a number of them are now using it daily."

IAN KEITH, Instructor,
New Plymouth Flying Club,
New Plymouth, New Zealand.

"Your machines seem to be as near fool-proof as any aircraft can be made. I have witnessed Rearwins stalled from heights of 30 feet, and they have dropped on their undercarriages and sustained no damage whatsoever. The maintenance of the Rearwins also make them ideal machines for school and private owners. The LeBlond engines have proved both reliable and economical and as regards oil, they are the cheapest engines to run we have ever had."

S. WILLIAMSON,
Air Taxi Company, Ltd.,
Capetown, South Africa.

"I have been extremely satisfied with my Rearwin airplane and she has occasioned a very great deal of favorable comment. I find she cruises easily at 115 miles per hour. Her climb and take-off are as good as advertised and gasoline consumption is in the nature of 20 miles and sometimes as high as 30 miles per gallon."

LYMAN CRAWFORD BROWN,
Toronto, Canada.

"I think my Rearwin is a wonderful airplane. One trip I made to Cajamarca, Peru, where the landing field is 8400 feet above sea level, and easily took off with a passenger. The field was only about 900 meters (2,952 ft.) in length, and until that time no airplane with less than 250 h.p. had ever attempted that flight. I am particularly satisfied with the slow landing speed, which is very helpful where fields are small and rough."

ALBERT GILDRED,
Gildred Corporation,
Lima, Peru.

"I would like to express my satisfaction with our Rearwin. The ship has made many friends here in Norway. Since we have had our Rearwin, neither the ship or the LeBlond motor have given any kind of trouble, in spite of hard flights with little or no service to ship or motor."

PETER WESSEL,
Wessel's Flyveselskap A/S2,
Oslo, Norway.

"While flying the Rearwin Speedster from Kansas City to California, I encountered all kinds of bad weather including very turbulent air, rain, snow, and bad icing conditions. The Speedster handled beautifully and although the gustiness was the most severe I have encountered, the ship rode through it in excellent shape. Cruising speed was very outstanding, my average being 132 m.p.h. Another outstanding feature is the fine take-off at high altitude. The Speedster got off quickly at Denver (5300 ft.) and Winslow (4900 ft.) and in spite of hot weather and soft sand at Albuquerque (5400 ft.) the take-off run was not over 450 feet. The entire performance of the Speedster is just as excellent."

D. W. HOFERER,
Hofco Pumps, Ltd.,
Long Beach, California.

"When I had comparatively little flying time, I decided to purchase an airplane to use for both business and pleasure. I cover a large territory as Division Manager for Motor Improvements, makers of Purolator oil filters, and felt that an airplane could be used to a good advantage. After investigating several makes, I decided the Rearwin Speedster was best for my purpose and purchased one. I have been very well pleased with the utility of this airplane and have been able to keep business appointments in Omaha, Wichita, Oklahoma City, Tulsa, Dallas, and similar cities. For example, I recently had a very important engagement in Wichita and was delayed in Oklahoma City longer than anticipated. In my airplane, I was able to fly to Wichita, 150 miles away, in about 70 minutes and couldn't have possibly made it any other way. Your airplane certainly is easy to fly; and with my limited experience, I have been surprised how simple it is to get around."

T. R. COLLIOUD,
Dist. Mgr. for Motor Improvements,
Kansas City, Missouri.

"In our ten years of school operation we have used all different types and models of airplanes for training, but in all our experience, we have never found a plane that so completely meets all the demands of a school operator as the Rearwin 70 h.p. Sportster. This plane flies better, lands better, and is nicer on the ground than any other plane we have flown. The LeBlond engine has been most satisfactory under all conditions with oil consumption about 1 quart per 20 hours. We have had no repair parts on the plane in 1350 hours of student operation and parts on the engine have been very few at a minimum cost."

HENRY VON BERG,
Pathfinder Flying Service,
Stockton, California.

"We are using our 70 h.p. Sportster for student instruction and single person charter work, one trip over 700 miles. We also use the Rearwin for hopping passengers and have carried as many as 76 in one day. We normally operate the airplane at Monte Vista (7800 ft.) and it gets off in less than one-half mile with full load. I recently flew a photographer up to 16,000 feet to take pictures of the Continental water sheds. We frequently fly it at 14,000 feet and have flown over Mount Blanc which is 14,107 feet. It is just as nice an airplane as I have ever flown at high altitudes, and I have flown for almost six years. We average 104 m.p.h. across country and the rate of climb off our field is about 450 feet per minute."

CLYDE ADAMS,
Monte Vista, Colorado.

"I have been flying the Rearwin Sportster for more than a year, and it is the best airplane on the market for our work. With a passenger in the ship, I have climbed 1000 feet per minute. We use the Rearwin in patrolling the forests of Puerto Rico and adjacent islands, and are continually using beaches, salt flats, and pastures. It takes a very strongly constructed plane to stand up under this kind of work and the Rearwin has the strength."

F. W. HADLEY, Supt. of Forests,
Dept. of Agriculture,
Govt. of Puerto Rico.

"The Rearwins are used daily for instruction, and I certainly do not know anything to beat them at this high altitude in any respect as trainers. Besides, they are very good for cross country and small fields."

COLONEL W. C. BROOKS,
Chief of Air Corps,
Republic of Honduras.

"From my experience around the country, I am convinced that for quality and all around use there is nothing in the class that will touch your ships. For proof, take a look at my Sportster—still flying with over 1500 hours on it and more than 20 new pilots. I suppose you know that most of that time has been had at a cost of less than $3.00 per hour."

WILLIAM ROCHFORD,
1624 Holman,
Houston, Texas.

"Today we are starting to give one of our Rearwin seaplanes a general overhaul. This ship has 600 hours, all on floats, and we have never had a motor or airplane failure. There are some 7000 landings on this ship, most of which were put on in student instruction. Ship and motor are still in perfect condition. Our other Rearwin seaplane has 500 hours. We are serving the most critical seaplane experts in the world including pilots of Air France and Lufthansa. These people know seaplanes, and they use our Rearwins exclusively for pleasure flying."

DAVID McMENAMIN,
Rio de Janeiro, Brazil.

# STUDENTS!! BUSINESS MEN!! PROFESSIONAL MEN !!

*Win*
**YOUR**
*Wings at*
**THE REARWIN FLYING SCHOOL**
**FAIRFAX AIRPORT**
**KANSAS CITY, KANSAS**

High above the smoke pall of the city there is fresh, clean air. High above the congested streets there are blue skies and solitude. From towering heights, a new perspective of the world and of men awaits your vision. To explore the magic of the sky and feel air turn solid under wings of speed is a challenge to any true sportsman and lover of the great outdoors.

Why not try YOUR hand at piloting? Thrill to the response of feather-soft controls and allow your eyes to feast on a hundred square mile terrestrial panorama at the tip of your tilted wing.

The Rearwin Sportster—2S Rating—90 H. P. Ken Royce Motor.
One type of ship used for training at Rearwin Flying School.

In aviation, as in any other profession or sport, it is of vital importance to receive your training from authorities who have proven their worth in their particular field. Whether you fly for profit or for pleasure you should demand the best in instruction and equipment.

Due to the fact that we are affiliated with Rearwin Aircraft & Engines, Inc., it is correspondingly easy for us to maintain a staff of superior pilots. This vast amount of knowledge and experience which is required in the manufacture of modern aircraft is in turn passed on to you as a student. No other flying school in this area has the same advantage.

**LEARN TO FLY THE RIGHT WAY**

As you will receive your training in equipment designed and manufactured at Rearwin Aircraft & Engines, it is now possible for us to offer a course of instruction in flying that cannot be surpassed in price or quality. Furthermore, the same careful, competent mechanics service and maintain our school planes. No other flying school in the country can boast of a higher safety record.

If you WANT this training, you can AFFORD it. A few dollars a week starts you on a life full of adventure and zestful living. The average student is usually well enough versed in the theory of flight to make his first solo hop after 9 or 10 hours of dual flight instruction. The modest price for 10 hours of flight instruction at the Rearwin Flying School gives you training which cannot be equaled at any other school, and the cost is only $3.75 a week which you pay as you go. Rearwin offers you the finest training at a price you can afford to pay.

**GET STARTED EARLY**

Competent and qualified pilots are now in demand with new flight jobs opening every day. With amazing rapidity, the frontier of aviation is being pushed into the far corners of the earth. The industry is calling upon intelligent and properly trained youth to keep pace with the tremendous expansion.

As a sport or recreation, flying is the most practical investment you can make. A plane stands ready whenever you care to travel, and operating costs are less than for driving your car or traveling by railroad. You arrive at your destination quickly and refreshed.

The Rearwin Flying School, which is affiliated with Rearwin Aircraft & Engines, Inc., is the only aviation school in this vicinity that is able to use flying equipment entirely manufactured by the parent company. Every airplane you

**Our Representative Will Be Pleased to Make a**

**REARWIN FLYING SCHOOL FAIRFAX AIRPORT**

will use is a product of Rearwin Aircraft & Engines, Inc. This feature alone affords a wide selection of flight equipment. The student gains a varied flight experience since the Rearwin factory is in current production on eight different models, both tandem and side-by-side, with motors ranging from 65 h. p. to 125 h. p., practically all of which are available for flight instruction. You are assured of late-type, up-to-date equipment at all times.

**FLIGHT EQUIPMENT**

All flying equipment used in the Rearwin Flying School is in the 2S Class, which includes all single engine airplanes weighing from 1300 pounds to 4000 pounds. Thus you are assured of a 2S license earned on Rearwin equipment at the Rearwin Flying School which enables you to pilot any single engine airplane up to 4000 pounds gross weight. All engines used in Rearwin Aircraft are dual ignition, assuring you safety, excess power, and dependability.

No piloting complications are involved if you ever desire to fly light aircraft as well as larger airplanes such as are used for all your flight instruction at the Rearwin Flying School. It is to your advantage to learn to fly on large airplanes that will enable you to pilot practically any aircraft after completion of the Rearwin Course. Get the proper training on heavy aircraft in the first place and you are equipped to meet any piloting demand.

The REARWIN method of flight instruction is styled closely after the Army's system of fundamental training. Our instructors insist on precision in all maneuvers. Here you will learn properly from the very beginning; and our constant supervision of your solo practice keeps you from developing bad habits in your flying technique.

**DETAILS OF FLIGHT TRAINING**

Our training program and methods of imparting knowledge of flight to the student are in accordance with proven accepted practices. The course of instruction includes FREE PRELIMINARY GROUND INSTRUCTION in the theory of flight and simple explanation of the aircraft as a unit, which is followed by actual flight training. Periodic instruction is continued after the student has completed his first solo flight in order to make him proficient in the operation of the airplane under varying weather conditions.

As one of our pilots has been designated by the U. S. Civil Aeronautics Authority to give both the written and flight examinations for the C. A. A. private license, you will have the advantage of receiving your training in a school one of whose instructors will act as the examiner for your pilot certificate.

**n Appointment With You at Your Convenience**

**KANSAS CITY, KANSAS** *Telephone* **FAIRFAX 1750**

**Model 9000 KR—Ken Royce 90 H.P.**
**$3,195.00**

# *The Rearwin Sportster* » » »

AND NOW—A *New* Rearwin Sportster! The new model powered with the dependable 90 h.p. Ken-Royce engine is even better than its predecessor, and incorporates improvements and features never before available in its class.

Look at the picture of this beautiful airplane. It's streamlined from spinner to rudder, and its combination of weight, wing area and horsepower gives it unusually high performance. It's economical too, averaging 22-25 miles to a gallon of fuel with low oil consumption.

Note that the cowling has been completely redesigned. Motor and exhaust manifold are encased in smart, effective NACA cowling. Full pressure baffling cools the motor. An ingenious method of forcing air past the cylinder fins, then out through a single opening in the bottom of the cowling is used on the new Sportster. This system, found on the latest military designs, assures a cool running motor even at full throttle in warm weather, and gives greater speed because there is less resistance than with conventional cowling.

Of improved design is the sloping, streamlined windshield, carefully formed from a single large sheet of transparent material. Better visibility than ever before is obtained by the elimination of the two channel strips which formerly divided the windshield into three sections.

The interior of the cabin, even more roomy than before, is entirely re-styled. The upper side walls and ceiling are beautifully upholstered with expensive fabrics to harmonize with the soft, luxurious seat backs and cushions. The control mechanism is out of sight beneath the floor. All fuel lines, fuselage members, and fittings are completely concealed providing a pleasingly smooth surface.

The instrument panel, now in a vertical position, makes it easy to see all instruments. Artistic walnut grain finish harmonizes with the rest of the luxurious interior.

If you are an operator, you'll find the new Sportster a profit maker. Its smart lines and beautiful cowling attract additional students and its powerful five cylinder 90 h.p. dual ignition motor gives them the long sought thrill of snappy take off and sky rocket climb at low hourly cost. With its class 2S rating, the Rearwin Sportster is excellent for primary instruction, for more advanced work, including cross country trips, for rental to licensed pilots, and for single passenger charter service. A Rearwin fills a multitude of requirements, yet its cost is surprisingly low. It is the airplane that meets the needs of flying schools everywhere for an "all-around" airplane.

If you are a Sportsman pilot, you'll be amazed at the attractiveness, unusual performance, and great utility of the new Rearwin Sportster. Its streamlining and smooth finish attract attention wherever you land. The 90 h.p. Ken-Royce engine gives you performance plus. You can go in and out of small fields even in hot weather or fly at high altitudes with full load. While it is absolutely safe for the beginner, the new Rearwin is no mere "round the airport" ship. With its NACA cowling, streamlined windshield and other improvements, it easily cruises 115 miles an hour. And its range of over 500 miles enables you to go on long cross country trips without wasting time on frequent stops for fuel. You may look farther and pay more, but you won't find more safety or more satisfaction than in the Sportster—the fastest ship in its class.

The new Rearwin Sportster Model 9000KR is built to the same exacting specifications as other Rearwin models. While the quality of workmanship and materials are as fine as those in any airplane at any price, the Sportster is an inexpensive airplane in first cost, operation, and maintenance. Its low price includes *full* equipment. Available on our easy payment plan.

## *Specifications and Performance*

### REARWIN SPORTSTER—MODEL 9000-KR
**Government Approved—Type Certificate No. 591**

| | English | Metric | | English | Metric |
|---|---|---|---|---|---|
| Model | 9000 KR | 9000 KR | Payload | 220 lbs. | 99.79 kg |
| Engine | Ken-Royce | Ken-Royce | Gross Weight | 1460 lbs. | 662.26 kg |
| Horsepower | 90 h.p. | 90 h.p. | Fuel Capacity | 24 gal. | 90.8 lit. |
| Wing Span | 35 ft. | 10.668 m | Fuel Consumption | 5 gal./hr. | 18.9 lit./hr |
| Length Overall | 22.25 ft. | 6.782 m | Oil Capacity | 2 gal. | 7.57 lit. |
| Height Overall | 6.75 ft. | 2.057 m | Maximum Speed | 125 m.p.h. | 201.2 k.p.h. |
| Wheel Tread | 72 in. | 1.829 m | Cruising Speed | 115 m.p.h. | 185. k.p.h. |
| Wing Area | 166 sq. ft. | 15.42 m sq. | Landing Speed | 38 m.p.h. | 61.1 km/hr |
| Power Loading | 16.2 lbs./h.p. | 7.35 kg/hp | Rate of Climb | 1000 ft./min. | 5.08 m/sec. |
| Wing Loading | 8.8 lbs./sq. ft. | 42.97 kg/m sq. | Cruising Range | 500 miles | 805 km |
| Empty Weight | 830 lbs. | 376.49 kg | Service Ceiling | 15,000 ft. | 4.572 km. |
| Useful Load | 630 lbs. | 285.77 kg | Luggage Compartment | 50 lbs. | 22.7 kg. |

### REARWIN SPORTSTER—MODEL 9000-KR
**Government Approved—Type Certificate No. 591**

### STANDARD EQUIPMENT

Airspeed Indicator, Altimeter, Tachometer, Oil Pressure Gauge, Oil Temperature Gauge, Switch, 2 Fuel Gauges, Exhaust Manifold, Carburetor Heater, DeLuxe (Ball Bearing Cabin Controls, Luggage Compartment Under Rear Seat, Speed Wing Tip, and Controls under Floor), Brakes, Parking Brake, NACA Cowling, Pressure Baffling, Carburetor Air Cleaner, Tail Wheel, Fire Extinguisher, Tool Kit, Cabin Door Lock—Yale type, 2 Luggage Compartments (50 lbs. total capacity), Dual Controls, Upholstered Cabin, Cushions and Seat Back, Manual, First Aid Kit.

### SPECIAL EQUIPMENT

Cabin Heater, Navigation Lights, Battery, Radio, Float Fittings, Electric Starter, Special Instruments, Wheel Pants

### SKIS—EDO FLOATS

The Big Rearwin Airplane Factory—30,000 sq. ft. of floor space for Rearwin students.

# Learn Aviation and Aviation Mechanics in an Airplane Factory!

● Aviation is the great industry of today and the future! Yet, it is a young industry with all the opportunities of a new, fast-growing industry. Those who enter this industry, with proper training, may well look forward to an opportunity, holding a responsible and good paying position.

For the young man who is eager to succeed, who has confidence in himself, and ambition, aviation offers practically unlimited possibilities. It is a tremendously fascinating industry and will become more so each year.

The first step is to seek proper training. Such training should be obtained where practically all phases of airplane construction and engineering are available, in addition to flying.

The famous Rearwin-built Ken-Royce—fast, speedy airplane. Winner of more than 100 performance tests!

# Easy to learn to Fly-!

● The average person has all the qualifications to fly successfully. There is no secret to flying—the principles are as simple as A B C once you master the fundamentals. Flying an airplane is just as simple as driving an automobile without the traffic hazards.

View in Student Wing Building Department

Rearwin Airplanes are the most desirable airplanes for student training. There are many reasons for this claim. The Rearwin Airplanes used in training students are the simplest and easiest planes to handle. They are remarkably responsive—easy to control, dependable always.

Students assembling airplanes; getting them ready to fly.

The Rearwin course of instruction is simplicity itself. You learn easily and quickly under the guidance of experts. They have ability to convey instruction in the manner that makes everything easy to understand.

Once you learn the simple controls you have unlimited confidence in your ability as a pilot. All this has been proved, in countless cases, with Rearwin instruction. This instruction is tremendously fascinating. Your interest increases each day until your course is completed, at which time you are qualified to apply for the government license which you desire. Private Pilot, Limited Commercial, or Transport. Regardless of the course you are interested in, whether a Private, Limited Commercial, or Transport, it will pay you to investigate the Rearwin Aviation School. Instruction is given on the latest type equipment by instructors who are especially trained for this work. Classroom instruction is given covering every phase of the aeronautical industry and with this instruction and the practical experience each student receives in the Rearwin factory, he is qualified to pass the examination given by the Department of Commerce for his particular license.

REARWIN SCHOOL OF AV

# AIRPLANE AND ENGINE MECHANICAL COURSE

There is an increasing demand for trained men in the aviation industry. Those who enter the Rearwin Mechanics Course and apply themselves, following the instructions diligently during the training period, should be fully qualified when the course is completed to accept a position in the aviation industry.

The Rearwin Airplane and Engine Mechanics Course requires six months' training. During this period students receive actual, practical experience building government approved airplanes. Students also receive practical shop experience in our factory, repairing and overhauling airplanes and motors, which are used in commercial flying.

R. A. Rearwin, President of Rearwin Airplanes, Incorporated, extends a personal invitation to any young man interested in his future to visit the Rearwin Factory and the Rearwin School—both in the same building. A visit to the Rearwin Plant will prove the many advantages offered by this institution. The cost of tuition in the Rearwin School of Aviation is unusually low, and the terms are most reasonable.

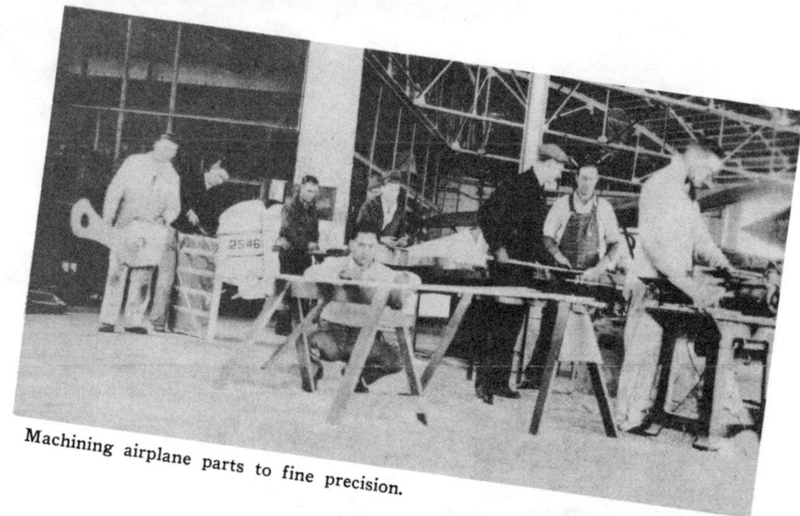

Machining airplane parts to fine precision.

Classroom instruction, covering every phase of airplane and engine mechanics, is given as part of the course. Upon completion of the course, students should be competent to pass written examinations given by the United States Department of Commerce.

Another view of students building airplane wings.

Our instructors have had long experience and their sole interest is in your development as a pilot.

IATION

FAIRFAX AIRPORT
KANSAS CITY, U. S. A.

The New Rearwin Speedster. Notice the advanced streamlines. A "modernistic" airplane, exceptionally high speed! Rearwin built throughout.

# YOU LEARN *Best* — WHERE AIRPLANES ARE BUILT

● With this close affiliation you gain the advantages of observation and practical experience in the fundamentals of airplane construction in an airplane factory where government approved airplanes are built. To every individual interested in aviation, this is, indeed a wonderful advantage.

Students enrolled in the Rearwin School of Aviation receive actual experience building new government approved airplanes as well as repairing and overhauling used airplanes and motors.

● Dormitory facilities are available for students. The Rearwin Dormitory is located on the second floor of the Rearwin Factory building—a modern building, constructed of fire-proof materials. The rates are very reasonable. Students find living in the Rearwin Dormitory just like a Club—convenient at all times and a real money saver, as there is no street car or bus fare to pay each day. You are right at the factory and school for all instruction.
Entertaining facilities are provided for students in the living room. Games are played for diversion, and aviation subjects of mutual interest are discussed informally. Lifetime friendships are formed in the Rearwin Dormitory.

## REARWIN SCHOOL OF AVIATION

(DIVISION OF REARWIN AIRPLANES, INC.)

FAIRFAX AIRPORT KANSAS CITY, U. S. A.

The
CLOUDSTER
by Rearwin

*1--Service With a Smile*—Now easier to service than ever! The Cloudster's newly designed two-piece engine cowling fits perfectly because it's made uniformly with dies in our 1000-ton hydraulic press. Although fastened securely in four places, the cowling can be raised in three minutes for quick and easy engine servicing. There's a special opening which saves additional time in checking the oil level.

The famous, time tested Ken-Royce 120 h.p. engine is your guarantee of motor dependability. Automatic pressure lubrication of rocker arm and valve mechanism has been added so that Ken-Royce engines now run absolutely clean with maintenance costs lower than ever. This improvement saves owners many dollars every hundred hours on grease jobs alone. In addition, increased lubrication efficiency of oil over grease will save a tremendous amount of wear and tear on engines and increase time between overhauls.

*Other major improvements in the Cloudster's power plant include:*

1. Austinetic steel exhaust valves with improved valve guides and new design valve springs.
2. Unusually hard cylinder barrels (400 Brinnel) assure many more hours between major overhauls.
3. Tappet adjustments now made in rocker arms. Tappets can now be adjusted with very little effort.
4. Finger type oil screens added to facilitate inspections. Can be removed in five minutes.
5. Oil consumption reduced to as low as ½ pint per hour, full throttle.

*2--Appointment With Beauty*—Interiors are more beautiful and luxurious than ever. Although the lowest priced seven-cylinder model in America, the Cloudster is a true luxury airplane. Windshield and all cabin windows are of expensive, long lasting "Plexiglass." Hardware is beautifully chrome plated and the instrument panel arranged for blind flying instruments and radio. Freedom of movement for the occupants is assured by gracefully curved sticks, either of which is quickly removable. Placement of sticks well forward enables women fliers to wear conventional dresses with perfect freedom.

You Get MORE for Your M

4
5
6
...E ...DSTER is Tops!
3--Three's Not a Crowd—There's all kinds of room in the new Cloudster! Inside width of 42 inches, and cabin height of 47 inches are greater than in many airplanes costing twice as much. Along with the Cloudster's beauty, safety, and performance, you'll like its extra roominess.
4--Cloudsters Go to Iran—From the many competitive training airplanes submitted, the Iranian Government picked Rearwin 120 h.p. Cloudsters—twenty-five of them—for its Aero Club. Why? Because the Cloudster has what it takes! On all points—appearance, dependability, construction, performance, economy of operation—the Rearwin Cloudster was first. These airplanes are being used half way around the world on fields a mile or more above sea level and over high, mountainous country. They have to be good—and the same features which appealed to the Aero Club will appeal to you. Whether you want an airplane for training purposes or private use, you'll find the Cloudster gives you more for your money every time.
5--Lucky Third Passenger—The right front seat folds far forward, making access to the rear seat easy. A tall man has plenty of head clearance due to the 47-inch distance from floor to ceiling. Built in for permanence, the third seat is well cushioned and beautifully upholstered. The thick chair height seat back and inviting arm rest make long trips a pleasure. Due to the seat location, the third passenger can easily converse with the other two cabin occupants.
6--Thrills For Three—A real three-place airplane, with room to spare and power to burn—these are two of the reasons more people are buying the three-place Cloudster than ever before. You'll find the Cloudster the yardstick of airplane value—the measure of what a modern airplane should be. It's the smartest and best performing airplane in the three-place field.
A Rearwin Model For Every Need!
Skyranger—cross country side-by-side—65 h.p. to 80 h.p. for private use and training. Speedster—famous tandem—125 h.p.—150 m.p.h. airplane. Sportster—popular tandem—70 h.p. and 90 h.p. for training and sport. Write for detailed information. Convenient Time Payment Plans available on all Rearwin models.
...oney with a Rearwin CLOUDSTER

We're proud of the Cloudster . . . we KNOW what it is and what it will do. We ask you to compare the specifications and performance with any other airplane in the Cloudster's horsepower and price class POINT-BY-POINT! Then ask for a demonstration. Ride in the Cloudster . . . fly it yourself! We know you'll agree with us that by any yardstick you choose, the CLOUDSTER "measures up!"

***The weight of 27 people in the Cloudster's strongly built cabin! On the front seat well over one and a half tons, equal to 19 people, at 170 pounds each. And on the rear seat almost three-fourths of a ton or the weight of 8 people—a total of over 4,600 pounds in the Cloudster. This picture proves better than words that the Cloudster has the strength to meet any test you will ever give it.***

## CONSTRUCTION

*Fuselage*: Four longeron design. Chrome-moly welded steel tubing for greater strength. Spruce fairing.

*Wings*: Selected solid spruce spars laminated at strut point; bushings at all bolt holes. Front spars 2⅜ inches thick, rear spars 1⅞ inches thick at strut point. Spruce truss-type ribs with strong plywood gussets, steel torsion braces, special steel alloy tie rods, and chrome-moly steel X braces for strut attachments. Duralumінum leading and trailing edges. Ball bearing control pulleys used throughout.

*Ailerons*: Metal construction, fabric covered. Carefully weighted for perfect balance in either smooth or rough air. Sealed self-lubricated ball bearings.

*Tail Group*: Chrome-moly welded steel tubular spars with steel channel ribs. Sealed self-lubricated ball bearings. Adjustable rudder tab. Duralumінum elevator trimming tab, controlled for sensitive longitudinal balance by Rearwin type micro-adjustment tab mechanism in cabin ceiling.

*Landing Gear*: Axle strut type with 80-inch wheel tread and oversize soft-action hydraulic shock unit. Combination full swivel and steerable hydraulic pneumatic tail wheel.

*Bearings*: All control system joints equipped with needle bearings or sealed self-lubricated ball bearings. Ball bearing pulleys used throughout control system.

*Covering and Finish*: Grade A fabric. Fourteen coats of highest quality clear and pigmented dope for a beautiful, lasting finish polished and buffed to a mirror-like surface. Standard color combinations are Stearman Vermillion with Insignia Blue trim or Insignia Blue with Red trim. Other colors at slight additional cost.

*Cabin*: Two extra large tight-fitting doors with sliding windows which can be fastened shut inside. Yale type locks on both doors. Full vision, specially molded Plexiglass windshield. Plexiglass door windows. Individual seats (3-place model). Trim stripe and thick rug to harmonize. Beautiful walnut grain instrument panel with lockable glove compartment and provision for blind flying instruments. Ash tray, assist cords, other conveniences. Two adjustable wing ventilators for fresh, clean air. Attractively designed control sticks, door handles, other hardware—all chrome plated.

*Fuel System*: Total capacity of 34 gallons safely placed in two 17-gallon wing tanks gives range of 600 miles. Two fuel gauges in cabin. Fuel switch on instrument panel.

### SPECIFICATIONS AND PERFORMANCE
### REARWIN CLOUDSTER MODELS 8125 (2-Place) AND 8135 (3-Place)
### GOVERNMENT APPROVED—TYPE CERTIFICATE No. 711

(Model 8090, with 90 h.p. Ken-Royce Engine, Specifications and Performance on Request)

| | English | Metric | English | Metric |
|---|---|---|---|---|
| Model | 8125 | 8125 | 8135 | 8135 |
| Engine | Ken-Royce | Ken-Royce | Ken-Royce | Ken-Royce |
| Horsepower | 120 h.p. | 120 h.p. | 120 h.p. | 120 h.p. |
| Empty Weight | 1100 lbs. | 498.8 kg. | 1140 lbs. | 517 kg. |
| Useful Load | 700 lbs. | 317.5 kg. | 760 lbs. | 344.7 kg. |
| Gross Weight | 1800 lbs. | 816.3 kg. | 1900 lbs. | 861.7 kg. |
| Baggage | 50 lbs. | 22.7 kg. | ***20 lbs. | †††9.1 kg. |
| Extra Equipment | **83 lbs. | ††37.6 kg. | *63 lbs. | †28.6 kg. |
| Fuel Capacity | 34 gals. | 128.7 lits. | 34 gals. | 128.7 lits. |
| Fuel Consumption | 7 gals./hr. | 26.5 lits./hr. | 7 gals./hr. | 26.5 lits./hr. |
| Oil Capacity | 3 gals. | 11.4 lits. | 3 gals. | 11.4 lits. |
| Wing Span | 34.146 ft. | 10.4 M. | 34.146 ft. | 10.4 M. |
| Length Overall | 21.5 ft. | 6.6 M. | 21.5 ft. | 6.6 M. |
| Height Overall | 7.33 ft. | 2.2 M. | 7.33 ft. | 2.2 M. |
| Wheel Tread | 80 in. | 2.03 M. | 80 in. | 2.03 M. |
| Wheels | 18x8x3 | | 18x8x3 | |
| Brakes | Goodyear | Goodyear | Goodyear | Goodyear |
| Wing Area (Inc. Ailerons) | 161.8 sq. ft. | 15.03 sq. M. | 161.8 sq. ft. | 15.03 sq. M. |
| Power Loading | 15 lbs./h.p. | 6.8 kg./h.p. | 15.8 lbs./h.p. | 7.16 kg./h.p. |
| Wing Loading | 10.1 lbs./sq. ft. | 49.3 kg./sq. M. | 11.73 lbs./sq. ft. | 57.3 kg./sq. M. |
| Maximum Speed | 135 m.p.h. | 217.2 k.p.h. | 135 m.p.h. | 217.2 k.p.h. |
| Cruising Speed | 120 m.p.h. | 193.1 k.p.h. | 120 m.p.h. | 193.1 k.p.h. |
| Landing Speed | 48 m.p.h. | 77.2 k.p.h. | 50 m.p.h. | 80.5 k.p.h. |
| Cruising Range | 600 miles | 965 Km. | 600 miles | 965 Km. |
| Rate of Climb | 910 ft./min. | 4.62 m./sec. | 860 ft./min. | 4.37 m./sec. |
| Service Ceiling | 16,300 feet | 4968 M. | 16,000 feet | 4877 M. |

*With 24 gallons of fuel.
**With 24 gallons of fuel, 143 lbs. of extra equipment.
***As 2-place, 190 lbs. of baggage and extra equipment.

†With 90.8 liters of fuel.
††With 90.8 liters of fuel, 64.9 kg. of extra equipment.
†††As 2-place, 86.2 kg. of baggage and extra equipment.

**REARWIN CLOUDSTER—MODELS 8125 (2-place) and 8135 (3-place) STANDARD EQUIPMENT: Airspeed Indicator, Altimeter, Tachometer, Oil Pressure Gauge, Oil Temperature Gauge, Compass, Dual Ignition, Switch, Two Fuel Gauges, Exhaust Manifold, Carburetor Heater, NACA Cowling, Pressure Baffling, Altitude Mixture Control, Plexiglass Windshield, Plexiglass Cabin Windows, Brakes, Parking Brake, Tailwheel—8-inch Pneumatic (Combination Steerable—Full Swivel), Navigation Lights, Battery, Ball Bearing Controls throughout, Two Cabin Doors with Yale-type Locks, Dual Controls, Complete Cabin Upholstery, Complete Carpeting, Paratex Cushions and Seat Backs, Glove compartment with lock, Fire Extinguisher, Tool Kit, Engine Manual, First Aid Kit, Safety Belts, Log Books, Luggage Compartment (8 cu. feet—On Model 8125). STANDARD COLOR COMBINATIONS: Insignia Blue with Red Trim; Stearman Vermillion with Blue Trim. SPECIAL EQUIPMENT: Cabin Heater, Generator, Landing Lights, Radio Receiver, Radio Transmitter, Electric Starter, Flares, Float Fittings, Wheel Pants, Special Instruments. ALSO SKIS AND FLOATS.**

**Rearwin AIRCRAFT & ENGINES, Inc.**
FAIRFAX AIRPORT . . . . . . KANSAS CITY, KANSAS

# Here's Proof the CLOUDSTER measures Up!

***Physician***—Dr. A. L. Cooper, *Scottsbluff, Nebraska.*
I have had my Cloudster up approximately one hundred fifty times, including a number of trips long enough to get definite information about its performance and flight characteristics. The more I have flown the Cloudster, the better I have liked it. I find it very easy to take off and land—it really takes care of itself in the air.

My wife and I enjoy trips in our Cloudster at every opportunity and we have found it flies so well even in rough air that we can keep planned schedules. I am sure flying a Cloudster is safer than driving a car, and it is distinctly more economical on trips beyond 100 miles. The Cloudster's performance is well up to your published specifications, and I have found the maintenance especially economical.

***Sportsman***—Herbert H. Unsworth, *Monterrey, Mexico.*
I purchased a Rearwin Cloudster because, after thoroughly checking the specifications of all other airplanes on the market, the Cloudster seemed to be the only one which would completely satisfy all my particular requirements. I needed a ship with plenty of power to clear 12,000 ft. peaks and one which could land and take off easily from poorly conditioned fields as high as 8,000 feet. Also, on most of my flights, I have to fly back home again on my original load of gasoline, so the great cruising range of the Cloudster is very important. The Cloudster gets you there so much faster than smaller ships and it's a comfort to have speed and power to go around or over any unforeseen bad weather. Having used the dependable LeBlond engine for seven years with complete satisfaction, I was naturally pleased that my Cloudster was powered with its improved successor, the Ken-Royce. Truly, the more I fly my Cloudster, the more I like and admire it.

***Engineer***—U. A. Whitaker, *New York, N. Y.*
I have been quite favorably impressed with my Cloudster. I have let about fifteen of my friends fly this ship, and most of them were men who have been used to heavier and more expensive equipment. They have all been impressed with its flying characteristics, and especially impressed with its quietness and comfort. Personally, I had, for several years, a much more expensive airplane which was unusually comfortable. I have found the Cloudster, however, just as comfortable to ride in, and it averages about the same air speed. The operating cost of the Cloudster is, of course, less than half that of my former airplane.

***Business Man***—Earl D. McKenzie, *Great Falls, Montana.*
I have been flying for nine years and the Cloudster is my fourth airplane. It has the nicest flying characteristics of any airplane I have ever flown—more stability, and no tendency to fall off at slow speed. My young daughter is enthusiastic about our Cloudster, and my wife now flys with me and greatly enjoys it. I fly a great deal cross-country, and have found all specifications very conservative. The Cloudster cruises nearly 125 m.p.h., uses exactly seven gallons of fuel an hour, and has a good rate of climb at high altitude. I have made several hops of over 400 miles, and still had plenty of gasoline left for over one and a half hours. Recently, I took off Great Falls airport (3,650 feet) and went up to 15,000 feet in 45 minutes with a load of 28 gallons of fuel and three people weighing 546 pounds and was still climbing when I leveled off. The Cloudster is a real three-place airplane with plenty of power for high altitude, and I am more than pleased.

***Flying School***—Capt. J. H. A. Treacy,
National Aircraft Pty., *Limited, Sydney, Australia.*
Congratulations to you in producing one of the finest aircraft in the world, namely, the Cloudster. This machine has been continuously in operation and has been training pilots with 100 per cent efficiency. Over a period of many months, our three Rearwins (one Cloudster and two Sportsters) have shown a nice profit and I am firmly convinced no other type of airplanes could stand up to this record under Australian conditions.

If your yardstick is PERFORMANCE, you'll find in the Cloudster features matched by no other airplane in its power or price class. The Cloudster is powered with the time-tested, dependable Ken-Royce motor, which assures plenty of power and pep for top notch performance under all conditions—small fields, high altitude, or hot weather. Just tap the throttle and the Cloudster is off with full load in 700 feet—up like a rocket, off like a bullet!

On controllability, the Cloudster stands aces high. It is so stable you can fly hands off indefinitely whether the air is smooth or rough. Because of ball bearing controls throughout, it is sensitive and responsive to your every touch. You'll find every hour at the controls a memorable experience.

The Cloudster is splendid for cross-country flying. It will carry you along at a cruising speed of two miles a minute and has a range of 600 miles, enabling you to make long hops between stops with plenty of reserve. When landing, the Cloudster glides down slowly and safely to a feather soft landing on its sturdy hydraulic gear. There's no performance quite like this in the air today. None so smooth, none so eager, none so satisfying as the Cloudster's.

If your yardstick is COMFORT, you'll revel in the luxury of the Cloudster, one of the most comfortable airplanes on the market, regardless of price. Entrance from either side to the roomy cabin is made easy by large doors; and in the spacious interior, restful individual seat cushions are as comfortable as your favorite lounge chair and seat backs are chair height for complete relaxation. Effective insulation gives quietness, keeps temperature even, and makes conversation easy and pleasant. Ventilator inlets in the wing leading edges provide an adequate supply of fresh, cool air under all weather conditions. Sliding windows, assist cords, ash tray, and lockable glove compartment are additional conveniences. There's no noise, no strain, no tensing for bumpy air in the Cloudster's restful cabin. Power from the quiet rubber mounted Ken-Royce engine flows steadily and smoothly with no vibration at any engine speed. Pilot and passengers fly hour after hour without fatigue.

If your yardstick is ECONOMY, you can't afford to own anything but the Cloudster. Sky-high in value, yet down to earth in price, one of the Cloudster's many economies is its initial cost. Compare the Cloudster—in performance, comfort, style, safety—with other airplanes. You'll find that again REARWIN gives more airplane value for every dollar invested. Maintenance cost is low, for the Cloudster is built to last—built to stand up under hard usage. And the Ken-Royce motor, with its new automatic overhead rocker box oiling system which eliminates hand greasing, cuts engine maintenance to lowest possible figure. Still another saving is in the low depreciation-high resale value found in all Rearwin models.

Operating costs are easy on the pocketbook, too. Owners report 18 miles per gallon while cruising two miles a minute with oil consumption of a quart per 1000 miles. You can fly a 3-place Cloudster for ½¢ per passenger mile!

Comparison of low first cost, low maintenance expense, low operating cost, and high resale value proves the real economy of the Cloudster.

If your yardstick is BEAUTY, see the flashing, streamlined styling of the Cloudster. When you eye the new Rearwin you'll know it's the most beautiful airplane of the year—and that it's also the most luxurious airplane in the medium price field. On the ground or in the air, the Cloudster's smart design and mirror-like rubbed finish are bound to catch and hold attention.

Outside and in, the Cloudster has a personality of its own, for its looks are as distinctive as its performance. Outside—smooth, glistening NACA cowling, streamlined landing gear and fairings, and hand-rubbed finish with lasting lustre. Inside—the rich quality of fine upholstery in attractive colors, gracefully curved chrome plated sticks, pedals, and hardware, perfectly appointed instrument panel with walnut grain finish, and a wealth of unusual style touches that contribute to lasting pride of ownership.

If your yardstick is UTILITY, here's the airplane that tops them all. Flying service operator? You'll choose the Cloudster because it's an inherently safe, "all around" airplane for instruction, passenger hopping, cross country rental, and fast, inexpensive charter service. Business man or sportsman pilot? If you love the feel of an airplane that wants to GO, spend half an hour at the controls of the new Rearwin Cloudster. Flying a beautiful, rugged Cloudster along your chosen sky path, over cities, rivers, and mountains will be one of the most satisfying sensations you ever experienced. Best of all, you arrive fresh and rested, ready for business or pleasure. A Cloudster enables you to cover a large business territory of several states quickly and safely—or brings your favorite play spot within close range. Whatever your purpose—instruction or charter, business or pleasure—you'll find the Rearwin Cloudster the utility airplane you want.

BY ANY YARDSTICK YOU CHOOSE, the CLOUDSTER "MEASURES UP." There's something about the Cloudster—the way it takes off, the way it handles, the way it streaks across country—that's different. Once you have flown the Cloudster, you'll be restless until you get your hand on the stick for keeps. Fly it and see for yourself.

# REARWIN INSTRUMENT TRAINER

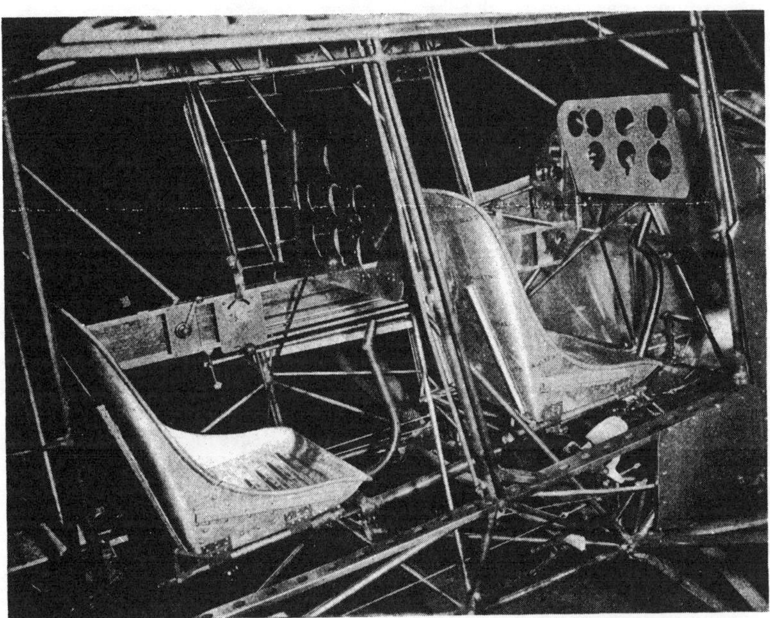

Tandem seating arrangement of the Rearwin Trainer. The view below shows the cockpits after the fuselage covering and other equipment has been installed

● An economical and efficient method of training pilots in instrument flying has been incorporated by Rearwin Aircraft & Engines in their Model 8135T. A development of the *Cloudster*, this new airplane is especially intended for flight and instrument training, particularly the latter since its removable instrument panel is arranged so as to provide all facilities for instrument flight work.

Departing from its recent custom of building side-by-side aircraft, Rearwin has adopted the tandem design in the new trainer, and has designed the cabin so that it is divided into two separate compartments, each with its own door and individualized equipment.

Fuselage is a truss-type structure of chrome molybdenum steel tubing, metal-covered aft to the front seat, and fabric-covered over the balance. This metal covering is readily removable from the underside of the fuselage. Doors are on the starboard side, and, in case of necessity, can be released from the airplane by pulling a handle on the right side of the fuselage; also, each door may be released individually from the front and rear compartments.

The instructor's seat is situated forward where visibility at the sides and ahead is excellent; the side windows are located considerably lower than in the 3-place *Cloudster* to provide additional downward visibility.

If desired the full 43″ width of the cabin can be used as instrument space. The normal instrument installation provides for a dual set of the more essential indicators. The flight instruments, mounted on centrally located and shock-insulated panels, include Sperry directional gyros and gyro horizons, compass, air speed, bank and turn, rate of climb, clock with sweep-second hand, and altimeter. Also in the flight group panel is a tachometer, while other engine instruments are to the left of the central group, and include oil pressure and oil temperature gauges, ice warning indicator, carburetor air temperature indicator, thermocouple, and selector switch and suction gauge. The electrical group, in the front cockpit, includes a generator field switch, ammeter, dash light, pitot heater, navigation and landing lights and temperature indicator switches, is on the left side just below the mixture and tab control group. The right hand side of the panel is reserved for additional instruments or radio equipment, *etc.* There are spare fuses, and a vacuum pump drive.

The rear panel is somewhat similar to the front panel except that with the exception of a tachometer, it has no engine instruments. The flight group is essentially the same as the front panel. The radio transmitting and receiving units, a Lear AMT-12 and AMR-12, are located to the left of the flight group within easy reach of the pilot's left hand. The rear cockpit electrical panel is located immediately under the radios and includes dynamotor, fixed antenna, phone jack, mike jack, simultaneous range filter, and dash light switch, as well as fuses. The throttle, mixture control, tab control and fuel shut-off are located immediately aft of the electrical panel. There is ample space to the right hand side of the flight group for additional instruments, if desired. The DF loop is centrally located above and slightly forward of the rear flight group within ready vision of the rear occupant. Dynamotor, battery, *etc.*, are located aft of the rear seat, with special provision made to permit ready access to these units.

Seats are Army type size and are adjustable about 4″ in a fore-and-aft direction, through a lever-actuated spring-loaded mechanism. The adjustment lever is located to the left of the seat. Cushions are readily removable and ample space has been provided for either back pack or seat pack type parachutes.

Dual toe-type brake pedals and dual stick controls are provided. The latter are ball or needle bearing mounted throughout. Rudder pedals are mounted in needle bearings on hardened and ground bushings.

Wings are of semi-cantilever type braced by vee struts and have spruce spars, spruce ribs, metal leading edges and single drag truss. An inverted tee type jury strut is employed. Ailerons are statically and dynamically balanced. Tankage for 34 gals. of fuel is provided in the wings.

Tail surfaces are welded chrome molybdenum steel structures employing tubular spars and channel ribs. All surfaces are fabric-covered. Elevators are statically and dynamically balanced and the starboard unit is equipped with a dural trimming tab controllable from the cabin by a micro-adjustment Rearwin type tab mechanism.

Landing gear is of the axle strut type with a 7″ vertical rise at the wheel; tread is 80″. Shock absorbers are of oil spring type while other equipment includes Goodyear 18 $\times$ 8 $\times$ 3 tires mounted on 3″ wheels, and mechanical brakes. A spring-oil tail wheel has been incorporated into the structure. This wheel is steerable and is controlled from the rudder pedals. Steering shock forces are dampened before reaching the rudder pedals. Beyond the steering range of about 30° the tail wheel becomes full swiveling automatically.

Particular attention has been paid to maintenance, especially in the primary structure, flight controls, engine controls and the engine installation. Seats may be readily removed as can the floor boards, providing complete access to the control and brake systems, *etc.* A large number of inspection holes have been provided.

A new type two-piece cowling employed hinges at the top and makes the entire engine compartment easily accessible. There is no inter-cowling except a small gill on each side of the firewall at the rear of the cowling. Magnetos, lubricating system, fuel strainer, vacuum pump, *etc.*, are readily accessible for inspection and maintenance. The cowling is retained in a fore-and-aft direction by steel fittings which fit over lugs cast integral with the rocker box caps. A small hinged door of sufficient size to readily permit filling the 3-gal. oil tank is on the right side of the cowling, thus eliminating the necessity for opening the engine hood for this purpose.

Model 8135T is powered with the Ken-Royce Model 7G engine, rated 120 hp at 2225 rpm, and equipped with rocker box pressure lubrication system and other recent refinements. Fuel consumption is 7 gals./hr.

The manufacturer believes that this airplane will find ready acceptance by the airlines, as well as private operators. The airplane is arranged so as to permit its use as a primary trainer by removing the rear instrument panel, as well as an instrument trainer.

The airplane's instrument arrangement was developed through the cooperation of Rearwin's engineering department and Pan American Airways which has purchased a number of the Model 8135Ts.

Specifications and performance data on the Rearwin Model 8135T powered with the 120 hp Ken-Royce Model 7G engine follow:

## SPECIFICATIONS

| | | |
|---|---|---|
| Wing span | 34 ft. 1.5 in. | 10.4 m. |
| Overall length | 21 ft. 6 in. | 6.6 m. |
| Overall height | 7 ft. 4 in. | 2.2 m. |
| Wing area | 161.8 ft.² | 15.03 m.² |
| Wing loading | 11.73 lbs./ft.² | 57.3 kg./m.² |
| Power loading | 15.8 lbs./hp. | 7.2 kg./hp |
| Empty weight | 1340 lbs. | 607.8 kg. |
| Useful load | 560 lbs. | 253.9 kg. |
| Gross weight | 1900 lbs. | 861.7 kg. |
| Fuel | 34 gals. | 128.7 lit. |
| Maximum speed | 135 mph | 217.2 kph |
| Cruising speed | 120 mph | 193.1 kph |
| Landing speed | 50 mph | 80.5 kph |
| Service ceiling | 16,000 ft. | 4877 m. |
| Rate of climb | 860 ft./min. | 262.1 m/min. |
| Cruising range | 600 mi. | 965 km. |

NC
255

the SKYRANGER
by Rearwin

A real cross-country 2S airplane, low in price but sky high in value—that's the new REARWIN SKYRANGER! Most smart things you buy are expensive—but not the beautiful and distinctive SKYRANGER. The same fine materials and pride of craftsmanship go into the SKYRANGER as into our expensive models. Long years of experience in the aviation industry, plus adequate production facilities, enable us to produce this truly De Luxe airplane in the low price field. New from nose to rudder, the SKYRANGER embodies all the latest technical structural developments, and combines these with appearance, comfort, and performance unsurpassed in its price class.

*The REARWIN SKYRANGER is a beauty from stem to stern. Trimming tab in right elevator provides longitudinal trim for 100 m.p.h. cruising speed. Streamlined large-area fin gives directional stability in rough air. Steerable tailwheel, standard on the SKYRANGER, guarantees easy cross wind taxiing and reduces wear on brakes.*

*Custom-built for comfort is the SKYRANGER'S stylish cabin. Thick, soft seat cushions and backs provide absolute relaxation on long cross country flights. Sliding windows in both doors give controlled ventilation. Luggage compartment has almost five cubic feet capacity. The sound-proofed cabin is amazingly quiet and complete absence of motor vibration makes "SKYRANGER flying" the thrill of a lifetime.*

The REARWIN SKYRANGER, a 2-place, side-by-side airplane, is as good under the cover as it is good looking—strong of fuselage and wings—an airplane built with exacting care. You'll find the SKYRANGER'S cabin sets new standards of comfort. Large doors make entrance and exit really easy, especially for women fliers. Gracefully curved, chrome plated sticks with onyx knobs provide freedom of movement for pilot and passenger, and insure sensitive control. Seat cushions and backs are scientifically moulded to an exact contour to increase comfort, and the seat back is chair height for complete relaxation. The REARWIN SKYRANGER is a comfortable and roomy airplane in which you can fly all day without fatigue.

The instant you seat yourself in the SKYRANGER, you will marvel at the unexcelled taxiing visibility for both pilot and passenger. As all fuel is safely placed in the wings, your view ahead is completely free, for the cowling lies well below the horizontal plane of your normal vision. In addition, windshield and window area much greater than on small airplanes provides you with unobstructed flight visibility so necessary when flying near or landing on busy airports.

You'll be amazed at the unusually safe flying characteristics and simple operation of the REARWIN SKYRANGER. This new design is actually a two-control airplane with respect to all flight maneuvers; the only time you need operate the rudder is during take-offs and landings. The REARWIN SKYRANGER literally flies itself. An outstanding safety feature you'll appreciate—the leading edge wing slots designed on latest N. A. C. A. data. These slots are similar to those used on expensive air liners and military aircraft. They guarantee complete and positive aileron control at slow speeds and even throughout the stall range, preventing unintentional spins.

You want to be able to make long hops between stops. The SKYRANGER'S standard fuel capacity is 24 gallons in two wing tanks; and its optional fuel capacity of 36 gallons in two wing tanks enables you to fly safely 750 miles, or across a quarter of the United States before landing.

The REARWIN SKYRANGER will appeal to your common sense as a really great *value*—low in cost, low in operation, high in resale value. Packed full of features you want, the SKYRANGER is the *most airplane* and gives *most pleasure* for your money.

You haven't known what a really modern, low priced, high quality 2S airplane should be until you've flown the REARWIN SKYRANGER. Come on—your greatest flying pleasure is still ahead! You belong in a REARWIN SKYRANGER today!

---

**The REARWIN SKYRANGER is priced fully equipped. And you can buy a beautiful new SKYRANGER on convenient time payments. Write for name of nearest dealer.**

**Also available with 80 h. p. engines.**

*Easy to service—The engine cowling on the SKYRANGER was especially designed for quick removal. Either section of the hood can be raised in one minute simply by unlocking three fasteners. If desired, the complete hood may be removed in an additional minute, thus making the entire motor accessible for servicing. The unusual amount of space behind the engine makes installation of battery or electric starter a simple matter.*

*The perfectly appointed and beautifully finished instrument panel typifies the up-to-the-minute design and styling of the REARWIN SKYRANGER.*

*Note that throttle, parking brake, carburetor heater and other controls are placed in the lower center of the panel within easy reach. The standard panel includes ash tray and large glove compartment equipped with Yale-type lock, and is easily arranged to accommodate a complete set of blind flying instruments. Removal of the glove compartment gives plenty of space for two-way radio installation. With the SKYRANGER, weight allowance for such items is no problem. There's 100 pounds for baggage and equipment.*

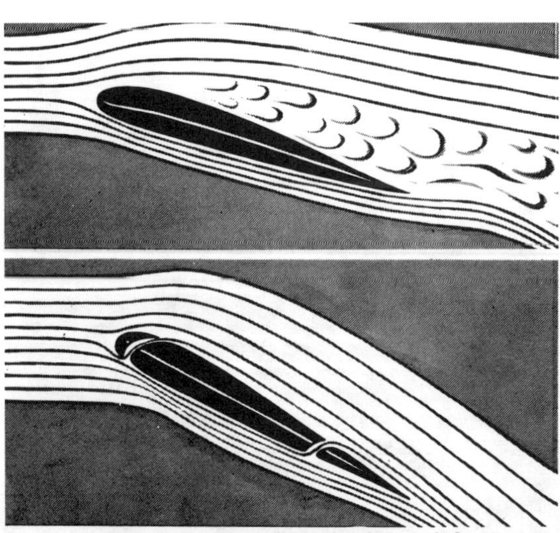

*Wing slots are an excellent safety feature which prevent unintentional spins by giving aileron control throughout the stall. See the turbulent flow of air over usual wing design in slight stall. Then observe the smooth flow of air over the REARWIN SKYRANGER'S slotted wing in spite of the increased angle of attack.*

*Almost two tons loaded in the SKYRANGER'S cabin! Three thousand pounds of lead in the SKYRANGER'S front seat and eight hundred pounds in the luggage compartment. Of course you'll never put a load like this in your SKYRANGER, but the picture is proof that the SKYRANGER can "take it." The entire structure—wings, fuselage, tail group, and landing gear are built with the best materials and workmanship obtainable.*

## REARWIN SKYRANGER—Models 165-175

### CLASS 2S RATING—STANDARD EQUIPMENT

Leading Edge Wing Slots, Airspeed Indicator, Altimeter, Tachometer, Oil Pressure Gauge, Oil Temperature Gauge, Compass, Switch, Two Fuel Gauges, Two Cabin Doors—with Locks, Rug, Paratex Cushions and Seat Backs, Complete Cabin Upholstery, Dual Controls, Glove Compartment with Lock, Brakes, Parking Brake, Steerable Tailwheel—6 inch, Exhaust Manifold, Exhaust Silencer, Carburetor Heater, Tunnel Cowling, Pressure Baffling, Altitude Mixer Control, Wood Propeller, Wiring for Navigation Lights, Safety Belt, First Aid Kit, Fire Extinguisher.

*Standard Color Combinations*: Insignia Blue with Red Trim; Stearman Vermilion with Blue Trim.

*Special Equipment*: Cabin heater, Navigation Lights, Landing Lights, Battery, Fuel Tanks with 36-gallon capacity, Dual Ignition (Standard on Model 175), Radio Receiver, Radio Transmitter, Electric Starter, Generator, Wheel Pants, Special Instruments. **ALSO SKIS AND FLOATS.**

# Rearwin SKYRANGER

## CONSTRUCTION

*Fuselage*: Four longeron design. Chrome-moly welded steel tubing for greater strength. Spruce fairing. Two cabin doors with sliding windows.

*Wings*: Selected solid spruce spars laminated at strut point and with bushings at all bolt holes. Spruce truss-type ribs with strong fibre gussets pressed in place. Steel tie rods and torsion braces. Duraluminum leading and trailing edges.

*Tail Group*: Chrome-moly welded steel tubular spars with steel channel ribs. Oilite bearings. Adjustable rudder tab. Elevator trimming tab, controlled by Rearwin type micro-adjustment tab mechanism in cabin roof.

*Landing Gear*: Axle strut type with 72-inch wheel tread and oversize soft-action hydraulic shock unit. Steerable tail wheel, spring mounted.

*Bearings*: Most control system joints equipped with ball, needle, or self-lubricating Oilite bearings.

*Covering and Finish*: Grade A fabric is used throughout, instead of light plane cloth. Ten coats of highest grade clear and pigmented dope give a beautiful, lasting finish. Standard color combination is Insignia Blue with Red trim outlined in gold. Stearman Vermilion with Insignia Blue trim outlined in gold is also available at no extra cost.

*Slots*: Fixed type leading edge wing slots of aluminum alloy construction. These slots assure safer flying by giving aileron control at slow speeds, thus preventing inadvertent spins. Available in no other airplane in SKYRANGER'S price class.

*Fuel System*: Total capacity of 24 gallons carried in two 12-gallon wing tanks gives range of 500 miles. Optional at slight additional cost 36-gallon capacity carried in two 18-gallon wing tanks giving 750 mile range.

### SPECIFICATIONS AND PERFORMANCE ON REARWIN SKYRANGER MODELS 165 AND 175

**U. S. Government Approved—Type Certificate 729 on Model 175**

| | English | Metric | English | Metric |
|---|---|---|---|---|
| Model | 165 | 165 | 175 | 175 |
| Engine | Continental | Continental | Continental | Continental |
| Horse Power | 65 h.p. | 65 h.p. | 75 h.p. | 75 h.p. |
| Wing Span | 34 ft. | 10.36 M. | 34 ft. | 10.36 M. |
| Length Overall | 21 ft. 9 in. | 6.63 M. | 21 ft. 9 in. | 6.63 M. |
| Height Overall | 6 ft. 7 in. | 2.00 M. | 6 ft. 7 in. | 2.00 M. |
| Wheel Tread | 74 in. | 1.88 M. | 74 in. | 1.88 M |
| Wing Area | 164.6 sq. ft. | 15.29 sq. M. | 164.6 sq. ft. | 15.29 sq. M. |
| Wing Loading | 8.2 lbs./sq. ft. | 40 kg./sq. M. | 8.2 lbs./sq. ft. | 40 kg./sq. M. |
| Power Loading | 20.77 lbs./h.p. | 9.42 kg./h.p. | 18 lbs./h.p. | 8.16 kg./h.p. |
| Weight Empty | 760 lbs. | 344.7 kg. | 760 lbs. | 344.7 kg. |
| Useful Load | 590 lbs. | 267.5 kg. | 590 lbs. | 267.5 kg. |
| Gross Weight | 1350 lbs. | 612.2 kg. | 1350 lbs. | 612.2 kg. |
| Baggage & Extra Equipment | 100 lbs. | 45.4 kg. | 100 lbs. | 45.4 kg. |
| Fuel Capacity | 24 gal. | 90.8 lits. | 24 gal. | 90.8 lits. |
| Fuel Consumption | 4 gal./hr. | 15.14 lits./hr. | 4.6 gal./hr. | 17.4 lits./hr. |
| High Speed | 105 m.p.h. | 169 km./hr. | 110 m.p.h. | 177 km./hr. |
| Cruising Speed | 95 m.p.h. | 153 km./hr. | 100 m.p.h. | 161 km./hr. |
| Landing Speed | 38 m.p.h. | 61 km./hr. | 38 m.p.h. | 61 km./hr. |
| Normal Range | 500 mi. | 805 km. | 500 mi. | 805 km. |
| Rate of Climb | 550 ft./min. | 2.794 m./sec. | 625 ft./min. | 3.175 m./sec. |
| Service Ceiling | 12,000 ft. | 3,658 M. | 14,000 ft. | 4,267 M. |

**There's a Rearwin Airplane for every need! Included are: *Speedster*—famous tandem—125 h.p.—150 mile an hour airplane. *Sportster*—popular tandem—70 h.p.—and 90 h.p. models for training and sport flying. *Cloudster*—all around favorite—side-by-side—90 h.p. and 120 h.p. airplane available as either 2 or 3 place.**

**For detailed information and descriptive folders, write or wire the factory. Convenient Time Payment Plans Available on all models.**

COMMONWEALTH
AIRCRAFT
TRADE MARK REG. U. S. PAT. OFFICE

Skyranger*
NC
COMMONWEALTH AIRCRAFT, INCORPORATED • NEW YORK • KANSAS CITY

The **SKYRANGER** is a thing of beauty throughout. Fine materials and pride of craftsmanship go into the **SKYRANGER.** Long years of experience in the aviation industry, plus adequate production facilities, enable us to produce this truly DeLuxe airplane in the low price field. The **SKYRANGER** embodies all the latest technical structure developments and combines these with appearance, comfort and performance unsurpassed in its price class.

The **COMMOI**
value—low
want, the **SI**

## A RE

The instan
visibility f
ahead is c
vision. In
provides
on busy

You'll be
**COMMON**
respect t
and lanc
feature
These sl
guarant
stall ra

Trimmi
100 mi
Standa
wind t

*Your greatest flying pleasure is still ahead . . .*

The **COMMONWEALTH SKYRANGER**—a two-place (side by side) airplane—is as good under the cover as it is good looking. Custom built for comfort is the **SKYRANGER'S** stylish cabin. Large doors make entrance and exit really easy. The luggage compartment has almost 5 cubic feet capacity. Seat cushions and backs are scientifically molded to an exact contour to increase comfort, and the seat back is chair height for maximum relaxation on long cross-country flights, while sliding windows in both doors give controlled ventilation. Gracefully curved, chrome plated sticks with onyx knobs provide freedom of movement for pilot and passenger, and insure sensitive control. The sound-proofed cabin is amazingly quiet and complete absence of motor vibration makes the **COMMONWEALTH SKYRANGER** a comfortable and roomy airplane in which you can fly all day without fatigue.

You
betw
fuel
fly
Unit

EAS
on
for
hoc
unl
co
dit
m
ar
m
a
**S**

ıWEALTH SKYRANGER will appeal to your common sense as a really great n cost, low in operation, high in re-sale value. Packed full of features you ıYRANGER is the most airplane and gives most pleasure for your money.

# ıL CROSS COUNTRY AIRPLANE

you seat yourself in the SKYRANGER, you will marvel at the unexcelled taxiing r both pilot and passenger. As all fuel is safely placed in the wings, your view ımpletely free, for the cowling lies well below the horizontal plane of your normal addition, windshield and window area much greater than on small airplanes ou with unobstructed flight visibility so necessary when flying near or landing ıirports.

amazed at the unusually safe flying characteristics and simple operation of the JEALTH SKYRANGER. This new design is actually a two-control airplane with all flight maneuvers; the only time you need operate the rudder is during take-offs ings. The COMMONWEALTH SKYRANGER literally flies itself. An outstanding safety ou'll appreciate—the leading edge wing slots designed on latest N. A. C. A. data. ıts are similar to those used on expensive air liners and military aircraft. They e complete and positive aileron control at slow speeds and even throughout the ge, preventing unintentional spins.

g tab in right elevator provides longitudinal trim for a cruising speed in excess of s per hour. Streamlined large-area fin gives directional stability in rough air. d equipment of the SKYRANGER is a steerable tailwheel guaranteeing easy cross xiing and reducing wear on brakes.

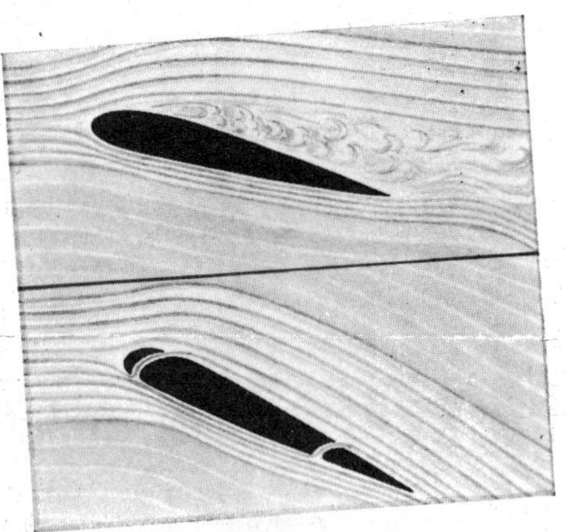

See the turbulent flow of air over usual wing design in slight stall. Then observe the smooth flow of air over the COMMONWEALTH SKYRANGER'S slotted wing in spite of the increased angle of attack.

# ʏou belong in a COMMONWEALTH *Skyranger* today*

vant to be able to make long hops en stops. The SKYRANGER'S standard apacity, 30 gallons, enables you to ı0 miles, or across a quarter of the d States before landing.

ʏ TO SERVICE — The engine cowling e SKYRANGER was especially designed quick removal. Either section of the l can be raised in a moment simply by cking three fasteners. If desired, the plete hood could be removed in an ad-ınal minute, thus making the entire or accessible for servicing. The unusual ount of space behind the engine accom-dates the starter and generator—stand-ı equipment in the COMMONWEALTH ʏRANGER.

The perfectly appointed and beautifully finished instrument panel typifies the up-to-the-minute design and styling of the **COMMONWEALTH SKYRANGER.** The throttle, parking brake, carburetor heater and other controls are placed in the lower center of the panel within easy reach. The standard panel includes ash tray and large glove compartment equipped with a lock and is easily arranged to accommodate a complete set of blind flying instruments. Removal of the glove compartment provides ample space for an optional 2-way radio installation. With the **SKYRANGER,** weight allowance for such items is no problem. There's 100 pounds allowance for radio and equipment.

# *Construction*

FUSELAGE: Four longeron design. Chrome-moly welded steel tubing for greater strength. Spruce fairing. Two cabin doors with sliding windows.

WINGS: Selected solid spruce spars laminated at strut point and with bushings at all bolt holes. Spruce truss-type ribs with strong plywood gussets pressed in place. Steel tie rods and torsion braces.

TAIL GROUP: Chrome-moly welded steel tubular spars with steel channel ribs. Oilite bearings. Adjustable rudder tab. Elevator trimming tab, controlled by Commonwealth type micro-adjustment tab mechanism in cabin roof.

LANDING GEAR: Axle strut type with 72-inch wheel tread and oversize soft-action hydraulic shock unit. Steerable tail wheel, spring mounted.

BEARINGS: Most control system joints equipped with ball, needle, or self-lubricating Oilite bearings.

COVERING AND FINISH: Finished Grade A fabric is used throughout, instead of light plane cloth, while pigmented as well as a number of coats of high grade clear dope together with rubbing give a beautiful lasting finish. An ample range of color combinations and contrasting trims are available.

SLOTS: Fixed type leading edge wing slots of aluminum alloy construction. These slots assure safer flying by giving aileron control at slow speeds, thus preventing inadvertent spins. Available in no other airplane in **SKYRANGER'S** price class.

FUEL SYSTEM: Total capacity of 30 gallons carried in two 15-gallon wing tanks gives range of 600 miles.

**COMMONWEALTH SKYRANGER**
**Model 185**
**STANDARD EQUIPMENT**

Leading Edge Wing Slots, Airspeed Indicator, Altimeter, Tachometer, Oil Pressure and Temperature Gauges, Compass, Switch, Two Fuel Gauges, Two Cabin Doors—with Locks, Rug, and scientifically designed Cushions and Seat Backs, Complete Cabin Upholstery, Dual Controls, Electric Starter, Generator, Dual Ignition, Glove Compartment with Lock, Hydraulic Brakes, Parking Brake, Steerable Tailwheel — 6 inches, Exhaust Manifold, Exhaust Silencer, Carburetor Heater, Tunnel Cowling, Pressure Baffling, Altitude Mixer Control, Wood Propeller, Safety Belt.

Standard color combinations are available.

Special Equipment: Cabin Heater, Landing Lights, two 18-gallon Fuel Tanks, Radio Receiver and Transmitter, Special Instruments, Wheel Parts, Adjustable Pitch Propeller.

## *Specifications and Performance*

**ON COMMONWEALTH SKYRANGER MODEL 185**

| | | | |
|---|---|---|---|
| Model | 185 | Gross Weight | 1450 lbs. |
| Engine | Continental | Baggage & Extra Equip. | 100 lbs. |
| Horse Power | 85 | Fuel Capacity | 30 gal. |
| Wing Span | 34 ft. | Fuel Consumption | 5 gal./hr. |
| Length Overall | 21 ft. 9 in. | High Speed | 114 m.p.h. |
| Height Overall | 6 ft. 7 in. | Cruising Speed | 103 m.p.h. |
| Wheel Tread | 74 in. | Landing Speed | 38 m.p.h. |
| Wing Area | 164.6 sq. ft. | Normal Range | 600 miles |
| Wing Loading | 8.81 lbs./sq. ft. | Rate of Climb | 650 ft./min. |
| Power Loading | 17.06 lbs./h.p. | Service Ceiling | 14,000 ft. |

★ THE NAMES SKYRANGER, TRIMMER, CLOUDSTER ARE TRADE MARKS, REGISTERED U. S. PATENT OFFICE

**COMMONWEALTH**
*Aircraft*, **INC.**

PLANT — KANSAS CITY CABLE ADDRESS "COMMONAIR"
**GENERAL SALES OFFICE — 521 FIFTH AVENUE, NEW YORK 17, N. Y.**

ALSO MANUFACTURERS OF "TRIMMER★" AMPHIBIAN AND "CLOUDSTER★" LANDPLANE

# AVIATION'S ADVANTAGES

Reprinted from February 1936 "Pilot" Magazine

By KENNETH R. REARWIN

● REFUTING GENERAL OBJECTIONS TO AIR TRAVEL

"SO YOU drive these flying machines, do you?" said Mr. Blotto on learning that I was a private pilot. "Well, I'll never fly. There's nothing to recommend it."

To me, recently returned from 5,000 miles of exhilarating carefree travel, his words were a red flag. Long ago I became tired of listening to people with preconceived ideas about aviation tell me how useless airplanes are. I suppose I replied a little too hotly to Mr. Blotto, but I think I woke him up. My belligerent mood has —or should—keep his eyes focused on the highway straight ahead most of the time. But in the air, it's different. After a little cross country experience, all I had to do was to check my posit-carried over, however, and I still have the urge to wage a battle against the barrier of closed minds. Mr. Blotto was, unfortunately, typical of too many Americans who, serene in ignorance, decry flying.

One of Blotto's first bright comments was, "Air travel is no pleasure, you can't see anything." Certainly in private flying you can see all there is. After all, if you really want to get an objective view of things, you must travel by plane. The car driver must ion occasionally with a sectional map, and settle down to enjoy myself. The topography of the entire country lay below us, and even at 100 m.p.h. the landscape unfolded slowly giving plenty of time to examine points of interest. I've been West before, but I had been restricted to hasty glimpses of swiftly passing fields and houses. Never before did I have the whole geographical panorama clearly presented. As we flew, we seemed to be over a huge relief map showing every detail, water sheds with all their tributaries, foothills increasingly steep leading up to gigantic mountains, towns and trees hugging the banks of rivers and canals. From the air I saw the true perspective of that vast region of West Texas. Between San Angelo and El Paso, the twin ribbons of a railroad track were our only connection with civilization. I felt secure with our 24 gallons of gas, but I realized as never before what broad reaches lie within the borders of Texas.

If Mr. Blotto had been driving his car on our schedule, he would not have had time to visit the places we did. The 140 miles from Ft. Stockton to Carlsbad were merely a matter of a late afternoon hop. We saw the Caverns and the following morning, flew westward again, over El Capitan mountain, that grim old Spanish soldier who guards the pass, and on to El Paso. We spent almost five hours in Old Mexico, bargaining over curios in Juarez, and still had ample time to fly on to Tucson before sunset. I wonder where Blotto and his car would have been by then?

From Tucson, winging westward over Yuma, we saw the sand hills of Eastern California where the desert scenes for the movies are taken. Finally we crossed a little irrigation ditch, and as if by magic, passed over into that wonderful agricultural paradise, Imperial Valley. Beneath us were rows and rows of evenly spaced orange trees and grape vines. Smoke from hundreds of brush fires sent a thin haze into the blue air. A few miles to the west we crossed another irrigation ditch and abruptly found ourselves out over sage brush again with a high range of mountains looming twenty miles ahead. From over these mountains at an altitude of 12,000 feet,

(Continued on page 4)

. . . recently completed 5000 miles of exhilarating carefree air travel.

Mr. and Mrs. Ken Rearwin of Kansas City.

. . . Gasoline averaged about 1c a mile. disproving the objection "It costs too much."

(Continued from page 3)

we could see the white stucco houses of San Diego with their bright green and red roofs. On the far side of the city lay Lindbergh Field, and beyond it the Pacific Ocean stretched out to meet the horizon. It was a wonderful view which I'll never forget.

From San Diego we flew up to Los Angeles, skirting a coastal fog which blanketed the shore a short distance inland. It lifted in time to give us a glimpse of the old mission San Juan Capistrano. In a little over an hour, we spanned the distance which meant days of weary travel to the Spanish friars.

After a few days in Los Angeles, we went northward over a sea of tumbled white clouds to Bakersfield, and on to San Francisco by way of Stockton. There we found an aerial sight long to be remembered. Approaching from the east, we flew over a low range of wooded mountains. On the other side of them we saw Oakland and Berkeley spread along the coast. Beyond them lay the Bay and across it, San Francisco's tall buildings clustered on a long promontory. As we passed over the Bay, we saw Alcatraz Prison, and waved a greeting to the boys on the Island. Something white fluttered in response. I thought it was Al Capone waving but my wife insisted it was only a bit of laundry hanging out to dry. We looked ahead and saw the new Golden Gate Bridge rapidly taking form. From the air, one realizes fully its colossal size. We circled Alameda, base of the China Clippers, and landed at San Francisco Bay Airdrome. A week later, we took off again on our way back to Los Angeles. It was great sport to pass by black dots of automobiles and long serpentine trains. Surely only Mr. Blotto would say you can't see anything from the air. That's the only place where you can get the complete picture. We ended our flight with a multitude of vivid mental images, with lasting impressions of many a beautiful scene.

Robbed of his first objection, Mr. Blotto offered triumphantly, "Well, it costs too much to fly." Disproving this objection was like taking candy from a baby.

Today, a well constructed two-place airplane such as our Sportster model, actually costs less to operate than a low priced automobile. The general public still doesn't realize this fact. People cling to the well intrenched idea that flying is expensive, despite the reductions in airplane prices and in the cost of flying time. Business men, however, are beginning to see that flying their own ships is really economical. Our Rearwin Sportster honestly averages 20 miles to a gallon of gasoline and has a lower rate of oil consumption than any automobile I have ever owned. Tires will last for hundreds of hours and the mileage attained before a top overhaul is as great as on an automobile. On the basis of the service given by our former models, we feel that today's Rearwin Sportsters will easily last 2000 hours—and that's a long time. Last fall on our trip West, my gasoline averaged about 20c a gallon with tax refunds, or just 1c a mile. It is a little hard to compare the cost of my return rail ticket and my flying expenses on the way out, because outward bound I followed an indirect course which led as far south as the Gulf of Mexico. However, the rail mileage from K.C. to Los Angeles is 1780 miles. Fare for my wife and me was $105.00, with Pullman and meals boosting the total to nearly $150.00. The air distance can be covered in a Rearwin Sportster for $30.00, which takes care of gas and oil, hangar, hotel for one night, and meals for two people. In addition to the cash saving, something has to be said about time saving. If a man's time is worth anything at all, flying is equivalent to money in the bank.

I was slightly disappointed in Mr. Blotto's next comeback. I felt he might have done a little better. "Pooh," he said, "maybe you do see the scenery, and maybe it is cheap. But look at the sort of fellows who fly. Young Dare-devils. It certainly proves what sort of an affair aviation is. Just look at the fliers." I hastened to tell him about the type of flier we encountered on our trip, and he had to back down. It's true that even I can remember when about the only person in our community interested in airplanes was the dare-devil type. You know—the young man who didn't feel that an ordinary car ran fast enough, so proceeded to strip down his auto, install a high speed transmission, or a high compression head in an effort to get more speed. Although this type of person was not the only one who turned to aviation, the opinion of the general public was that anyone interested in airplanes must be harum-scarum.

Today the picture has changed. There is a new type of flier. He is usually a young up-and-coming business or professional man but he may be a progressive fellow in his fifties when he learns to pilot his own sihp. These new aviation enthusiasts enjoy the relaxation of flying, but most of them are also interested in the great saving of time which is now available. They kill several birds with one stone by covering long distances in a short time at exhilarating speeds. We have sold Rearwin Sportsters to many such people. To list a few—a partner of a successful accounting firm who travels between branch offices in his own plane; a prominent official in America's largest lumber company who covers a large territory by plane; a lawyer in the East who flies everywhere for cases. And there are many more.

Occasionally I meet someone like Mr. Blotto who talks about the inconveniences of flying—how airplanes aren't as dependable as automobiles, that there are always little things needing fixing, how poorly located air-

(Continued on page 5)

## AVIATION'S ADVANTAGES

(Continued from page 4)

ports are. In short, this type of person "just can't be bothered" with flying.

My home town of about 20,000 population is well located at the cross roads of two hard surfaced main highways. But fifteen years ago dirt roads connected it with other nearby places. On Sundays, we often drove to a small town, about 40 miles away to visit relatives. At that time even forty miles was quite a jaunt. First we looked in Saturday's paper to see what the weather was supposed to be. Next we called the local telephone office to find out how the roads were "up the line." Finally if all the signs and omens were favorable, we started out to cover 40 miles in a little less than two hours—with luck. Rarely did we make a round trip without one or more flat tires, and often we had engine trouble before arriving safely home that night. Our experiences were duplicated by thousands of others. But we didn't give up automobiles and automobile trips. Not at all; we thought them great sport.

I grant that airplanes, when used for short distances, are a little more trouble than automobiles. But look at the tremendous time and mileage saving on longer trips; think of the great advances in airplane construction and airport facilities in the last few years. Thanks to wide awake city aviation committees and recent Federal funds, the nation is fast being covered with good landing fields. And with modern economically operated airplanes, flying is constantly being made even more pleasurable.

Mr. Blotto entirely overlooked the fact that the hospitality and helpful friendliness which fliers receive away from their home airports more than compensates for any possible inconveniences. No matter what the size of the field or how late one arrives, he can always be sure of a warm welcome. Of course all of us like the large, easily accessible fields, but I think we too often take for granted the hospitality which we receive everywhere. After all, that's something P.W.A. funds can't provide and without which the finest airport in the world isn't worth much.

Finally Blotto burst out with his secret difficulty. "I'm afraid of 'em," he said. "They kill people off like flies. They're not safe!"

In the face of an increasing number of highway fatalities, all of us in aviation are constantly being told that autos are reasonably safe, airplanes unsafe. I usually drive between 50 and 60 miles an hour—and although I never pass on hills or curves, always slow down at dangerous intersections, and otherwise try to be careful, every time I drive any distance whatever I have one or two close shaves that leave me a bit shaky, contemplating what might have happened.

Manufacturers of automobiles no longer tell us that cars are safe, but they do spend a great deal of money trying to prove how much less chance there is of dying in today's wreck compared with that of a few years ago. For example, when your car is crowded off the highway and rolls over half a dozen times, you will merely be smashed around inside an all steel body instead of being shoved through a caved-in top. You are also offered the choice of having your throat cut off by a piece of broken glass or getting a brain concussion by smashing your head against a shatter proof windshield. Nevertheless, dangerous as the highways are, with their drunken drivers, road hogs, careless drivers, speed demons, over-size trucks and the like, I still use an automobile on very short trips. But from now on, if I can possibly arrange it, I'm going to stick to the flying of my own plane. I know I'm much safer.

However, the fact that riding in automobiles is no longer safe does not prove that flying is safe.

Why do people like Mr. Blotto have the impression that airplanes are dangerous? I believe one reason is the unfortunate publicity which all airplane wrecks receive. Of course wrecks are news and should be published, but I can't see any reason for splashing the information all over the front page for days. If Mr. and Mrs. John Smith and their three children are killed in an automobile wreck on some Saturday night, they will merely be added to the numerical total of fifty or sixty killed every week-end by automobiles and listed in a small paragraph on page three. If a week later, Mr. Smith's brother is killed in a private plane or on an airliner, we are shown pictures of the deceased and his life history is printed on the front page. In fact he is mentioned in so many consecutive issues that I'm not always sure whether one or half a dozen Mr. Smiths were killed. Once an airplane wreck occurs the newspapers make sure that it is lastingly imprinted on the public's mind.

A large percentage of plane accidents involve military craft. Mr. Blotto does not realize that speedy attack planes land very fast and are bound to have trouble when forced to come down in small fields or rough country. The public forgets that military planes must do a great many acrobatics and manuevers that aren't exactly safe. Army and navy pilots also often make long flights in bad weather to simulate war conditions. But to Mr. Blotto, an airplane accident, military or civil, is an airplane accident, "for a' that."

While civil mishaps are becoming more and more infrequent, they of course do still occur. But I believe that if we discount the number of wrecks in old, often unlicensed ships, and the absolutely unnecessary ones in storms and fogs, the total of civilian fatalities becomes amazingly low.

After all, almost any piece of machinery can be made dangerouns by its human operator, and the airplane is no exception. I for one am firmly convinced that when properly handled in decent weather, the airplane is as safe or safer than any other means of transportation.

# Hello, Southwest!

**Two members of an aviation family take a five thousand mile jaunt and discover happy days.**

**By MRS. KENNETH REARWIN**

THE era of the airplane is here to stay. You can choose your forms of flight and either flee from them, or fly in them. At first I tried the former course, but there wasn't a chance for me in the midst of an airminded family. With outward smiles and inward fears I climbed in behind my husband for a five thousand mile jaunt through the unfamiliar Southwest. It was my husband's first cross country flight over new territory, and it was the longest trip either of us has ever made by air. It was a trip full of surprises that we will never forget. But every one of those surprises was pleasant. Of course we had our share of funny experiences. Not knowing the initials of Mr. Johnson of Palacios, Texas, and mispronouncing the name of the town, we tried to call him long distance. After a protracted wait, the operator reported that Mr. Johnson was in the tub, but would hurry. He did. And then, after a nightmarish conversation, we finally discovered we were talking to a very different Mr. Johnson of Columbus, Texas—and would we please stop playing practical jokes and exposing him to pneumonia?

In all other respects, however, the trip was a complete success. I have gone through the traditional "ten lessons" and emerged a new woman. I gaze with pity at those who cannot combine business with pleasure and accompany their husbands on business trips by plane. It wasn't long before my enthusiasm for air travel became whole hearted and deep.

Together, my husband and I noted with satisfaction unmistakable signs that aviation is due for an increased boom. Regardless of the situation in the rest of the country, aviation in the Southwest is bound to prosper for three reasons. There we found the Ideal Time, the Ideal Place, and the Ideal Persons.

**MR. AND MRS. KENNETH REARWIN**
**A five thousand mile trip netted eight airplane sales.**

THE time is ideal because this is the twentieth century when people are accustomed to particular demands. They want speed, they want safety, they want comfort, they want economy—and they want all these with the minimum of effort. The airplane is the answer. We found many proofs that the average citizen is beginning to regard flying as a logical, economical, imperative means of transportation. The Southwest is full of new types of fliers—business men, professional men, salesmen, whole families. Flying is no longer a sport, a thrill, a flash of news. It has become a part of every day life. Even the children cry for it. One four-year-old proudly exhibits proof of his hundred hours passenger time. In Stockton, California, Joan Von Berg is as airminded as her parents. Familiar with all home port ships, she confidently expects a hop in visiting planes. If denied, she yells. Needless to say, we thought it advisable to take her up! In San Angelo, Texas we met a charming youngster whose chief delight is posing on the propeller of her father's plane. She obligingly sat for her picture on the front of our ship, the only difficulty being in coaxing her to leave. Perhaps the mothers have something to do with the children's attitude. One woman flies with her little girl to a nearby city to shop. She says she feels safe from the hazardous highways, and knows she can get home in time for dinner. We ourselves can honestly vouch for air travel in regard to speed. We felt like Olympians, high above a landscape of beauty, covering five hundred miles in five hours or less. On landing, we had the better part of the day to enjoy our new surroundings and to work. Equally important, we had our untapped energy to expend. In coolness, we sped over scorching plains; snug and dry, we flew in rain; when mountain winds were coldest, we were warm. I soon found, however, that one of the greatest appeals to my miserly soul was the amazing economy of it. Twenty miles to the gallon, without fail! Our car keeps me in a constant condition of I. O. U. Me for the air, where the poor woman has her chance for travel! Proud possessor of an aeronautical vocabulary, I remarked to Ken: "No more 'ceiling zero' for the airplane industry. The depression fogs are lifting."

AVIATION in the Southwest is endowed with an ideal place. With present demand and the natural advantages at hand, expansion in the field is inevitable. I used to live in New York, where one goes "way out west" to Chicago. The vast distances in the southwestern states amazed us both. Nevertheless, we were equally amazed at the ease with which we went unerringly from place to place. My husband confessed that before we started, he had a mild suspicion that we'd probably wander far off our course three or four times. But with the Department of Commerce sectional maps and a reasonably accurate compass, the navigation could be done by an absent-minded professor on his first hop. We thought it would be a task to keep an accurate course unless we had had several hundred hours of flying to our credit. My husband met several people who shared our mistaken idea. They complained of private flying because you have to have hundreds of hours before you dare to go anywhere. It's an impression that we were charmed to prove false. The brisk business activity in cities like Oklahoma City, Dallas, Fort Worth, San Antonio, Phoenix, and San Diego necessitates frequent and rapid journeys on the part of the business man. Weather conditions are excellent the year round, if what we experienced was a fair sample. The land is naturally adapted for good airports with little expense.

It is small wonder that in San Antonio, Hangar Six, Inc. has more students than two instructors can handle; that in Burbank, Huntington and Ross report that they scarcely need a hangar, because their ships are out on charter trips day and night. Everywhere operators testify to an improvement in both student and charter business. If you are curious as to the sales of airplanes, let me point with false modesty to the fact that we sold eight. And if I had not insisted on so many sidetrips for pleasure alone, I'm sure the score would be still higher.

Last but not least, I want to point out that the scenery in the Southwest is as varied and imaginitive as reports of a $700 airplane. Each state left an individual impression of beauty that we shall always remember. In Oklahoma, the fields lay like huge pieces of linen spread out with artistry to dry. Above Texas, we looked down upon meandering streams, snow white cotton fields, and forests of oil derricks that stood up stiffly like mechanical trees. New Mexico we remember as a graphic study in geology, and a land of glorious sunset clouds. Abrupt ranges over tinted desert made Arizona appear to be a geometrical masterpiece in light and shadow. California held up to our gaze the fruited lands that men have created, the dark dry mountains above them, the limitless ocean beyond them. No traveller could ask for more than perfect weather, a rapid journey, and an ever-changing landscape to divert. The flier in the Southwest has all these.

WHATEVER boosting the airplane needs, the people of the Southwest are ready and eager to give. In the first place, the type of men and women interested in flying is high. They are creating good will for the industry through their own personalities. They are deeply engrossed in their work, full of enthusiasm. They are hard workers and steady pushers. We saw airport projects, abandoned during lean years, being resumed through their efforts. We saw good publicity being given through the valuable service of ambulance planes. Everywhere, new demand is being created by increased student enrollment. Charter service, too, is growing, and with it will come familiarity with airplanes and real appreciation of them. The whole attitude of fliers is conducive to success.

Landing at sundown many an evening, I indulged myself in a fire of criticism. Too many airports nestle in a labyrinth of high wires, power lines, and trolley poles. In California, removal of dangerous obstructions is soon to begin. I know that many a student flier, and seasoned pilot as well, will join me in a brief blessing over such constructive action. Few towns in the Southwest are too small to have an aviation committee, and we heard many of them swearing to take arms against these hazardous networks. Everywhere we went, we commented to each other on the courtesy as well as the industry of our new acquaintances. If I were Mr. Prospect on my first cross country trip, the hospitable spirit that prevails would win me over as quickly as anything else. We "strangers in a strange land" were treated as old friends, driven to and from the airports, given hotel information, shown about the city, provided with weather reports—a hundred and one little things that filled our travels with pleasant memories. The competent servicing and attractive appearance at most airports gave me a feeling of enjoyment and confidence from the very first. Even in places like Carlsbad, New Mexico, where there is no hangar, the flier is well cared for. There's a former pilot by the name of Lester Stroup who is a one-man airport and crew. We came in at dusk, circled over town, and landed. In a few moments, Les was on hand to take us to town, to get stakes to tie the ship down, to provide a guard for the night, to lead us to the best hotel, and to lend us his car to drive to the famous Caverns next day. There is a true spirit of aviation in the Southwest, and I insist that it will do as much for future expansion as good weather conditions, and increased need.

If you have a wife who is afraid to fly, take her on a five thousand mile trip. When she sees the coziness, the speed, the economy, and the safety of air travel, she won't want to drive or take the train again. A hop around the airport on Sunday afternoon may be all right for some, but it was not until I actually went somewhere by plane that I realized what it was like. My husband and I are more than satisfied with what we saw. After all, when children play in ships at the age of two, and clamor for rides at the age of four, you can be pretty sure that it's begun to be in the blood of the nation. There's perfect visibility ahead for flying, and a tail wind is hurrying aviation along a clearly charted course to increased success.

**Even in remote sections landing fields are common.**

## *Appendix D*

# References and Further Reading


*Aircraft Year Book*. New York: Aeronautical Chamber of Commerce, Inc., 1928-1942.

*Antique Airplane Association News*. Robert L. Taylor, ed. Blakesburg, IA: Antique Airplane Association, 1960-1996.

*Aviation and Aero Digest*. New York: Aeronautical Digest Publishing Corp., 1924-1941.

*Aviation History In Greater Kansas City.* Kansas City, KS: Cub Flyers Publications, 1978.

Bowers, Peter M. "Yesterday's Wings, The Rearwin Sportster." *AOPA Pilot*. Washington, D.C.: Aircraft Owners and Pilots Association, March 1975.

Bowers, Peter M. "Yesterday's Wings, The Skyranger." *AOPA Pilot*. Washington, D.C.: Aircraft Owners and Pilots Association, June 1976.

Cooper, Ann L. *On The Wing*. Mt. Freedom, NJ: Blackhawk Publishing Co., 1993.

Crawford, Robert. "West Coast By Rearwin Sportster." *The Sportsman Pilot*. New York: Sportsman Pilot, Inc., August 15, 1935.

*Fairfax Facts*. Kansas City, MO: Fairfax Airport, Inc., 1930-1932.

Hooper, Friea. "Rearwin Had Humble Beginnings." *Pacific Flyer*. Oceanside, CA: Pacific Flyer Newspapers, Inc., December 1988.

Juptner, Joseph P. *U.S. Civil Aircraft*, vols. 1 - 9. Fallbrook, CA: Aero Publishers, Inc., 1960-1980.

*Kansas City Kansan*, 1929-1946.

*Kansas City* (MO) *Star*, 1929-1946.

Komons, Nick A. *Bonfires To Beacons*. Washington, D.C.: Smithsonian Institution Press, 1977.

Kurt, Franklin T.; "The Sportsman Test Pilot Flies The 85-Horsepower LeBlond Rearwin Sportster." *The Sportsman Pilot*, vol. xv, no. 1. New York: Sportsman Pilot, Inc., January 15, 1936.

Kurt, Franklin T. "The Sportsman Test Pilot, Flying The Speedster." *The Sportsman Pilot*, vol. xix, no. 2. New York: Sportsman Pilot, Inc., February 15, 1938.

Miller, William E. "The Rearwin Story." *Antique Airplane Association News*, vol. iv, no. 11. Blakesburg, IA: Antique Airplane Association, June 19, 1961.

Mosley, Zack T. *Brave Coward Zack*. St. Petersburg, FL: Valkyrie Press, 1976.

Neprud, Robert E. *Flying Minute Men*. New York: Duell, Sloan and Pearce, 1948.

Nichols, Ruth S. *Wings For Life*. New York: Lippencott Publishing Co., 1959.

Ong, William. *Ride The High Wind*. Kansas City, MO: Pilot News Press, 1957.

Pratt, Don. "Porterfield Collegiate." *American Aircraft Modeler*. Reno, NV: Potomac Aviation Publications, August 1969.

"Progress of Civil Aviation in the United States, 1929-1939." *Civil Aeronautics Journal*, vol. 1, no. 20. Washington, D.C.: U.S. Department of Commerce, October 15, 1940.

"Rearwin: Aviation's Elder Manufacturer." *Kansas City Aviation*. Kansas City, MO: The Suburban Pilot, Inc., November 1981.

Rearwin, Kenneth R. "Aviation's Advantages." *The Pilot*. Los Angeles: Pilot Publishing Co., February 1936.

Rearwin, Mrs. Kenneth. "Hello Southwest." *Southwestern Aviation*. Fort Worth, TX: Southwestern Aviation Publishing Co., December 1935.

*Rearwin Register*, vols. 1-18. Blakesburg, IA: Rearwin Club, 1981-1996.

Rummel, Robert W. *Howard Hughes and TWA*. Washington, D.C.: Smithsonian Institution Press, 1991.

*Salina* (Kansas) *Journal*, 1906-1969.

Salvay, M.E. "Rearwin M-6000 Speedster." *Model Airplane News*. Wilton, CT: Air Age, Inc., September 1972.

Salvay, M.E. "Rearwin Skyranger." *Model Airplane News*. Wilton, CT: Air Age, Inc., November 1970.

Taylor, Robert L. "A Short Rearwin History." *Aviation Quarterly*, vol. 1, no. 4. Arlington, VA: Airtrails, Inc., 1974.

Thaden, Louise. "The National Women's Air Derby." *Aviation Quarterly*, vol. 1, no. 3. Arlington, VA: Airtrails, Inc., 1974.

"They Make Their Bow." *The Sportsman Pilot*. New York: Sportsman Pilot, Inc., February 15, 1940.

Underwood, John W. "Those Wonderful Rearwins — Some Great Birds." *Air Progress*. Canoga Park, CA: Challenge Publications, January, 1968.

*Western Flying*. Los Angeles, CA: Occidental Publishing Co.

*The Wichita* (KS) *Beacon*, June 1929.

# Index

by Lori L. Daniel